"This book is of immense value to public relations, its scholarly inquiry, and professional practice. However, those in a wide range of disciplines will find the volume to be both enlightening and delightful reading. The author describes the significant role in U.S. westward expansion of the brave women who had migrated over five to six months via the 2,000-mile Oregon Trail to subsequently settle in the Willamette Valley. This exhaustively researched book provides evidence of a feminist orientation when these women had assumed needed roles as caretakers/advocates, community builders, and civilizers, as well as when they had provided an emotional connection for social cohesion and complicity. Pompper's research provides conclusive evidence that the women of the Oregon Trail were not fragile or delicate, nor were they subservient to and dependent upon men. Rather, they became essential leaders during this arduous journey and in the nascent settlements of the Willamette Valley. The author observes that there was a reason that women's suffrage was first successful in the West.

These women became among the first historians to have recorded the Western experience. However, using feminist theory, network theory, and social constructionism, the author argues that they also were pioneers in public relations – precursors to today's public relations practitioners in formal organizations. Pompper calls for a revisionist history as well as expanded historiographical methods to include such examples in public relations history. How we learn history influences how we think about ourselves and our career choices, and existing public relations history has been highly gendered – not a welcoming space for women or for people of color. Pompper argues that if public relations were more broadly defined to incorporate informal community work, new opportunities would exist for theorizing about public relations. The author concludes that public relations history must be expanded to include marginalized voices, such as the women community builders who had enabled the wagon trains and their destination settlement communities to connect with their past, to make sense of a new present, and to plan for the future. Then, the gaps that have been caused by patriarchal perspectives would no longer limit present-day understanding of public relations."

—*Dr. Dean Kruckeberg*, *APR, Fellow PRSA, Professor,*
Department of Communication Studies,
University of North Carolina at Charlotte

"*Community Building and Early Public Relations: Pioneer Women's Role on and after the Oregon Trail* is well researched and a pleasure to read. More importantly, the book provides a much-needed approach to opening up new spaces for thinking about public relations history. It offers deep insights into diverse practices of public relations by giving voice to women's missing stories. Pompper traces women's contributions to early community building and civil society. Public relations students and practitioners will benefit from this text because they will better understand how our field helped shape the communities in the American frontier."

—*Professor Maureen Taylor, Ph.D.*, Head of Discipline, Public Communication, School of Communication, University of Technology Sydney

"In *Community Building and Early Public Relations*, Donnalyn Pompper presents history from a different perspective, at the grassroots and with a lens focused firmly on women. She takes a deep dive into understanding relationship-building from the bottom up, demonstrating that in their efforts to survive as pioneers in the Oregon territory, women developed elements of what has become standard PR practice, offering a more nuanced understanding of the field. Based on evidence from women's own private writing, Pompper also documents the violent side of homesteading, its effects on indigenous people, thus drawing attention to an overriding question about PR: can practitioners ever balance client interests with those of the public"

—*Karen Miller Russell*, University of Georgia

"This 'herstoriography' of pioneer women in the mid-1800s examines their voices through a contemporary lens. The review of their diaries and journals reveals the roles they served as community builders, caretakers, advocates, and social leaders. A vital step toward gender inclusion in public relations history, the stories provide outstanding insight for 'herstoric' revisionism. The book is an essential course supplement for current texts and, by challenging earlier narratives, it provides a critical benchmark for social, racial, and gender inclusion in future editions."

—*Pam Creedon*, Professor Emeritus, School of Journalism and Mass Communication, University of Iowa

"This is a novel, field-widening contribution to the 'herstory' of public relations in the U.S., which offers an additional conceptual model drawn from analysis of the nineteenth-century Oregon Trail."

—*Tom Watson Ph.D.*, Emeritus Professor, Bournemouth University; Founder of the International History of Public Relations Conference

Community Building and Early Public Relations

From the start, women were central to a century of westward migration in the U.S. *Community Building and Early Public Relations: Pioneer Women's Role on and after the Oregon Trail* offers a path forward in broadening PR's Caucasian/White male-gendered history in the U.S. Undergirded by humanist, communitarian, critical race theory, social constructionist perspectives, and a feminist communicology lens, this book analyzes U.S. pioneer women's lived experiences, drawing parallels with PR's most basic functions – relationship-building, networking, community building, boundary spanning, and advocacy.

Using narrative analysis of diaries and reminiscences of women who travelled 2,000+ miles on the Oregon Trail in the mid-to-late 1800s, the author uncovers how these women filled the roles of *Caretaker/Advocate*, *Community Builder of Meeting Houses and Schools*, served a *Civilizing Function*, offered *Agency and Leadership*, and provided *Emotional Connection for Social Cohesion*. Revealed also is an inevitable paradox as Caucasian/White pioneer women's interactional qualities made them complicit as colonizers, forever altering indigenous people's way of life.

This book will be of interest to undergraduate and graduate PR students, PR practitioners, and researchers of PR history and social identity intersectionalities. It encourages us to expand the definition of PR to include community building, and to revise linear timeline and evolutionary models to accommodate voices of women and people of color prior to the twentieth century.

Donnalyn Pompper (Ph.D., Media & Communication, Temple University) teaches courses in and researches public relations, corporate social responsibility, and social identity. Overall, her research provides routes for enabling people, globally, to achieve their maximum potential at work, to embrace their intersecting social identity dimensions (e.g., age, ethnicity, gender), and to critically examine these issues across mass media representations.

Pompper is an internationally recognized and award-winning scholar. She holds the Accredited Public Relations credential from the Public Relations Society of America. Prior to joining the academy, she worked as a public relations manager and journalist, bringing 25 years of practical experience to the classroom and her research. She worked in public affairs management at

Campbell's Soup Company, marketing public relations management at Tasty Baking Company, where she created the public relations department, and as an account manager at Lewis, Gilman & Kynett (Philadelphia's then-largest public relations/advertising firm). She also worked as a daily newspaper freelance reporter at *The Philadelphia Inquirer* and the *Courier-Post*, as well as news editor at a weekly New Jersey newspaper chain.

Routledge New Directions in PR & Communication Research
Edited by Kevin Moloney

Current academic thinking about public relations (PR) and related communication is a lively, expanding marketplace of ideas and many scholars believe that it's time for its radical approach to be deepened. Routledge New Directions in PR & Communication Research is the forum of choice for this new thinking. Its key strength is its remit, publishing critical and challenging responses to continuities and fractures in contemporary PR thinking and practice, tracking its spread into new geographies and political economies. It questions its contested role in market-orientated, capitalist, liberal democracies around the world, and examines its invasion of all media spaces, old, new, and as yet unenvisaged.

The New Directions series has already published and commissioned diverse original work on topics such as:

- PR's influence on Israeli and Palestinian nation-building
- PR's origins in the history of ideas
- a Jungian approach to PR ethics and professionalism
- global perspectives on PR professional practice
- PR as an everyday language for everyone
- PR as emotional labor
- PR as communication in conflicted societies, and
- PR's relationships to cooperation, justice, and paradox.

We actively invite new contributions and offer academics a welcoming place for the publication of their analyses of a universal, persuasive mindset that lives comfortably in old and new media around the world.

Public Relations, Branding and Authenticity
Brand Communications in the Digital Age
Sian Rees

Paradox in Public Relations
A Contrarian Critique of Theory and Practice
Kevin L. Stoker

For more information about this series, please visit www.routledge.com/Routledge-New-Directions-in-Public-Relations–Communication-Research/book-series/RNDPRCR

Community Building and Early Public Relations

Pioneer Women's Role on and after the Oregon Trail

Donnalyn Pompper

LONDON AND NEW YORK

First published 2021
by Routledge
2 Park Square, Milton Park, Abingdon, Oxon OX14 4RN

and by Routledge
52 Vanderbilt Avenue, New York, NY 10017

Routledge is an imprint of the Taylor & Francis Group, an informa business

© 2021 Donnalyn Pompper

The right of Donnalyn Pompper to be identified as author of this work has been asserted by her in accordance with sections 77 and 78 of the Copyright, Designs and Patents Act 1988.

All rights reserved. No part of this book may be reprinted or reproduced or utilised in any form or by any electronic, mechanical, or other means, now known or hereafter invented, including photocopying and recording, or in any information storage or retrieval system, without permission in writing from the publishers.

Trademark notice: Product or corporate names may be trademarks or registered trademarks, and are used only for identification and explanation without intent to infringe.

British Library Cataloguing in Publication Data
A catalogue record for this book is available from the British Library

Library of Congress Cataloging-in-Publication Data
A catalog record has been requested for this book

ISBN: 978-0-367-22401-1 (hbk)
ISBN: 978-0-429-27471-8 (ebk)

Typeset in Bembo
by Taylor & Francis Books

Contents

List of Illustrations	xi
Foreword	xii
KARLA K. GOWER	
Acknowledgments	xv
Primary Sources	xvi
Introduction: Opening New Spaces in Public Relations History to Include More Women	xvii

PART I
Overview   1

1 (Re)discovering the Past in Order to Understand Public Relations History Today   3

2 Re-examining the American West's Lure and Women's Role Representations   29

PART II
Gendering and Expanding Roles as Early Public Relations Work   55

3 Interrogating Pioneer Women's Role as *Caretaker/Advocate*   57

4 Exploring Public Relations from the Care Perspective: Pioneer Women's Role as *Community Builder of Meeting Houses and Schools*   80

5 *Civilizing Function*: Pioneer Women and Religion   101

PART III
Ideologies, Women's Work, and the Female Frontier   115

6 Understanding Pioneer Women's *Agency and Leadership*   117

7 Expanding Women's Role: *Emotional Connection for Social Cohesion*   137

8 Concluding Thoughts and Direction for Discovering More Women's Voices for Public Relations History   160

Index   177

Illustrations

Figures

1.1	Oregon Trail, 1846	4
1.2	Buffalo Bill Center of the West, Cody, Wyoming; Whitney Western Art Museum, "Madonna of the Prairie" by WHD Koerner, 1921; 25.77.	19
2.1	Four-Cent U.S. Homestead Act Postage Stamp	31
2.2	Parting of the Ways	41
2.3	Oregon Trail Wagon Ruts	42
2.4	Oregon Trail Ruts State Historic Site	42
2.5	Pioneer Mother Statue	44
3.1	Amelia Stewart Knight	60
3.2	Ada McColl collecting Buffalo Dung	64
3.3	Jane (Jennie) Paul Eakin Hanna's Headstone, Pioneer Cemetery, Eugene, Oregon	65
3.4	Independence Rock	66
4.1	Cecilia Adams	88
5.1	Keturah Belknap and Husband	109
6.1	Abigail Scott Duniway	124
7.1	Chimney Rock	144
7.2	Amelia A. Hammond Hadley's Journal	145

Table

0.1	Texts Examined	xxvii

Foreword

Karla K. Gower[1]

Much of the history of American public relations remains to be written, but Donnalyn Pompper's account of the role of pioneer women in community building via public relations gets us a step closer. Not only does the book explore early public relations activities by women, but it also focuses on an important but seldom researched area of the field – community building.

Researching and writing public relations history can be problematic. Pioneer women in the U.S. would not have even heard the term "public relations." Can we still describe what they were doing as public relations if that's not what they saw themselves doing? According to L'Etang (2008), the answer to that question is yes. In fact, doing so is necessary for "more richly textured understandings of the discipline" (p. 329).

While defining public relations seems to be a perennial issue, the Public Relations Society of America currently defines it as "a strategic communication process that builds mutually beneficial relationships between organizations and their publics" (www.prsa.org/about/all-about-pr). Others describe it as "the management of communication between an organization and its publics" (Grunig & Hunt, 1984, p. 8). That it is a management function within an organization fits well with the early public relations histories that gave credit to Ivy Lee and Edward Bernays as the "fathers" of public relations. Those histories privileged a corporate point of view. In this perspective, large monopolistic enterprises such as railroads, oil companies, and, especially AT&T, used public relations to convince the public that they were operating in the public's best interest. In equating public relations with whiteness, maleness, and power, the early histories necessarily excluded minorities and women and discounted the contemporaneous efforts of activists, unions, and religious groups, among others. Anything that might "look" like public relations prior to the late nineteenth century was referred to as an antecedent or as some kind of proto-PR (proto-public relations), suggesting that it was not "real" public relations (Cutlip, 1995). Real public relations was corporate-centric and had a decidedly modernist, progressive bent.

But it is clear from more recent studies that public relations existed before it was co-opted by corporations and professional practitioners. That is, it was a practice before it was a function in an organization or thought of as a profession. In that sense, it is, as Myer (2021) argues, a form of public communication through which an organization or individual attempts to affect attitudinal or behavioral change. As such, it does not depend on the self-identification of the communicator. Treating public relations as a practice allows non-professional communicators prior to 1900, especially people outside the traditional sites of power, to be included.

Public relations historians have called for the voices of ordinary people, including minorities and women, to be heard. Their activities and lived experiences can and should be considered public relations. Including their stories can help broaden and deepen our understanding of the development of the field as well as move us in new directions in the future, especially important if public relations is to remain relevant in an ever-changing society. Pompper's research into Oregon's pioneering women answers that call.

As she notes, it was exceptional circumstances that enabled ordinary women to find their voice in the nineteenth century. Research suggests that women experienced the trail differently from men. The hardships the men faced on the trail were offset by the lure of financial gain and a sense of independence. Women, on the other hand, viewed those same dangers as threatening their families' way of life. Once these women arrived in Oregon, their roles expanded. They became influential in building communities, participating in economies in ways they had not been permitted to in the east (Faragher, 1979). Along the trail and once settled, these pioneer women engaged in community building, a public relations activity that has received limited scholarly attention.

Community building is the "integration of people and the organizations they create into a functional collectivity that strives toward common or compatible goals" (Hallahan, 2004, p. 46). The role of public relations in community building is "one of helping both organizations and publics build a community where dialogue and mutual understanding can take place" (Valentini, Kruckeberg, & Starck, 2012, p. 874). Kruckeberg & Starck (1988) in their original community-building theory suggested several ways that public relations could help develop a sense of community, ways that are echoed in Pompper's findings: "helping individuals in the community to overcome alienation; helping individuals find security and protection through association with others; actively taking part in community projects promoting progress; and helping foster personal friendships" (Valentini, Kruckeberg, & Starck, 2012, p. 875).

Application of the community-building theory requires looking at public relations through a humanist communitarian lens rather than the modernist/progressive one typically used by public relations historians. That forces us to view the work of the pioneer women "in the context of an overall human story" (L'Etang, 2014, p. xx), a woman's story. The "female frontier" was different from the frontier dominated by white men and celebrated in American culture (Holmes, 1983). Pompper focuses on that difference in experience from a public relations perspective. She reminds us that public relations is not just about institutions, publics, men, and power. It can also be about communities, relationships, women (and people of color), and empowerment.

Of course, that does not mean public relations in the pursuit of community building is always ethical. The taming of the frontier was not just about fighting Mother Nature; it also involved conquering indigenous peoples. Pompper is ideally suited to tackle this duality. Her previous work on feminism and diversity gives her the ability to recognize, and the willingness to grapple with, the paradox of building community while at the same time colonizing indigenous communities. Dualism is a constant presence for public relations practitioners. We advocate for our clients' interests while also seeking to serve the public's interest; yet those interests are not always going to be aligned. But we have not come to terms with that fact, even in our history. Ignoring unethical aspects of our past will not make them go away. We need to come to terms with those dimensions to move forward.

In giving a voice to the pioneer women of the Oregon Trail and recognizing their community-building efforts as an example of early public relations, Pompper broadens our view of public relations and reminds us that at its heart, it is about human communication and human relationships.

Note

1 Karla K. Gower, Ph.D., University of Alabama

References

Cutlip, S. M. (1995). *Public relations history: From the 17th to the 20th century. The antecedents.* Hillsdale, NJ: Lawrence Erlbaum Associates.

Faragher, J. M. (1979). *Women and men on the Overland Trail* (2nd edn). New Haven, CT: Yale University Press.

Grunig, J. E., & Hunt, T. (1984). *Managing public relations.* New York: Holt, Rinehart & Winston.

Hallahan, K. (2004). "Community" as the framework for public relations theory and research. *Communication Yearbook*, 28, 233–279.

Holmes, K. L. (1983). *Covered wagon women* (Vol. I). Lincoln, NE: University of Nebraska Press.

Kruckeberg, D., & Starck, K. (1988). *Public relations and community: A reconstructed theory.* New York: Praeger.

L'Etang, J. (2008). Writing PR history: Issues, methods and politics. *Journal of Communication Management*, 12, 319–335.

L'Etang, J. (2014). Public relations and historical sociology: Historiography as reflexive critique. *Public Relations Review*, 40, 654–660.

Myers, C. (2020). *Public relations history: Theory, practice and profession.* New York: Routledge.

Valentini, C., Kruckeberg, D., & Starck, K. (2012). Public relations and community: A persistent covenant. *Public Relations Review*, 38, 873–879.

Acknowledgments

I am grateful to many who supported this project. Endowed Chair in Public Relations funding enabled me to purchase books and travel to conferences, so I especially thank the School of Journalism and Communication, University of Oregon. I also am indebted to Linda Long, Curator of Manuscripts, Special Collections and University Archives, University of Oregon Libraries, for her support. At the Oregon Historical Society in Portland, OR, thanks to Scott Daniels, Reference Services Manager, for help in sharing information about photograph resources. I am grateful for the photograph resources of the University of Oregon, Buffalo Bill Center of the West, Randall Brown, Kansas State Historical Society, and Wyoming State Historical Society.

Many thanks also to the support of graduate assistants available through the School of Journalism and Mass Communication at the University of Oregon, including Tugce Ertem Eray, Farah Azhar, and Irene Awino. Their help with accessing library books and note taking was invaluable. Thanks also to the School of Journalism and Communication faculty support expert Tami Oar, for copying, and Gail Tinkham for loaning pioneer books – with both offering words of encouragement.

Thanks, too, to colleagues Dr. Laura Pulido for advice about feminist historical geography, Dr. Debra Merskin for insights about Oregon's Native American communities, Tom Lundberg for help with camera equipment, and to friends Peter Clark, Nika Helmer, Hana Marino, Jordan Marx, and Dennis Peck for politely listening to stories about this research project. Last, but not least, I am grateful for the support of my Eugene-based, fellow East-coast native friend, Michael DeLuise, for help with acquiring permissions for important photographs.

I dedicate this book to Mrs. Mildred Schaible (1915–2010), who taught us the "Sweet Betsy From Pike" song in third grade, inspiring my interest in pioneer women.

Primary Sources

Adams, Cecilia E., & Blank, Parthenia. Diary Manuscript, 1852. "The Oregon Trail diary of twin sisters Cecilia Adams and Parthenia Blank." Oregon Historical Society, Portland, OR.

Belknap, Keturah. Diary Manuscript, 1848. Oregon Historical Society, Portland, OR.

Cooper, Arvanza A. Spillman. Reminiscence Manuscript, 1901, "Our journey across the plains from Missouri to Oregon, 1863." Oregon Historical Society, Portland, OR.

Evans, S. D. Reminiscence Manuscript, 1863, "A trip from Washoe, Nevada, to Douglas County, Oregon in 1861." Special Collections and University Archives, University of Oregon Libraries, Eugene, OR.

Goltra, Elizabeth Julia Ellison. Journal Manuscript, 1853. Special Collections and University Archives, University of Oregon Libraries, Eugene, OR.

Hadley, Amelia A. Hammond. Diary Manuscript, 1851. "Journal to Oregon of Travails." Special Collections and University Archives, University of Oregon Libraries, Eugene, OR.

Hanna, Jane (Jennie) Paul Eakin. Diary Manuscript, 1866. Special Collections and University Archives, University of Oregon Libraries, Eugene, OR.

Knight, Amelia Stewart. Diary Manuscript, 1853. In L. Schlissel (2004). *Women's diaries of the westward journey*. New York: Schocken Books.

Loughary, Harriet A. Journal Manuscript, 1864. Special Collections and University Archives, University of Oregon Libraries, Eugene, OR.

Newell, J. A. Reminiscence Manuscript, 1901. The Margaret Bannard Letters. Special Collections and University Archives, University of Oregon Libraries, Eugene, OR.

Rudd, Lydia Allen. Diary Manuscript, 1852. Special Collections and University Archives, University of Oregon Libraries, Eugene, OR.

Thomas, Julia. Reminiscence Manuscript, 1907. Special Collections and University Archives, University of Oregon Libraries, Eugene, OR.

Introduction
Opening New Spaces in Public Relations History to Include More Women

In order to understand pioneer women's community-building role on and after the five–six-month westward trek with their family to settle in Oregon, first it is important to examine U.S. nationalism as the backdrop. The dynamics involve a complex set of issues with many parallels to aspects of modern ethical and strategic public relations practice. The western half of the North American continent was occupied by communities of indigenous peoples, but Caucasian/White people who had descended from European emigrants felt it was their right as racial-and-cultural superiors to expand U.S. territory across the Mississippi and to the Pacific Ocean. The Oregon Treaty with Great Britain in 1846 when President James K. Polk acquired Oregon Country from Britain sharpened the U.S. border to the north and debates about war with Mexico to the south increased. U.S. Southerners sought more lands for cotton cultivation, which meant expanding slavery across the Mississippi River. Many Northerners opposed adding more slave states to the Union, however. Industrial capitalists – especially railroad companies – sought to enhance their profits with expanded geography.

Simultaneously, financial panic and cholera and malaria outbreaks in the East transformed mere curiosity about the West in the 1840s into action for survival. When the westward pioneer movement began, Oregon was a territory and fewer than 20,000 Caucasian/White U.S. citizens lived west of the Mississippi River (Burns, Duncan, & Burns, 1997). But by the end of the nineteenth century, about half a million people had emigrated West. As 1846 began, three years before the Gold Rush, thousands of Americans were on the move West – eager to bring Oregon, Texas, and California territories into the Union. Bolstered by a belief that they were obligated to expand U.S. boundaries to the Pacific coast and incentivized by the Homestead Act of 1862 which meant free land after working it for five years, pioneers became swept up in this nationalism wave that changed the landscape and altered the life path of Native American communities forever. While the land to the eastern side of the Mississippi in the U.S. had long been claimed and settled, the Louisiana Purchase lands were still being explored. Lewis and Clark's Corps of Discovery in search of a Northwest Passage was widely publicized, and then gold was discovered in California in 1848. The phrase, *Manifest Destiny*, was coined by newspaper editor John O'Sullivan, in 1859: "the manifest destiny of the American Republic" (Pratt, 1927, p. 797). The migration was kicked into high gear and women played a key role as community builders.

From the start, women were central to a century of westward migration. Lewis and Clark had journaled about two Native American women without whose help the 1804–1806 Corps of Discovery may not have achieved its goal of journeying westward to the Pacific Ocean. These relationships also advanced another of the explorers' goals – drawing indigenous peoples into political and economic alliances with the U.S. Ken Burns' (Burns, Duncan, & Burns, 1997) narration in the PBS documentary, *Lewis & Clark: The Journey of the Corps of Discovery*, offered: "At two times of greatest need, they were saved by women." These were a Shoshone woman, Sacajawea, and a Nez Perce woman, Watkuweis. Sacajawea traveled with the explorers as an interpreter helping to secure horses for travel over mountains and showed them how to gather roots and berries for food. Watkuweis advocated for the explorers and eventually convinced a chief not to kill Lewis and Clark in today's Idaho.

Soon the emigration floodgates opened and the Anglo-American women who walked and rode 2,000+ miles to Oregon Country/Territory lived according to a nineteenth-century cult of domesticity, or cult of true womanhood. The standard by which women were regarded focused on "piety, purity, submissiveness, and domesticity" (Welter, 1966, p. 59) as they clung to a domestic role in the private sphere as mother, daughter, sister, and wife. Once the Overland Trail journey began – whether continuing on to California or Oregon – women quickly discovered that they must adjust to meet the demands of new circumstances. As findings for the study revealed in this book suggest, women's lived experiences of the Oregon Trail journey and settlement in Oregon's Willamette Valley and beyond facilitated the expansion of the role of women as much more complex people – *Caretaker/Advocate, Community Builder of Meeting Houses and Schools*, as embodying the *Civilizing Function*, and providing *Emotional Connection for Social Cohesion and Complicity*. Each of these roles, as thematically emerged among women's first-person texts, is explored in depth throughout the chapters of this book with the aim of adding new dimensions to our understanding of early public relations work in the form of community building. While applauding this addition to public relations history, a critique is offered to probe the dynamics of a paradox where on one side is women's community building and outreach work and on the other their complicity as colonialists who negatively impacted indigenous communities. This contradiction necessitates addressing the hard truths about the violent side of Oregon's homesteading history, while reflecting on ethical public relations practice – even in its early community-building antecedent. There is a powerful parallel with the work of today's public relations professionals who strive to serve those for whom they advocate while remaining true to the field's broader ethical commitment to society.

This introduction backgrounds a study of women's community-building role on the Oregon Trail journey and settlement in Oregon's Willamette Valley and beyond, setting the stage for research findings with these interrelated subtopics: 1) Expansionism, Manifest Destiny, and Media, 2) How Does One Learn History?, 3) Revisionist History, 4) Learning about Professional Public Relations History, 5) Formal Research Method, 6) Examining Women's First-Person Texts, and 7) Chapter Synopses.

Expansionism, Manifest Destiny, and Media

The U.S. westward migration allure saga began in the nineteenth century when economic, technological, cultural, and political conditions interplayed with religion/faith systems, ethnicity/race issues, and socioeconomic social identity dimensions. A historical economist underscored the impact of the two U.S. economic depressions of 1873–1978 and 1893–1897 as inspiring geographic expansion westward, especially earmarking the 1880s as "a decade of buoyant growth" (Williamson, 1974, p. 93). Moreover, a transportation revolution with improved canals, roads, and railroads – along with European immigration swelling U.S. urban centers beyond capacity – increased the romance of westward expansion as opportunity (Riley, 2004). The U.S. frontier period was from the mid-1810s until the outbreak of World War I in Europe in 1914, although the U.S. Census Bureau declared the frontier "closed" in 1890 with an average of two residents per square mile (Riley, 2004, p. 7). One western historian characterized the 1841–1869 time period as a critical change "era of decision," shaped by westward expansion, the Civil War, the end of slavery, and the early steps toward industrialization and urbanization in the U.S. (Holmes, 2008, p. 21).

In 1803, U.S. President Thomas Jefferson doubled the size of the U.S. when he bought the Louisiana Territory from France: 828,000 square miles of land from the Mississippi River to the Rocky Mountains (east-west) and Gulf of Mexico to Canada's border (south-north). He sent Meriwether Lewis and William Clark in 1803–1806 to explore the Louisiana Purchase. Their Corps of Discovery involved pushing westward across the Rocky Mountains through present-day Wyoming, Montana, and Idaho, and navigating the Columbia River to the Pacific Ocean. The Louisiana Purchase was a land deal that eventually resulted in carving the massive lands into 15 U.S. states, bringing about an invasion into indigenous communities. Manifest Destiny ranks among the most enduring of American cultural myths (Cross, 1995), as amplified by nineteenth-century media, and came to mean a conviction among Caucasian/White Americans, Canadians, and Europeans that "God intended them to migrate to and to shape to their own ends the frontiers West" (Riley, 2004, p. 8). Critical historians (and others) have called this belief that U.S. migration West was a right or duty "colonization or even colonialism" (Riley, 2004, p. 7), given that the land *was* already inhabited by Native Americans. The impact of colonialism has to a large extent been forgotten and many people have become complicit with it, such as by not problematizing commemorations.

Eighteenth-century newspapers supported the migration West with sensational stories, especially weekly newspapers funded by land or railroad companies that were designed to stimulate land booms and publish paid advertising about "proving up notes" legally required as part of the homesteading processes (Riley, 1988, p. 6). The media promoted westward expansion by amplifying publicity about touring lecturers and promoting guidebooks projecting images of the American West as a promised land (Riley, 2006). The railroad-underwritten rhetoric (Cutlip, 1995) embraced expansionism and promoted Oregon and California in "glowing terms" (Jeffrey, 1998, p. 38). Newspapers especially amplified the theme of land just waiting for cultivation by printing settlers' letters back home to railroad companies (Riley, 1994). However, it was *New York Tribune* publisher, Horace Greeley, who is best known for promoting Western settlement as a "safety valve" for New York City's population growth, high unemployment, and daily influx of 1,000 immigrants (Sloan, Stovall, & Startt, 1989, p. 177). Historians of the nineteenth-century westward movement have unearthed significant evidence supporting the role of the media in advancing the phrase oft credited to Horace Greeley: "Go West, young man, and grow up with the country" (Taylor, 2015). This erupted into a rallying cry for support of the Homestead Bill promoting western expansion and settlement. Greeley's excitement filled the *New York Tribune*: "Young men! Poor men! Widows! Resolve to have a home of your own! If you are able to buy and pay for one in the East, very well, if not, make one in the broad and fertile West!" (Robbins, 1942, p. 206). For the rest of his life as *New York Tribune* editor and politician, Greeley campaigned for an agrarian utopia by promoting agriculture and the establishment of Land Grant universities, the passage of land reform and homestead acts, the restriction of slavery from western territories, and the building of the transcontinental railroads (Cross, 1995). Other newspapers across the Union also played a role in Oregon Fever (Schlissel, 2004).

With the media promoting the idea and government providing the incentive, it is easy to see why 350,000 Eastern and Mid-western emigrants heeded the call, setting out on a 2,000+ mile journey from home in search of something better in the form of free land, freedom, better health, adventure, or proving their own mettle. Men, women, and children of all ages crossed wide windswept plains, three great mountain ranges, and several dessert areas. Pioneers departed in waves over consecutive years throughout the nineteenth century once the spring rains had subsided with plans to be in Oregon before the snows began. For married women, the decision may have felt less democratic as husbands sold their home and belongings to fund the trip (Butruille, 1993). According to nineteenth-century law, a wife had to live where her husband dictated – meaning that while some women agreed to a 2,000+mile trek across unknown lands to Oregon, married women "couldn't not go" (Butruille, 1993, p. 3). The Homestead Act also stated that a married couple would be given more land than a single person (and an unmarried woman couldn't get any at all). Some women's diaries and letters clearly reflected mixed feelings about the journey West, as some joined their husbands under protest (Jameson, 1988).

Before unfolding narratives from pioneer women's diaries, journals, and reminiscences – and offering their stories as community-building precursors to early public relations work – I first invite a deeper look at how we learn history to critique how public relations history has been shaped over the last few decades.

How Does One Learn History?

We learn about the past from people who have experienced it themselves and by discovering the findings and opinions of experts such as historians and other authorities as communicated through artifacts such as books, museums, and more. How we learn history is a research arena far less traveled than investigations of how we learn mathematics, languages, or science (Miller & Stearns, 1995), but I posit that understanding how we learn history is quite important because it reveals the role of influences in shaping how we think about ourselves, career choices, and the past that comes with the territory.

Each generation reinterprets its nation's heritage through a viewfinder of contemporary conditions. Until the twentieth century, most historians were uninterested in *theoretical* reflections of history (Wehmeier, 2015). Rather, stories in history included few women, a phenomenon in Nigeria called the history of "the great man," used to typify the age in which men lived to "sum up and represent humanity … greatness and what determines it" (Adejunmobi, 1979, p. 350). With such telling of history in the U.S., the focus was on key dates and stories about central figures and events to provide readers with explanations of why things happened. These techniques provided a citizenship-building foundation for good decision-making through lessons underscoring efficacy of democratic institutions, the superiority of Americans, and the inevitability of progress. More recently, examining history through a contemporary lens has revealed themes across U.S. history teaching that have emphasized economic opportunity, participation in politics, belief in reform, population mobility, status for women, concern for the welfare of others, toleration of differences, respect for the rights and abilities of individuals, and worldwide responsibility (Waller, 1978). Fitch (2016b) opined that in the highly gendered history of public relations, women's historical contributions have seldom been recognized and have often been marginalized – such as with the early U.S. professional public relations work of Doris E. Fleischman, who barely emerges from the shadows of her husband, Edward Bernays, celebrated for being a self-promoter. It has been speculated that she was the ghostwriter at the firm they were partners in the early twentieth century (Heath & Coombs, 2006).

In recent decades, new techniques and more broad-minded critical approaches have significantly changed how we go about writing history. First, historiographical methods for analyzing the theory behind writing history emerged in the 2000s. Experiential learning techniques encourage students to engage with history and to think and ask questions about human experience rather than just memorizing facts (Savagian, 2009). Social constructionist historians like White (1973) emphasized context as shaping the interpretation of facts in history in order to "[bring] meaning to the flow of facts" (Wehmeier, 2015, p. 91). Second, because certain events and achievements have not made it to the pages of history, research undergirded by Marxist, feminist, postmodernist, and post-colonial critique are slowly shaping the telling of history (Southgate, 1996). For example, even though researchers' interest in historiography seems to be on the rise, there remains a lack of "herstorical perspective" (L'Etang, 2015, p. 355) and a "sketchy" history of women in public relations (Creedon, 1989, p. 26). Also, postmodernists view first generations of history as outdated due to the emphasis on positivism. Foucault (1972) pointed out that history, as discourse, is shaped by power relations which ultimately define *which* stories of history are told and *how* they are told. From a constructivist standpoint, history is in flux and a "permanently contested terrain" shaped by critique and revision (Wehmeier, 2015, p. 95).

Revisionist History

Examining history in a contemporary light enables us to see both the past and the present with a hindsight that fuels a critical view of people and events as they unfolded long ago. *Historiography* is a concept describing the analysis of the theory and history of historical writing (Wehmeier (2015). Thus, (re)discovering the past is a theme explored in this book in order to add a more equitable, fair, and well-rounded facet to the U.S. history of public relations that heretofore has relied on telling limited narratives steeped in twentieth-century industry and the development of the mass media. Discovering the past is rooted in a critique of why a certain event or person never made it to the pages of history in the first place. For those who study and practice public relations, culling through events of the past is an exercise that requires a broadening of the popular definition of *public relations* and calls for a critique of the way in which founding of the profession has been framed almost exclusively by the work of three Caucasian/White men. We may better understand the practice and theorizing in the present of public relations through historical studies of its development (Gower, 2006). Calling for a more radical consideration of public relations historiography, McKie and Xifra (2012) called for a postmodern approach that examines phenomena from bottom to top rather than top down.

In historiography, revisionist history offers a re-interpretation of the historical record. *Revisionist history* usually means challenging established and traditional views held by professional scholars about a historical event, introducing new data, incorporating developments from other fields, considering new perspectives gained by the passage of time, or reinterpreting the motivations and decisions of the people involved. Some revisionists call into question moral teachings amplified in the telling of history, such as European colonization of the Americas and Reconstruction in the U.S. following the Civil War. Historical revisionism also means simply introducing new evidence or interpretations. McPherson (2003), former president of the American Historical Association, described revision as "the lifeblood of historical scholarship [and] history [as] a continuing dialogue between the present and the past." Revisionism makes history "vital and meaningful" (McPherson, 2003), drawing parallels with U.S. Supreme Court decisions that take contemporary application and meaning making into account. Feminist studies scholars routinely engage in adding new and additional interpretations of history from women's perspectives given that a feminist research agenda is concerned with empowering women. Trained historians interpret accounts and classify their significance. I do not profess to be a historian. Yet, my training as a communication and public relations scholar enables me to offer new interpretations of professional public relations precursors in *the context of* the function of early community-building in public relations. Waller (1978) encouraged each generation of teachers to "re-examine its teaching of history" (p. 201) and for *revisionists* to amend the focus on which history is taught.

Learning about Professional Public Relations History

While many public relations researchers have reflected on the historiography of public relations (e.g., McKie & Xifra, 2014; Olasky, 1987; Pearson, 1992; Szyszka, 1997), perhaps the best way to investigate how public relations history is told is to examine the field's textbooks written to educate college students to be tomorrow's professional practitioners and researchers. Conventional approaches to public relations history suggest that as a tool of persuasion and conflict resolution, it is "as old as civilization" (Kruckeberg & Starck, 1988, p. 4).

The timing for benchmarking the history of public relations is established in public relations textbooks, as well as in practitioners' speeches and memoirs, and in obituaries (Fitch, 2016a). Cutlip's (1995) *History of Public Relations: From the 17th to the 20th Century* offers a benchmark set by navigators who promoted the land and people of Virginia to audiences back home in sixteenth-century England. Watson (2013) suggested that the public relations field emerged in reaction to press agentry persuasion tools used to convince non-indigenous Americans to travel and settle in the West (Kruckeberg & Starck, 1988). Some public relations researchers tend to time stamp the emergence of professional public relations with the end of the U.S. Civil War in 1865 and with the commercial growth of the mass media in the early twentieth century – both benchmarks occurring after "the frontier disappeared" (Kruckeberg & Starck, 1988, p. 5). Many scholars accept that "*public relations* – as the concept is used today – is seen primarily as a twentieth century phenomenon" (Kruckeberg & Starck, 1988, p. 6). Other U.S. public relations scholars tend to build on this standard by positioning public relations as a profession that has progressed over time and become increasingly sophisticated and ethical in the process (e.g., Gower, 2006, 2007; Grunig & Hunt, 1984). For example, this linear model suggests that professional public relations techniques emerged following a period of press agentry when corporations needed to tell their side of the story after muckrakers' newspaper and magazine exposés about the negative effects of industrial and commercial expansion. Not all U.S.-based researchers subscribe to the linear framework, however. Some have written that the stages of the manipulation, information, and then mutual influence/ understanding of public relations have co-existed all along (e.g., Aronoff & Baskin, 1983).

Generations of college students rely on learning about the past from textbooks which feminist theory critiques suggest have embedded shortcomings. It is not unusual to find "narrowness and inadequacies" among conventional historical narratives (Morrissey, 1992, p. 134) – so that conventional college textbooks may "come close to ignoring women entirely" (Riley, 1994, p. xii). In public relations, Cutlip, Center, and Broom's popular *Effective Public Relations* (1952), now in its 11th edition, is a bestseller on Amazon.com, with a slight title change to *Cutlip & Center's Effective Public Relations* and now authored by Glen M. Broom and Bey-Ling Sha (2013). This textbook is on the Public Relations Society of America's (PRSA's) Accredited Public Relations exam "shortlist" for exam study resources, www.praccreditation.org/resources/ recommended-texts/index.html (B.-L. Sha, personal communication, October 28, 2019). Broom and Sha's (2013) chapter devoted to public relations history has changed a bit over the years and now briefly mentions the twentieth-century achievements of Doris E. Fleischman and Betsy Plank. A scan of the book's index for *women* lists only two, both from the eighteenth century – a Caucasian/White woman who published anti-British plays and poems and an African-American woman author and former slave. Cutlip's (1995) textbook devoted exclusively to public relations history liberally covers contributions made by a series of men, including Amos Kendall, member of U.S. President Andrew Jackson's kitchen cabinet and several other male political leaders and supporters.

Altogether, public relations history seems to have two fathers, but noticeably absent from recorded public relations history telling are detailed stories about the mothers. Rather, male public relations practitioners such as Ivy Lee and Edward Bernays long have been attributed with founding U.S. public relations practice early in the twentieth century on account of their ability to help organizations to motivate the public in ways favorable to them. Ivy Lee (1877– 1934) is said to have invented the public relations profession when he opened a consultancy in 1904. The other oft-credited "father of PR" figure is Edward Bernays (1891–1995), whom it is said invented the public relations profession in the 1920s. This benchmark made sense given twentieth-century's Progressivism with attention to increasing efficiency in the workplace and on the farm, fighting for social reform to combat poverty, responding to the growth of the mass media, and a growing spirit of optimism (Gower, 2007). Bernays is credited with writing the first public relations textbook (DiStaso, 2019) and teaching the first public relations class in 1932 (Broom & Sha, 2013). When Ewen (1996) wrote his "social history of public relations," (p. 5), he had the benefit of interviewing 104-year-old Bernays before his passing in 1995 as well as examining Bernays' lifetime body of writing. In 1990, *Life* magazine had published a biography of Bernays and included it in a special issue dedicated to the *one hundred most influential Americans of the twentieth century*. Similarly, Ivy Lee's turn from journalist to spokesman for the Rockefeller family in 1914 when he was hired to perform damage control cemented his place in public relations history (Hallahan, 2002). Hiebert's (2017) biography of the "father of public relations" explained how Lee provided opinion leaders with Standard Oil's perspective following exposés by muckraking Progressive Era journalists like Ida Tarbell whose investigative journalism eventually led to the breakup of Standard Oil's monopoly. Lamme (2015) persuasively argued that both Lee and Bernays strategically crafted their public personae and were skilled at shaping their own legacies beyond serving clients.

The findings of a deconstructionist critique of the five most popular public relations textbooks suggested that the framing of public relations in a modernist approach was due for postmodernist updating. The traditional linear advancement model promotes a "PR progress myth" (Duffy, 2000, p. 312) as a line that connects a progression of persuasion tools throughout Antiquity (e.g., Christianity), then leaps forward to Ivy Lee's advocating for John D. Rockefeller Jr. when dealing with striking coal miners in 1914. Such bookends offer a limited, modernist history of public relations as "an almost seamless story of the evolution and continuing improvement of public relations practice" (Duffy, 2000, p. 297). Alternatively, a postmodern pedagogy might see public relations history as a "series of stories told from different perspectives and focus on the concrete experiences of public relations workers" by adding "previously muffled voices and heretofore unseen viewpoints" (Duffy, 2000, p. 313). Supplementing the historical record of public relations with women's community-building contributions prior to the twentieth century could enable students to critically de-institutionalize a limited view of the profession. Incidentally, standard college/university textbooks on Western history also ignored women prior to the 1990s for the most part (Riley, 1994).

Many public relations textbooks around the globe offer a limited view of public relations history embedded with U.S.-centric examples (Fitch, 2016a). In Europe, this perspective on the history of public relations merely echoes U.S. corporate and government communication activities (L'Etang, 2008; McKie & Munshie, 2007). While serving as the editor of *Journal of Public Relations Research*, Linda Hon told an audience of Association for Education in Journalism and Mass Communication (AEJMC) members during the 2004 annual convention in Toronto that, overall, too little research is emerging on public relations history. Similarly, Lamme and Russell (2010) argued for a "broad, long-term view" of a time before industrialization and of additional contexts such as "the political and sociocultural sphere" (p. 281). We have much to learn about the roles women played in the development of professional public relations because public relations history has not been a welcoming space for women or people of color. Failure to incorporate women's contributions to the development of our field has grave implications, including a stymying effect on the integration of theories across disciplines. Incorporating women's achievements in our history could encourage other disciplines to cite our research and provide role models for our students who are predominantly women in the U.S. The results of not including women in public relations history made it clear over a decade ago that public relations research was "at a crossroads" and that we must explore new options while "questioning our knowledge base" (Gower, 2006, pp. 177, 178).

One way to address the shortcomings of our field's history and to better understand our present is to look at "why public relations developed in the first place" (Gower, 2006, p. 181). While most U.S.-based public relations history researchers have grounded history telling in the development of industry and the mass media, the study reported in this book examines the roles of individual women who traveled the Oregon Trail throughout the nineteenth century and settled in present-day Oregon, a community-building journey of physical, emotional, and practical dimensions. History studies steeped in examining women's lived experiences as evidence of community-building precursors to professional public relations practice means formal organizations and the mass media are not required to background early public relations work.

In particular, three important, inspired, and inspiring edited collections have begun filling the gaps in public relations history beyond the achievements of Caucasian/White men (Straughan, 2007), through entry points other than U.S.-centric perspectives (St. John III, Lamme, & L'Etang, 2014), and as a critique of the ways both the past and present can power imagined futures (Somerville, Edwards, & Ihlen, 2019). Gibbons (2008) described essays in Straughan (2007) as adding "illuminating detail to the underreported history of women in public relations' development" (p. 202). McCoy (2008) applauded emphases that "women played a significant role in the development of public relations … before Ivy Lee and Edward Bernays hung out their shingles and laid claim to the profession" (p. 123). St. John III and colleagues' (2014) edited collection builds upon the International History of Public Relations Conference momentum by moving beyond traditional models for a "very welcome scholarly addition to the expanding field of public relations history" (Watson, 2014). The most recent collection of essays on public relations history engages with four key themes – challenging managerial corporatism, difference and diversity, the political sphere, and nationalism and identity (Somerville, Edwards, & Ihlen, 2019). Together, these books should prove useful for faculty looking to offer a broad understanding of public relations practice and its history. When teaching the introductory public relations course in the U.S., many faculty members supplement the popular traditional textbooks with lived experiences and voices that are minimal or non-existent among so many pedagogic resources (Ertem-Eray & Pompper, 2020). So, we must ask: Is it appropriate to talk about the work of public relations before the term was invented? L'Etang (2008) opined that it is, adding that doing so is necessary to contextualize the *public relations* concept, to locating it as a form of human communication, and to offering a means of connecting public relations to "more richly textured understandings of the discipline" (p. 329). This is not to say that writing public relations history is without theoretical and methodological challenges. Recognizing both the opportunities and the limitations of historical paradigms and methods must be acknowledged.

Why Study Pioneer Women's Oregon Trail Experience?

The decision to investigate the community-building work of Oregon Trail pioneer women as "particular in the context of an overall human story" (L'Etang, 2014, p. xx) is one shaped by the author and her point of view on history. In other words, writing about history is a series of interpretations of key texts – in this case, diaries, journals, and reminiscences – underscoring the fact that there never will be what public relations historian L'Etang (2014) called a "universal or right history" (p. xxi). The means of addressing this subjectivity issue include steeping history writing in theory building and the "scale of time" (L'Etang, 2014, p. xxi), or contextualizing people and events amidst epochs or social change (Ewen, 1996). Invoking Bloch's (1954) formative training, L'Etang (2014) also recommended making history writing processes as transparent as possible. In research findings reported here, this advice is used to make a historical explanation "intelligible" by revealing "basic pattern[s]"

Table 0.1 Texts Examined

Pioneer Woman	Diary	Journal, Daybook	Reminiscences[2]
Cecilia E. Adams[1]	1852		
Keturah Belknap	1848		
Parthenia Blank[1]	1852		
Arvazna A. Spillman Cooper			1863/1901
Mrs. S. D. Evans			1861/1863
Elizabeth Julia Ellison Goltra		1853	
Amelia A. Hammond Hadley	1851		
Jane (Jennie) Paul Eakin Hanna	1866		
Amelia Stewart Knight	1853		
Harriet A. Loughary		1864	
J. A. Newell			1848/1901
Lydia Allen Rudd	1852		
Julia Thomas			1859/1907

[1] Twin sisters
[2] Oregon Trail travel year/year reminiscences put to paper

(Berlin, 1974, pp. 162–163) in women's lived experiences as recorded in their first-person texts.

Formal Research Method

Outlined next is the structure built for investigating the phenomenon of Oregon Trail community-building women as a precursor to formal public relations practice. Personal diaries and journals offer a unique opportunity to discover an author's inner voice "as a way to explore ambivalent, everyday experiences and interrogate the role of diaries as a form of confessional or measurement of private life" (Harvey, 2011, p. 664). L'Etang (2010) posited that public relations is an anthropological activity, so investigating texts of the past in order to provide revisionist accounts of public relations history makes sense. Attempting to differentiate between the operationalizations of *diary, journal* and *log*, Mallon (1984) resolved that they're "hopelessly muddled" (p. 1). Travers (2011) related *journal* to a daily newspaper concept and considered the *diary* as a much more intimate form since putting thoughts on paper appears to calm some people, enabling them to focus "in an almost meditational way" (p. 215). A *reminiscence* may be likened to a *reflection*, which is "the process of internally examining and exploring an issue of concern" (Boyd & Fales, 1983, p. 99). Each of these text forms offers a repository for experiences and feelings. Comparatively, gender differences emerged between nineteenth-century pioneer men who wrote in diaries about "fight, conflict and competition and ... hunting" while women wrote in diaries about "family and relational values" (Faragher, 1979, p. 14). Oregon Trail pioneer women's private writing, as their informal talk, contradicted the notion that nineteenth-century women were completely submissive, pure, and fully occupied with leisure domesticity (Jameson, 1987). With reference to pioneer women's diaries, Riley (2004) explained that the women were "somewhat educated" so they recorded their thoughts and experiences to chronicle what they found significant or to share a personal record with family "back East" or in Europe (p. 2).

Methodologically, examining diaries, journals, and reminiscences requires significant amounts of time and extreme attention to detail in order to evaluate Oregon Trail pioneer women's motives and actions. A field of history called the *new social history* amplifies lived experience of the past (Morrissey, 1992) and treats those experiences as data. Examining diaries as source materials benefits qualitative method researchers exploring historical phenomena from a practical standpoint (Alaszewski, 2006; Coxon, 1996). Phenomenological research methods and pedagogy scholar, Max Van Manen (1990), has encouraged discovery of patterns, or themes, among lived experiences in texts. Furthermore, "impressionist tales," characterized by ethnographer John Van Maanen (1988, p. 103), have been likened to "reflexive accounts" (Elliott, 2005, p. 164) among feminist method researchers (e.g., Ribbins & Edwards, 1997). Some women who kept diaries of their Oregon Trail journey provided exceptional detail (like impressionist painters) that "draw[s] the audience into an unfamiliar story world and allow[s] it ... to see, hear, and feel" what an ethnographic fieldworker might experience (Van Maanen, 1988, p. 103). Like others who have studied diaries as text and preserved "variances in spelling" (Webber, 1990, p. 13), I made no changes and preserved typos, misspellings, and grammatical errors in this analysis. Both twin sisters Cecilia E. Adams and Parthenia Blank wrote a diary in 1852 and even though some stenographers are confident they can discern between the two women's writings, I consider the diary as one text and combine the authors' names when citing it. The text available for analysis features notes by those who typed the handwritten words and used different typefaces and noted lost pages at the beginning of the diary (Webber, 1990). Questions about the freedom of women's voices and intentions also must be considered. For example, it is impossible to determine all the factors influencing individual first-person accounts. Spacks (1975) noted that pioneer woman Arvazna Angeline Cooper worried about her writing appearing "so personal as to seem egotistical" so she switched to writing in the third person.

Throughout this book, I've given careful thought to labels used to describe people and lands, as I worked to offer respectful analysis. When citing specific research, I used those authors' labels of social identity dimensions (e.g., gender, ethnicity, religion, etc.). As for myself, I use *emigrants, pioneers, frontierspeople, European descendants, Mid-westerners, Easterners*, and *Caucasians/Whites* to describe those who traveled the Overland Trails in general and Oregon Trail in particular. Butruille (1993) used *pioneer* to describe people only after they settled, but I tend to use *pioneer* across the experience of travel and settlement. Yet, I concur that the use of *immigrant* and *emigrant* is grounded in whether people were coming or going – or departing or arriving. I refer to *Native Americans* and *indigenous peoples* interchangeably, reserving *Indians* and *American Indians* for quoted material of others. Regarding names attached to the land, I use *Oregon Country* and *Oregon Territory* before U.S. statehood and then *Oregon* when the lands were incorporated into the Union as the thirty-third state on February 14, 1859.

I used Van Manen's (1990) hermeneutic phenomenological technique to discern patterns among Oregon Trail women's diaries (seven), journals/daybooks (two), and reminiscences (four) archived at the University of Oregon Knight Library, Special Collections, in Eugene, Oregon, to identify themes that bind together stories of their community-building journey.

According to Van Manen (1990), themes are best handled when they emerge among voices characterizing lived experiences. I and a female doctoral student read all the texts independently and together to get a sense of the data, making notes along the way. Historical writing goes beyond the telling of a story and following L'Etang's (2008) advice offers reflexivity in history writing. We both are women of higher education with terminal degrees, she is in her 30s and was born in Turkey and I am in my 50s and was born in the U.S. Women's voices, their individual perceptions, stories, and hand-drawn doodles chronicling experiences in their own hand constituted the unit of analysis.

Then, consistent with Glaser and Strauss' (1967) grounded theory approach to qualitative data, notes – beginnings of emergent patterns/themes – were recorded on index cards which were placed in piles and reshuffled as needed. The number of index cards was reduced and consolidated down to an essence, with proposed labels ongoing as some theme labels were rejected, resurrected, and modified along the way.

Notes on the cards were then transferred to an Excel spreadsheet and organized in columns reflecting emergent theme labels on the index cards. Finally, all the texts were re-read and examples of each theme were noted on the Excel spreadsheet, according to Van Manen's (1990) selective technique of pondering statements and phrases that seem particularly revealing or remarkable. Anomalies also were noted, as advised by Miles and Huberman (1994) and closely attended to and integrated into findings for enhanced understanding and nuance. The goal was to portray the lived experiences of women as they performed community-building work. According to Wehmeier (2015), performing reflective historiography is telling stories about "ways to construct a historic picture consisting of events and their multipolar and multi-layered narratives that should be seen as discourse" (p. 106).

Examining Women's First-Person Texts

One's life writing may take several forms. When investigating nineteenth-century women's experiences, diaries often constitute the only means by which we can reconstruct many women's use of language (Hoffman & Culley, 1985), and often the only form women were allowed to practice (Huff, 1989). Diaries, daybooks, and journals – as recordings of everyday intimate experiences – constitute "artistry as a form of autobiography" (Bunkers, 1990, p. 115). Also, diaries are filled with descriptions of intimate moments that may be likened to a "therapeutic encounter" (Birch & Miller, 2000, p. 189). While diary entries may appear to be random or aimless, Hogan (1991) posited that the diary as a feminine form constitutes important engendered autobiography as text for analysis.

Critical textual analysis approaches are useful for investigating the diary, journal, and remembrance forms as text. Central to the purpose of study findings revealed throughout this book, diaries are "about community, not hierarchy, about communication, not authority" (Huff, 1989, p. 6) and the diary enables researchers to ask questions, make connections, and establish community among diarists' lived experience recordings (Rich, 1979). Journals, too, are "that profoundly female, and feminist genre" (Rich, 1979, p. 217). Reminiscences are a form of remembering after time has passed and this too constitutes important feminist research text. Systematically examining these forms to assess women's lived experiences as each unfolded in the nineteenth century served as the text analyzed.

There are several important considerations when examining first-person texts for research, such as concerns about accuracy or subjectivity. Researchers must consider at least four sets of limitations associated with using diaries, journals, daybooks, and reminiscences as data for historical analyses. First, the voices captured are those of literate, "educated (middle) classes" (Norwood, 1988, p. 163), which means voices of women of the lowest socioeconomic classes may not be represented. As Méndez-González (1987) noted, women of poor, slave, or laboring classes do not tend to leave diaries. Without doubt, some of the texts analyzed were written by women of elementary education levels, as evidenced by misspellings and grammatical shortcomings. Second, diarists choose to tell a certain perspective on events (Harvey, 2011). Third, it is customary to detect a change in a diarist's behavior over the course of recording in a diary. Similarly, reminiscences written in hindsight years after the Oregon Trail journey may be shaped by events of the day, or be cast in a "rosy glow" after the trip (Jeffrey, 1998, p. 37) or "rosy hue" that may not have matched reality (Riley, 1994) as women writing after the event tended to be more positive about the frontier experience than those who wrote diaries during migration (Norwood, 1988). Finally, nineteenth-century women used the margins of their diaries to add thoughts, often lacking in grammar, spelling, or punctuation accuracy, but what may seem like "unforthcoming writing may actually contain a wealth of concrete information about the texture of women's lives" (Carter, 1999, p. 56). Historians have found that some original handwritten dairies, journals, and letters that were typed (bonus for readability!) also were edited/censored by the typist, perhaps to spare a family embarrassment. For example, some historians have contrasted original documents with transcribed pages and discovered references to pregnancy and sex have been censored (Butruille, 1993). Estimating how many families removed a "woman's ramblings" from their papers before donating them to archives, libraries, or historical societies is impossible (Riley, 1994, p. xii). Despite these shortcomings, feminist historians have applauded the "Renaissance of the American feminist movement of the 1960s" for amplifying women's voices across history (Riley, 1994, p. xii). Enduring female gender myths and stereotypes may be attributed to long supported ignorance of the cultural import of women's diaries and strategic attempts to suppress pioneer women's documents "to keep women's voices subordinate to male-directed history" (Riley, 1994, p. xii).

Digging into long-ago events by scouring library archives also presents challenges for those who write about public relations history. First, researchers are at the mercy of library administrators who have decided what to acquire and how to file it, label it, and preserve it. Second, researchers must be prepared to spend vast amounts of time reading and re-reading through archived materials to discover those which are relevant and useful for a particular project. Third, researchers must expand their traditional reading bandwidth to discover important contexts to explain the roots of public relations and roles of individuals representing specific social identity groups, such as women. Finally, reading original source materials objectively in order to discern women's true feelings about their conditions and to separate these from a researcher's personal expressions of sympathy or frustration is a challenging task (Riley, 1994).

In the current study's investigation of the community-building experiences of women who traveled the Oregon Trail and settled in Oregon Country/ Territory, women are the main characters of the diaries, journals, and reminiscences and not secondary or support players. Investigating public relations history research by using first-person narrative texts enables a backward reflection that must be placed in context when drawing parallels with present-day public relations practice. Historical documents serve as "important guides for feminism because they provide alternate understandings of gender relations today" (Corn, 2014). The process of writing women into the past involves negotiating a complex interplay of social identity differences in a broad context of social and spatial conditions out of which authors landscape and produce one another (Scott, 1992). The chronicling of early development of the U.S. public relations field took place before feminist theory was introduced to the public relations body of knowledge to explain and predict gender-power dynamics in practice and research (Hon, 1995). I suggest that examining public relations beyond industrial development and the founding of large organizations, and before the explosion of the mass media enables researchers to escape the narrow bounds of men's work in the twentieth-century public sphere. Exceptional circumstances enabled ordinary women to find their voice in the nineteenth century.

Chapter Synopses

The study reported in this book unfolds across three main units: 1) *Overview*, providing the backdrop for a critique of how the grounding of professional public relations history's roots in the twentieth century has excluded women's voices, 2) *Gendering and Expanding Roles as Early Public Relations Work*, revealing key themes of women's roles as *Caretaker/Advocate* (meal preparer, healer, childcare provider, livestock care provider, conflict negotiator, ambassador/liaison), as *Community Builder of Meeting Houses and Schools*, and as embodying the *Civilizing Function* – which involved developing skills shaped by new circumstances that ultimately influenced social change through community building, and 3) *Ideologies, Women's Work, and the Female Frontier*, understanding the way pioneer women forged *Emotional Connections for Social Cohesion* provided agency and leadership on the Oregon Trail and beyond while homesteading.

Chapter 1: "(Re)discovering the Past in Order to Understand Public Relations History Today" explores the ways public relations and the writing of public relations history has defined the practice, critiques the implications of gaps in public relations history, offers the study's research question, introduces the community-building framework, provides the study's theoretical underpinning (feminist theory, feminist historical geography, network theory, social constructionism), and outlines history's sources for women's voices.

Chapter 2: "Re-examining the American West's Lure and Women's Role Representations" looks at the lure of the American West, addresses frontier history's representations of women/femininity, offers the context of Oregon statehood through the Homestead Act of 1862, unfolds the lure of the American West as it shaped collective memory, incorporates gendering and examining ways we make meaning about gender and race as part of history about the West, explores the challenges of the Oregon Trail journey which impacted women's perspectives, incorporates collective memory about pioneer women, and considers women's voices as historians.

Chapter 3: "Interrogating Pioneer Women's Role as *Caretaker/Advocate*" broadly explores female gender roles in the nineteenth century with the Civil War as a backdrop, examines the blurred and broken lines of gendered division of labor, and introduces the theme of Oregon Trail women's *Caretaker/Advocate* role.

Chapter 4: "Exploring Public Relations from the Care Perspective: Pioneer Women's Role as *Community Builder of Meeting Houses and Schools*" addresses how adopting a care perspective enabled pioneer women to transition to settlement and then network, becoming community organizers and planners, as well as entrepreneurs in developing commerce.

Chapter 5: "*Civilizing Function*: Pioneer Women and Religion" explores the part women played in taming the wilderness, adapting their religion and spiritual life, embarking on missionary work, and offering moral guidance, the use of religion for recovery and relationship building, and a critique of religion's uneasy fit with race in Oregon's history.

Chapter 6: "Understanding Pioneer Women's *Agency and Leadership*" challenges traditional historical accounts by illustrating women's leadership on the plains through suffrage, including women's decision-making for network building, strategic planning for endurance, and managing to stay alive and thrive.

Chapter 7: "Expanding Women's Role: *Emotional Connection for Social Cohesion*" explores the female frontier and the recording of the landscape, while simultaneously harboring apprehension toward Native American people and communities. This paradox underscores the violent side of Oregon's homesteading history, and invites exploration of the ways ideology, stereotyping, and captivity narratives shaped women's lived experiences.

Chapter 8: "Concluding Thoughts and Direction for Discovering More Women's Voices for Public Relations History" offers the significance of research findings, provides advice for moving forward with the expansion of U.S. public relations history enterprise, explains the ways in which the expansion of public relations history impulse could be made global, and concludes with some final thoughts.

Chapter 1 gets the journey started with a critique of the ways the limited understandings of public relations' past also has limited the ways we currently think of public relations practice and women's roles as practitioners.

References

Adejunmobi, S. A. (1979). The biographical approach to the teaching of history. *The History Teacher*, 12(3), 349–357.

Alaszewski, A. (2006). *Using diaries for social research*. London: Sage.

Aronoff, C. E., & Baskin, O. W. (1983). *Public relations: The profession and the practice*. St. Paul, MN: West Publishing Co.

Berlin, I. (1974). Historical inevitability. In P. Gardiner (ed.), *The philosophy of history* (pp. 162–163). Oxford: Oxford University Press.

Birch, M., & Miller, T. (2000). Inviting intimacy: The interview as therapeutic opportunity. *International Journal of Social Research Methodology*, 3(3), 189–202.

Bloch, M. (1954). *The historian's craft: Reflections on the nature and uses of history and the techniques and methods of historical writing*. Manchester: Manchester University Press.

Boyd, E. M., & Fales, A. W. (1983). Reflective learning. *Journal of Humanistic Psychology*, 23(2), 99–117.

Broom, G. M., & Sha, B-L. (2013). *Cutlip & Center's effective public relations* (11th edn). Upper Saddle River, NJ: Prentice-Hall.

Bunkers, S. L. (1990). Subjectivity and self-reflexivity in the study of women's diaries as autobiography. *Auto/biography Studies*, 5(2), 114–123.

Burns, K. (Writer), Duncan, D. (Writer), & Burns, K. (Director) (1997). *Lewis & Clark: The Journey of the Corps of Discovery*. Washington, DC: Public Broadcasting Service.

Burns, R. (Writer), & Burns, R. (Director) (1992). The American Experience [Television series episode]. In J. Crichton (Executive Producer), *The Donner Party*. Boston, MA: WGBH Public Broadcasting Service.

Butruille, S. G. (1993). *Women's voices from the Oregon Trail: The times that tried women's souls and a guide to women's history along the Oregon Trail*. Boise, ID: Tamarack Books, Inc.

Carter, K. (1999). An economy of words: Emma Chadwick Stretch's account book diary, 1859–1860. *Acadiensis*, 29(1), 43–56.

Corn, G. (2014). Elementary feminisms: How useful is a feminist approach to history for historians? Accessed August 14, 2019, from https://thefeministwire.com/2014/10/useful-feminist-approach-history-historians.

Coxon, A. (1996). *Between the sheets: Sexual diaries and gay men's sex in the era of AIDS*. London: Cassell.

Creedon, P. J. (1989). Public relations history misses "her story." *Journalism Educator*, 44(3), 26–30.

Cross, C. F. (1995). *Go West young man! Horace Greeley's vision for America*. Albuquerque, NM: University of New Mexico Press.

Cutlip, S. M. (1995). *Public relations history: From the 17th to the 20th century. The antecedents*. Hillsdale, NJ: Lawrence Erlbaum Associates.

DiStaso, M. (2019). Undergraduate public relations in the United States: The 2017 Commission on Public Relations Report. *Journal of Public Relations Education*, 5(3), 3–22.

Duffy, M. E. (2000). There's no two-way symmetrical about it: A postmodern examination of public relations textbooks. *Critical Studies in Media Communication*, 17(3), 294–315.

Elliott, J. (2005). *The researcher as narrator: Reflexivity in qualitative and quantitative research*. Thousand Oaks, CA: Sage.

Ertem-Eray, T., & Pompper, D. (2020). Reconstructing the PR history time machine: Missing women and people of color in introductory textbooks. Paper presented at

the Association for the Education in Journalism and Mass Communication Conference, San Francisco, CA, August 6–10, August 6.
Ewen, S. (1996). *PR! A social history of spin*. New York: Basic Books.
Faragher, J. (1979). *Women and men on the Overland Trail*. New Haven, CT: Yale University Press.
Fitch, K. (2016a). *Professionalizing public relations: History, gender and education*. London: Palgrave Macmillan.
Fitch, K. (2016b). Feminism and public relations. In J. L'Etang, D. McKie, N. Snow, & J. Xifra (eds), *Routledge handbook of critical public relations* (pp. 54–64). Abingdon: Routledge.
Foucault, M. (1972). *The archaeology of knowledge and the discourse on language*. New York: Pantheon Books.
Foucault, M. (1980). *Power/knowledge*. Brighton: Tavistock.
Gibbons, S. J. (2008). Review of *Women's use of public relations for Progressive-era reform: Rousing the conscience of a nation*, D. M. Straughan (ed.), *Public Relations Review*, 27(3), 202–203.
Glaser, B. G., & Strauss, A. L. (1967). *The discovery of grounded theory: Strategies for qualitative research*. Chicago, IL: Aldine Publishing Group.
Gower, K. K. (2006). Public relations at the crossroads. *Journal of Public Relations Research*, 18(2), 177–190.
Gower, K. K. (2007). Introduction. In D. M. Straughan (ed.), *Women's use of public relations or Progressive-era reform: Rousing the conscience of a nation* (pp. 1–8). Lewiston, NY: Edwin Mellen Press.
Grunig, J. E., & Hunt, T. (1984) *Managing public relations*. New York: Holt, Rinehart and Winston.
Hallahan, K. (2002). Ivy Lee and the Rockefellers' response to the 1913–1914 Colorado coal strike. *Journal of Public Relations Research*, 14(4), 265–315.
Harvey, L. (2011). Intimate reflections: Private diaries in qualitative research. *Qualitative Research*, 11(6), 664–682.
Heath, R. L., & Coombs, W. T. (2006). *Today's public relations: An introduction*. Thousand Oaks, CA: Sage.
Hiebert, E. R. (2017). *Courtier to the crowd: Ivy Lee and the development of public relations in America*. New York: PR Museum Press.
Hoffman, L., & Culley, M. (eds) (1985). *Women's personal narratives: Essays in criticism and pedagogy*. New York: Modern Language Association of America.
Hogan, R. (1991). Engendered autobiographies: The diary as a feminine form. In S. Neuman (ed.), *Autobiography and questions of gender* (pp. 186–212). London: Frank Cass.
Holmes, K. L. (2008). *Best of covered wagon women*. Norman, OK: University of Oklahoma Press.
Hon, L. (1995). Toward a feminist theory of public relations. *Journal of Public Relations Research*, 7, 27–88.
Huff, C. (1989). That profoundly female, and feminist genre: The diary as feminist practice. *Women's Studies Quarterly*, 17(3/4), 6–14.
Jameson, E. (1987). Women as workers, women as civilizers: True womanhood in the American West. In S. Armitage, & E. Jameson (eds), *Writing the range: Race, class, and culture in the women's West* (pp. 145–164). Norman, OK: University of Oklahoma Press.

Jameson, E. (1988). Toward a multicultural history of women in the Western United States. *Signs*, 13(4), 761–791.

Jeffrey, J. R. (1998). *Frontier women: Civilizing the west? 1840–1880*. New York: Hill & Wang.

Kruckeberg, D., & Starck, K. (1988). *Public relations and community: A reconstructed theory*. New York: Praeger.

Lamme, M. O. (2015). Where the quiet work is done: Biography in public relations. In T. Watson (ed.), *Perspectives on public relations historiography and historical theorization: Other voices* (pp. 48–68). New York: Palgrave Macmillan.

Lamme, M. O., & Russell, K. M. (2010). Removing the spin: Toward a new theory of public relations history. *Journalism Monographs*, 11(4), 281–362.

L'Etang, J. (2008). Writing PR history: Issues, methods and politics. *Journal of Communication Management*, 12(3), 319–335.

L'Etang, J. (2010). Making it real: Anthropological reflections on public relations, diplomacy, and rhetoric. In R. L. Heath (ed.), *The Sage handbook of public relations* (2nd edn) (pp. 145–162). Thousand Oaks, CA: Sage.

L'Etang, J. (2014). Writing PR history: Issues, methods and politics. In B. St. John III, M. O. Lamme, & J. L'Etang (eds), *Pathways to public relations: Histories of practice and Profession* (pp. xix–xxxviii). Abingdon: Routledge.

L'Etang, J. (2015). "It's always been a sexless trade;" "It's clean work;" "That's very little velvet curtain:" Gender and public relations in post-Second World War Britain. *Journal of Communication Management*, 19(4), 354–370.

Mallon, T. (1984). *A book of one's own: People and their diaries*. London: Picador Books.

McCoy, J. R. (2008). Review of *Women's use of public relations for Progressive-era reform: Rousing the conscience of a nation*, D. M. Straughan (ed.), *American Journalism*, 25(2), 123–125.

McKie, D., & Munshi, D. (2007). *Reconfiguring public relations: Ecology, equity and enterprise*. Abingdon: Routledge.

McKie, D., & Xifra, J. (2012). Re-resourcing PR history's next stage: New historiography and other relevant stories. Presentation to the International History of Public Relations Conference, Bournemouth University, July 11–12, July 11.

McKie, D., & Xifra, J. (2014). Resourcing the next stages in PR history research: The case for historiography. *Public Relations Review*, 40, 669–675.

McPherson, J. (2003). From the president: Revisionist historians. Accessed January 14, 2020, from www.historians.org/publications-and-directories/perspectives-on-history/september-2003/revisionist-historians

Méndez-González, R. (1987). Distinctions in Western women's experience: Ethnicity, class, and social change. In S. Armitage & E. Jameson (eds), *Writing the range: Race, class, and culture in the women's West* (pp. 237–251). Norman, OK: University of Oklahoma Press.

Miles, M. B., & Huberman, A. M. (1994). *Qualitative data analysis* (2nd edn). Thousand Oaks, CA: Sage.

Miller, M. M., & Stearns, P. N. (1995). Applying cognitive learning approaches in history teaching: An experiment in a world history course. *The History Teacher*, 28(2), 183–204.

Morrissey, K. G. (1992). Engendering the West. In W. Cronon, G. Miles, & J. Gitlin (eds), *Under an open sky: Rethinking America's western past* (pp. 132–144). New York: W. W. Norton & Company.

Norwood, V. (1988). Women's place: Continuity and change in response to Western landscapes. In L. Schlissel, V. L. Ruiz, & J. J. Monk, *Western women: Their land, their lives* (pp. 155–181). Albuquerque, NM: University of New Mexico Press.

Olasky, M. N. (1987). *Corporate public relations: A new historical perspective*. Hillsdale, NJ: Lawrence Erlbaum Associates.

Pearson, R. (1992). Perspectives in public relations history. In E. Toth & R. Heath (eds), *Rhetorical and critical approaches to public relations* (pp. 152–174). Hillsdale, NJ: Lawrence Erlbaum Associates.

Pratt, J. W. (1927). The origin of 'Manifest Destiny'. *The American Historical Review*, 32(4), 795–798.

Ribbins, J., & Edwards, R. (1997). *Feminist dilemmas in qualitative research: Public knowledge and private lives*. Thousand Oaks, CA: Sage.

Rich, A. (1979). *On lies, secrets, and silence*. New York: Norton.

Riley, G. (1988). *The female frontier: A comparative view of women on the prairie and the plains*. Lawrence, KS: University Press of Kansas.

Riley, G. (1994). *Frontierswomen: The Iowa experience*. Ames, IA: Iowa State University Press.

Riley, G. (2004). *Confronting race: Women and Indians on the frontier, 1825–1915*. Albuquerque, NM: University of New Mexico Press.

Riley, G. (2006). Sesquicentennial reflections: A comparative view of Mormon and gentile women on the westward trail. In D. L. May & R. L. Neilson (eds), *The Mormon History Association's Tanner Lectures: The first twenty years* (pp. 153–171). Urbana, IL: University of Illinois Press.

Robbins, R. M. (1942). *Our landed heritage: The public domain 1776–1936*. Princeton, NJ: Princeton University Press.

Savagian, J. C. (2009). Toward a coherent curriculum: Teaching and learning history at Alverno College. *The Journal of American History*, 95(4), 1114–1124.

Schlissel, L. (2004). *Women's diaries of the westward journey*. New York: Schocken Books.

Scott, J. W. (1992) Experience. In J. Butler & J. W. Scott (eds), *Feminists theorize the political* (pp. 22–40). New York: Routledge.

Sloan, W. D., Stovall, J. G., & Startt, J. D. (1989). *The media in America: A history*. Worthington, OH: Publishing Horizons, Inc.

Somerville, I., Edwards, L., & Ihlen, Ø. (2019). *Public relations, society, and the generative power of history*. Abingdon: Routledge.

Southgate, B. (1996). *History: What and why – ancient, modern and postmodern perspectives*. London: Routledge.

Spacks, P. M. (1975). *The female imagination*. New York: Alfred Knopf.

St. John III, B., Lamme, M. O., & L'Etang, J. (2014). Realizing new pathways to public relations history. In B. St. John, III, M. O. Lamme, & J. L'Etang (eds), *Pathways to public relations: Histories of practice and profession* (pp. 1–8). New York: Routledge.

Straughan, D. M. (ed.) (2007). *Women's use of public relations or Progressive-era reform: Rousing the conscience of a nation*. Lewiston, NY: Edwin Mellen Press.

Szyszka, P. (ed.) (1997). *Auf der Suche nach Identität: PR-Geschichte als Theoriebaustein* (*In Search of identity: PR history as a theory building block*). Berlin: Vistas.

Taylor, S. J. (2015). "Go West, Young Man": The mystery behind the famous phrase. *Hoosier State Chronicles: Indiana's Digital Historic Newspaper Program*. Accessed January 22, 2020, from https://blog.newspapers.library.in.gov/go-west-young-man-the-mystery-behind-the-famous-phrase

Travers, C. (2011). Unveiling a reflective diary methodology for exploring the lived experiences of stress and coping. *Journal of Vocational Behavior*, 79, 204–216.

Van Maanen, J. (1988). *Tales of the field: On writing ethnography*. Chicago, IL: The University of Chicago Press.

Van Manen, M. (1990). *Researching lived experience: Human science for an action sensitive pedagogy* (2nd edn). Albany, NY: State University of New York Press.

Waller, R. A. (1978). A thematic approach to teaching United States history. *The History Teacher*, 28(2), 201–210.

Watson, T. (2013). Keynote speech to the International History of Public Relations Conference, Bournemouth University, June 24–25, June 24. Accessed October 27, 2019 from https://microsites.bournemouth.ac.uk/historyofpr/files/2010/11/Tom-Watson-IHPRC-2013-Keynote-Address4.pdf.

Watson, T. (2014). Introduction. In T. Watson (ed.), *Asian perspectives on the development of public relations: Other voices*. Basingstoke: Palgrave Macmillan.

Webber, B. (1990). Introduction and contemporary comments. *The Oregon Trail diary of twin sisters Cecilia Adams and Parthenia Blank in 1852*. Medford, OR: Webb Research Group.

Wehmeier, S. (2015). Historiography (and theory) of public relations. In T. Watson (ed.), *Perspectives on public relations historiography and historical theorization: Other voices* (pp. 85–114). New York: Palgrave Macmillan.

Welter, B. (1966). The cult of true womanhood, 1820–1860. *American Quarterly*, 18, 152–174.

White, H. (1973). *Meta-history: The historical imagination in nineteenth-century Europe*. Baltimore, MD: Johns Hopkins University Press.

Williamson, J. G. (1974). *Late nineteenth-century American development: A general equilibrium theory*. New York: Cambridge University Press.

Part I
Overview

1 (Re)discovering the Past in Order to Understand Public Relations History Today

What would happen if we defined *public relations* more broadly to incorporate informal community-building work prior to the nineteenth century? In short, the view would be more diverse, equitable, and inclusive. It also would be supportive of new opportunities for theorizing about the development of public relations as a field and academic discipline. For example, adding to public relations history the voices of nineteenth-century U.S. women during and after one of the most significant events on the North American continent – the Oregon Trail – could inspire researchers in other nations to consider similar projects and expand public relations history globally. For many years, public relations history has been framed as male gendered and women have been conspicuous by their absence. The gaps in formative thinking about how patriarchy shapes the past simultaneously limit present-day understanding of public relations practice and the ways public relations work is gendered.

As will be revealed, women played instrumental community-building roles as pioneers, emigrants, settlers – and colonialists. The East-West wagon "road" that took roughly 400,000 Caucasian/White emigrants to the Pacific coast's present-day states of Oregon and California was known generally as the *Overland Trail*. This name came from the Overland Stage Company, which transported mail and passengers throughout the nineteenth century (Faragher & Stansell, 1975). Eventually, a shorter and safer westward route of 2,000+ miles became known as the *Oregon Trail*, taking people from Missouri, Iowa, and Nebraska to Oregon Country/Territory. The California Trail and the Oregon Trail meandered West together for the first 1,000 or 1,200 miles from the Missouri frontier to Fort Hall (Feltskog, 1969). From a social class standpoint, the trails' first émigrés were moderately prosperous, Caucasian/White U.S.-born farming families. Subsequent waves of travelers emigrated from Northern Europe and Canada. By the time the Civil War ended in 1865, several thousand African Americans also migrated West when they were freed from slavery and could join the journey westward to claim land for their own (Freedman, 1983).

Throughout the 1800s, many changes altered North American lives and lands. Missionaries and French Canadians who had retired from the Hudson Bay Company fur trade were the earliest Caucasian/White settlers in Oregon's

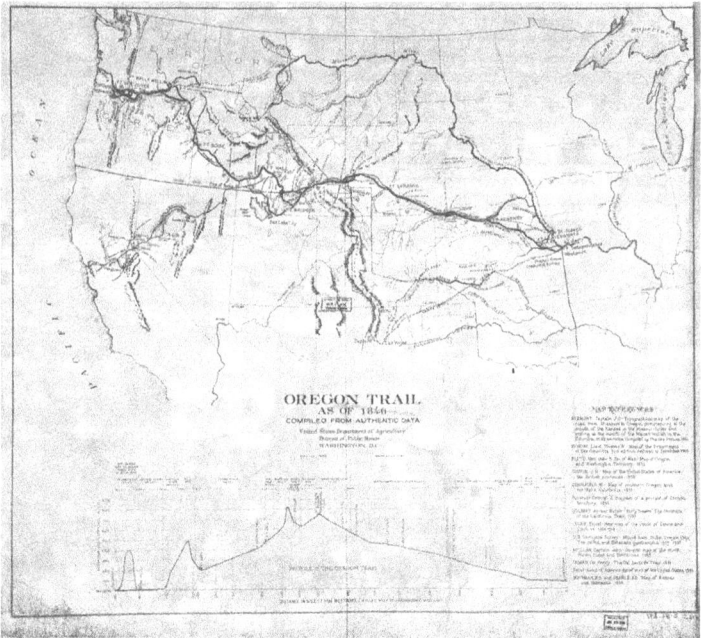

Figure 1.1 Oregon Trail, 1846
Source: Public Domain.

Willamette Valley – an area measuring 100 miles long and 20–30 miles wide – bounded by the Cascades mountain range, the Coastal Range, and the Calapooya Mountains (Robbins, 2002a). Today, the Willamette Valley extends from Portland to Eugene, Oregon. A Provisional Government was formed in this lower Columbia River region of the 1840s in conjunction with a series of meetings in the fall of 1843 as Caucasian/White settlers learned that large numbers of emigrants were coming to Oregon Country/Territory. The government body was created to be independent of the U.S. and Great Britain. Eventually, the lands of indigenous peoples were expropriated through the treaty process and much of Oregon was considered part of the public domain and available for settlement. The Oregon Donation Land Law "validated white settlers' claims in the Willamette Valley" and served as a green light for hundreds of settlers into the Umpqua and Rogue Valleys (Robbins, 2002b). Oregon Trail emigrants began filing into the fertile Willamette Valley in earnest in the early 1840s, after traversing Oregon's Blue Mountains and floating down the Columbia River (LaLande, 2005). The Donation Land Claim Act, passed in the U.S. Congress in September 1850, "enabled citizens to acquire free, farmable land" (Atwood & Gray, 2003). Oregon's Willamette Valley features a mild climate and geography that enabled emigrants to "escape frontier hardships," offering women somewhat gentler conditions than in some other western regions (Prescott, 2012, p. 338).

This book offers the findings of a research project about the lived experiences of Oregon Trail pioneer women and invites readers to consider community building as early public relations before mass media fully developed into a global enterprise and before there were really large organizations or institutions. It offers a context for thinking about the degrees of public relations work's formality and the ways we define it over time. This investigation is built on a foundation of considering the public interest to "develop mutual understanding" (J. E. Grunig & White, 1992, p. 53) and sharpens a focus on public relations' community-building function (Kruckeberg & Starck, 1988). The study also was inspired by L'Etang's (2016) argument that public relations history constitutes more than a focus on occupational development, but is enriched by understandings from a social development standpoint. At its roots, public relations serves "society at large" (Kruckeberg & Starck, 1988, p. xii), benefits society through facilitating dialogue – its "ideal social role" (J. E. Grunig & White, 1992, p. 53). Also, public relations research is committed to the community (Sha, 2019). All in all, this foundation supported an investigation of informal community-building work performed by women on the Oregon Trail and in Oregon as homesteaders and settlers.

The diaries, journals, and reminiscences of women who traveled the Oregon Trail and settled in Oregon offer empirical evidence of the ways nineteenth-century pioneer women fulfilled a community-building function. Their first-person documents detail organizing work, conflict negotiation, relationship building, a civilizing function, social cohesion, emotional connections, and more. Examining women's lived experiences is a sharp departure from decades of formal chronicling of public relations history which has generally ignored women's contributions and instead begins with the work of Caucasian/White males whose paths are steeped in contexts of advocating for profit-centric organizations and shaping public opinion by amplifying their mass mediated messages. Because women were acknowledged only for the "more customary and comfortable beliefs" about their "place," such as in the performance of domestic duties (Riley, 1984, p. 251), Western women's diaries and letters were not widely published nor were women welcome at lecture circuits in the early 1900s (Riley, 1984). Consequently, historical accounts of the West have been filled by and with Caucasian/White male, hyper-masculinized, colonizing images. Perhaps this is because most nineteenth-century Americans and Europeans were unable to trade in biased images of women for accurate representations of them as "rational, capable beings," (Riley, 1984, p. 251).

Moreover, confusion, ignorance, and discomfort explains the degrees of inattention to lived experiences among Native Americans in U.S. history across waves of colonization. Historians and popular culture have tended to offer what Riley (1984) called "selective experiences" (p. 252) as a means to control or "neutralize its effects, deny or obscure the death itself" (Dennis, 2014, p. 282). For generations, historical accounts and popular media representations have perpetuated myths about nineteenth-century pioneer travels with limited views that fail to fully interrogate relationships among indigenous peoples and Caucasian/Whites (Riley, 1984).

In recent decades, public relations scholarship has accepted a critical lens to broaden its body of knowledge to acknowledge important aspects of diversity, equity, and inclusion in the profession with research into the dimensions of social identity. One useful tool for adapting this approach to historical topics is to engage with historiography, which Bentele (2015) qualified as being reflective and a legitimate means for contextualizing phenomena. Studies acknowledging the experiences and impacts of people of color (e.g., Logan, 2016; Pompper, 2005; Vardeman, Kennedy, & Little, 2019; Waymer, 2012) have been added to the public relations theory-building enterprise. Yet, historical accounts of women's contributions have been woefully inadequate (Lamme, 2015). U.S.-based, public relations textbook history chapters consistently consider public relations primarily as a twentieth-century phenomenon and position the achievements of Caucasian/White males as the starting point for public relations professionalization. The study reported in this book incorporates historiography techniques and offers a meta-level reflection on the ways we define *public relations* – in order to correct an egregious oversight in public relations history. It posits that a limited definition of *public relations* has been a logical outgrowth of hegemonic, male-powered perspectives that have failed to incorporate women's achievements in developing the public relations profession.

What follows in Chapter 1 is scaffolding for this book with theoretical underpinning and research question: 1) Defining Public Relations and Writing Public Relations History; 2) Implications of Gaps in Public Relations History, Reflexivity, and Research Question; 3) Communitarianism and (In)formal Relationship Building; 4) Theoretical Underpinnings; 5) History's Sources for Women's Voices; and 6) Summary.

Defining Public Relations and Writing Public Relations History

Tracing the history of public relations invites problematizing the ways we define it. In recent years, senior scholars who research public relations history have pointed out that because *public relations* is difficult to define, pinpointing its origins is also complex (e.g., Gower, 2006; Lamme & Russell, 2010). Bentele (2015) cautioned researchers to avoid a form of relativism when considering history as "only a series of interpretations" and held that "all public relations are descended from forms of communication, but not all types of communication can and should be understood as public relations" (p. 20). Study findings reported in this book suggest that expanding the historical roots of public relations as community building offers new space for adding the lived experiences of heretofore marginalized voices.

Interest in public relations history has been growing. In the 1950s, practitioners' perspectives filled textbooks with profiles and "uncritical accounts" (Fitch & L'Etang, 2017, p. 118). Attention to public relations history has been increasing since 2009, when Tom Watson launched the annual International History of PR Conference at the University of Bournemouth. Moreover, Watson created new publication opportunities in the 2010s with special history-themed issues of *Public Relations Review* and *Journal of Public Relations Research*. His efforts have been characterized as inspiring "the professionalization of PR historical work" (Fitch & L'Etang, 2017, p. 119).

After examining research presented at these conferences and elsewhere, a taxonomy was created to organize the direction of public relations history. Bentele (2013) offered three blends of public relations history investigation: 1) national public relations histories, 2) historical development of organizations, and 3) meta-theoretical or -methodological approaches to public relations historiography. There seem to be two major approaches to public relations historiography – one that examines facts and events, and another that offers models and theories. Among the facts-and-events approach to public relations historiography, public relations tools or methods used for economic or political ends have precursors dating back to 1800 B.C. with a Sumerian bulletin educating farmers about growing crops (Heath, 2005) and evidence of the inner workings of the Greek polis from around 1000 B.C. (Bentele, 2013). It is a framework that offers two mutually exclusive meta-perspectives – either that public relations is "as old as the history of humankind itself" (Bentele, 2015, p. 25), or that it began with Europe's industrialization (Ronneberger & Rühl, 1992) in the late nineteenth century (Gower, 2006), or with early-twentieth-century industrialization in the U.S. (Broom & Sha, 2013). Over all timeframes, L'Etang (2014) and others have noted that public relations history has been constructed from a U.S.-centric standpoint. Lamme and Russell's (2010) monograph breaks from a "dependence on linear interpretations" (p. 281) of public relations' past by incorporating examples of persuasion techniques used in public relations over the course of 2,000 years.

Even though experts disagree as to when, where, or how public relations first began, the Public Relations Society of America (PRSA) and many U.S.-based researchers have adopted the simplicity of J. E. Grunig and Hunt's (1984) four models characterizing public relations development. Moreover, it may be hypothesized that the temptation throughout the twentieth century to benchmark the launch of professional public relations with any century other than that present one – with an emphasis on economic underpinnings – was too strong to resist. The four models set up public relations history as a progression; an evolutionary march from early-twentieth-century press-agentry developed in tandem with mass media and profit-centered industry – toward ethical, professional practice. By contrast, Vasquez and Taylor's (2001) five-stage framework for considering professional public relations' development in terms of foundations, expansion, institutionalization, maturation, and professionalization promotes a broader timescape for incorporating elements of relationship and community building in the U.S. and beyond – avoiding an impulse to steep public relations in Western contexts. Fitch and L'Etang (2017) posited that public relations researchers do not always ground their history work within wider historical or social context. So, the research project reported in this current book was inspired by the Vasquez and Taylor (2001) model and findings are offered to inspire others around the globe to retrace history's steps in both U.S. and non-U.S. areas in search of other *foundations* that may have contributed to public relations development. For example, beyond U.S. shores, public relations phenomena have been examined in pre- and Christian biblical times (Sriramesh, Kim, & Takasaki, 1999), in late-nineteenth-century Germany (Wilcox, Ault, & Agee, 2014), and more. The developing nations of Latin America, Asia, and Eastern Europe's emerging democracies are experiencing the *foundations* stage (Vasquez & Taylor, 2001).

In the U.S., the origins of for-profit public relations have been rooted in the onset of the industrial revolution, the growth of railroads, and corporations' expansion during the late nineteenth and early twentieth centuries (Logan, 2014). According to Bentele (2015), J. E. Grunig (1996) outlined in an unpublished paper a critique that traditional public relations historiography has been Caucasian/White- and male-dominated (p. 7). So, whether researchers support the approaches and categories outlined above, or some other labeling of public relations "antecedents" (Cutlip, 1995), "protohistory" (Watson, 2013), "seedbed era" (PRSA, 2019) or "beginnings" (Broom & Sha, 2013) prior to the twentieth century, research findings reported in subsequent chapters of this book provide an important means of recognizing the contributions of pioneer women in shaping what we have come to acknowledge to be community-building and early public relations work.

Implications of Gaps in Public Relations History, Reflexivity, and Research Question

Considering public relations predominantly within a framework of formal organizations, mass media, and Caucasian/White male, gender power dynamics has limited the writing of public relations history. A significant outcome of confining the founding of public relations to the early twentieth century means excluding the contributions of women and people of color when their stories are left out merely because during their time, they were predominantly relegated to the private sphere and margins. This limitation privileges the lived experiences of Caucasian/White men operating largely in the public sphere. Critical race theory builds on the insights of radical feminism to identify socioracial hierarchies and redress historical wrongs to make society better (Delgado & Stefancic, 2001). Like critical race theory, feminism is increasingly diverse – yet at its heart is a mission to expose women's oppression and propose solutions for eliminating it (Tong, 2009).

Those who write about U.S. history have their own standpoint and opinions about the past that shapes the ways they analyze and contextualize stories. Standpoints also shape how one frames the passage of time passage as advancement, critiques the impact on indigenous peoples and the planet, and offers morality lessons for improving living conditions in the present and the future. Among feminist historians of the U.S. West, it is widely believed that myths and stereotypes about women as fragile and insignificant were perpetuated in an "attempt to keep them subordinate to male-directed history [and these] must be identified and revised" (Riley, 1994, p. xii). Similarly, adding the voices of pioneer women and their community-building work to the chapter on public relations history could avoid such a claim in our field. The goal of the study reported in this book is to discover the voices and lived experiences of the pioneer women of the nineteenth century in the West by answering this research question – *What roles did women on the Oregon Trail play that may be considered early public relations community building?*

Responding to this research question and adding a new dimension to the chapter on public relations history chapter contributes to the well from which we draw information to educate public relations students. To explore and improve the state of public relations education in the U.S., the Public Relations Commission on Undergraduate Education regularly surveys public relations practitioners and educators. Recent findings suggest that some educators said this knowledge is "valuable because it provides context and a solid understanding of how public relations has evolved" (Commission, 2018, p. 28). Among practitioners, as employers who hire entry level public relations staff, 16% those who completed the questionnaire *strongly agree* and 32% percent *somewhat agree* that an outcome of undergraduates' education should include "understanding the history of public relations so as to provide context and explain how public relations has evolved" (Commission on Public Relations Education, 2018, p. 30).

In addition to attending to history in the curriculum, the Public Relations Commission on Undergraduate Education also recently recommended updating undergraduate core courses to emphasize *ethics* (Commission on Public Relations Education, 2018; DiStaso, 2019). Public relations practitioners in the U.S. are held to industry standards based on the core values of ethical practice (PRSA, n.d.) To many, this includes having a healthy dose of respect for diversity, equity, and inclusion, and all social identity dimensions; a position crucial to public relations practitioners in their advocacy role (Brunner, 2017). Some important numbers shed light on the relevance of expanding the pages of public relations history. At the last count, 50.8% of the U.S. population is female (U.S. Census, 2010b). Also, the number of female public relations practitioners is reported to be about 85%, up from 27% in 1970 (George, 2013). Finally, 70% of public relations students in the U.S. are women (U.S. Department of Education, 2018). If stakeholders, practitioners, and students are largely female, it is logical that textbooks on public relations history must give greater attention to women, beyond the token one or two currently mentioned (Ertem-Eray & Pompper, 2020). Too few representations of women among public relations history pages means that public relations practitioners often have no background in their chosen occupation's actual history (L'Etang, 2014). Maslow's (1970) hierarchy of human needs model introduced a psychological perspective on the human need to *belong* and be part of a community or in relationships with others after an individual's physiological and safety needs are met. The effects the inability of women and underrepresented groups to *see someone like me* employed in certain fields/industries or represented in books have been widely noted and offered as a critique of the ways Caucasian/White homophily is perpetuated and promoted as some "neutral one-size-fits-all" perspective (Brook, Ellenwood, & Lazzaro, 2016; Broughton, 2019, p. 260).

Communitarianism and (In)formal Relationship Building

The humanist, communitarian approach to exploring public relations phenomena involves examining concern for and attention to maintaining a living environment for everyone's benefit (Starck & Kruckeberg, 2001). This theoretical framework embraces social and historical elements as a means of restoring a sense of community today – while technology increasingly replaces face-to-face communication. Communitarianism also offers a useful framework for reading nineteenth-century women's diaries, journals, and reminiscences as pioneer women chronicled their community-building experiences in supporting others. Most formal definitions of *community relations* rely on organizational standpoints and external communication perspectives. For example, Neff (2013) defined *community relations* as a management function and roots its practice in using communication to ensure that both organizations and their publics co-exist. Yet, Neff (2013) also referred to community relations metatheory as "speech act as affected by the self, the episode, the relationship, and culture" (p. 172). Thinking of community relations as only a means of warding off adverse public opinion that can threaten the prosperity of organizations short-changes the value of community relations to relationship building. In other words, the more informal dimensions of communication for community building outside of organizations deserves greater scrutiny.

Indeed, an underdeveloped conversation in public relations research and theory building is the degrees of formality associated with effective public relations beyond organizational settings. Kruckeberg and Starck (1988) lamented that public relations research about community relations is "grossly deficient and inappropriate" (p. 25). According to the seminal work of Burns and Stalker (1961), which J. E. Grunig (1992) referenced when building public relations excellence theory, there are two basic types of organizations – the *mechanical* organization with formal rules and vertical centralized decision-making at the top, and *organic* organizations which are horizontal, less formal, less stratified, and decentralized. Some clues as to how public relations performs informally beyond organizations may be taken from the work of public relations researchers who have borrowed liberally from the interpersonal communication literature (e.g., Stafford & Canary, 1991) in order to identify communication strategies for achieving mutual understanding, compromise, and common goals. The current study suggests that these same strategies of access, positivity, openness, assurance of legitimacy, networking, and task sharing (Hon & J. E. Grunig, 1999; J. E. Grunig, 2006) also factor into community building for quality relationship building outside of organizations.

The formality concept in public relations research has usually been linked to organizational settings. For example, organizations that have "formalized relationships with strategic publics" means the greater the likelihood that public relations will be "excellent" (L. A. Grunig, J. E. Grunig, & Ehling, 1992, p. 83). However, L. A. Grunig (1992) incorporated Robbins' (1987) ideas about *culture* as a substitute for formalization since culture increases behavioral consistency and culture "controls the mind and soul as well as the body" (Robbins, 1987, p. 362). This addition to theorizing about formality in public relations research also opens a window to considering community building beyond organizations.

Perhaps wherever people organize with a common mission, culture guides the creation of mutually agreed upon rules and supports the ways people network interpersonally to build relationships. Recent organizational communication scholarship explores the order among social settings even when people are not part of formal organizations. For example, Ahrne and Brunsson (2010) broadened the concept of *organization* to include some aspects of order that exist outside organizations – *partial organization* – going beyond simple networking processes. When considering *organization* as a particular kind of social order, it is not a stretch of the imagination to think of informal sets of people as incorporating partial organizing characteristics. Hence, *organization* as "a decided order" makes distinguishing between *organization* and *environment* "less dramatic" so that organization exists outside formal institutions, and includes one or more elements of membership, hierarchy, rules, monitoring, and sanctions (Ahrne & Brunsson, 2010, p. 84). Preferring the term *community engagement*, Johnston and Lane (2019) examined the under-researched perspective of focusing on the role of public relations in identifying and involving authentic voices even if they are more "quiet or silent" (p. 436) in conjunction with socially situated problems. Privileging these more subtle voices is useful for the current study's investigation of the ways emigrant women on the Oregon Trail and as homesteaders organized to build community in their challenging new environments. Webber (1990) characterized the role of Overland Trail women of the nineteenth century as "*possibility thinkers* of their time who looked forward to new opportunities in a new land" (p. viii, italics in original). Themes that emerged among original first-person texts are explained in subsequent chapters to detail the ways pioneer women communicated across differences when survival of their family and community hung in the balance.

Applying communitarianism to a historic phenomenon – beyond contexts of industry, formal organizations, and mass media – requires looking at fundamental relationship building in *informal* contexts. Emphases on public engagement beyond organizational settings to examine intercultural connections using Gudykunst's (1995, 2005) anxiety and uncertainty management theory as a means of supporting relationships across diverse audiences (Ni & Wang, 2011) and social networking sites (Men & Tsai, 2014) have become a hallmark of the relationship building research on strategic publics. For example, we know that authenticity and perceptions of transparency are essential to cultivating quality relationships and boosting public trust (Rawlins, 2009), as are degrees of community investment, credibility, commitment, mutuality, openness, and trust (e.g., Seltzer, Gardner, Bichard, & Callison, 2012).

In subsequent chapters of this book, these relationship building elements – as part of community building – are addressed with examples illustrating the work pioneer women performed on the Oregon Trail and across Oregon's Willamette Valley. As westward journeying pioneers traveled 2,000+ miles (Butruille, 1993) to Oregon, they were bound geographically only by mountains, prairies, rivers, desert, and the open air (rather than the bricks and mortar of formal organizations). As a group traveling together en masse, emigrants were dependent on women's caretaking, leadership, advocacy, emotional support, partnership, and friendship for survival. Once settled in Oregon, pioneers networked and got to work building more formal structures. Women played central roles in these tasks.

For those less comfortable with supplementing the traditional benchmark of Ivy Lee's and Ed Bernays' contributions to formal professional public relations as "founding fathers," L'Etang (2014) invited readers to consider how enlightening it is to explore the possibilities of expanding the chapter on public relations history "in order to contextualize the concept and locate it as a human communication practice" (p. xxxi). L'Etang (2014) also rhetorically pondered "[why] no mothers yet!" (p. xxviii). In the words of Stuart Hall (1969), this is one of those journeys that promises to take readers toward a better understanding and appreciation of praxis. As educators, our guiding light must be to continue discovering ways to positively impact students who happen to be overwhelmingly female at the moment.

This chapter now turns attention to major theoretical frameworks undergirding the analyses of Oregon Trail pioneer women's diaries, journals, and reminiscences. I use a feminist criticism approach, given its flexibility for blending with other theory strands and overall "melding of various disciplines" (Huff, 1989, p. 6), as examined in these next subsections of feminist theory, feminist historical geography, network theory, and social constructionism.

Theoretical Underpinnings

In addition to Vasquez and Taylor's (2001) five-stage framework for public relations development and the communitarianism concept for community building, four major theory strands shape the study reported in this book.

Feminist Theory: A feminist approach to history shows that gender inequalities are neither universal, nor only contemporary, nor fixed. Rather, using a feminist theory lens to look at recorded history promotes resurrecting from obscurity the lives, experiences, and ideas of women to offer alternative understandings on gender relations today (Corn, 2014). The study findings are situated in a feminist theory framework and involved using Van Manen's (1990) hermeneutic phenomenological technique for discovering themes/patterns among handwritten pages chronicling women's lived experiences. When established gender roles and inequalities are revealed as socially constructed within a certain historical context, then feminists argue that gender inequalities are open to change. Feminist Western historian, Jeffrey (1979), initially sought to discover the ways women used the frontier as a means to liberate themselves from stereotypes and behaviors she considered "sexist" (p. xv). The use of a feminist theory lens also invites re-examinations and potentially the rewriting of entire historical narratives. Examining history using a feminist theory lens promotes the transformation of historical writing and understanding. Yet, "projecting feminism onto the past" has its challenges, such as when researchers presume that historically significant women identify with feminism (Golombisky & Holtzhausen, 2005, p. 12). To avoid this outcome, Burt (1998) suggested providing "dispassionate descriptions and analyses of women's experience and role in history" (p. 19).

When feminist historians of the late nineteenth and early twentieth centuries found that women were largely absent from history books, they inspired new research that continues to impact the ways we think of gender and intersections with other social identity dimensions, such as ethnicity/race. Feminist scholars of the 1970s began problematizing the causes and implications of women's secondary status by recovering women's history (Byerly, 2018; Matthews, 1986). The goal has been not only to critique the ways that recorded history is socially constructed with significant gaps, but to illustrate the ways a feminist approach broadens the understanding of historical events. By the early 1990s, some wondered why all women were not feminists acting as if they had been emancipated from subordination (Ferree & Hess, 2000). Applying feminist theory to historic phenomena facilitates the exploration of meaning making according to women (Reinharz, 1992) and contributes to social justice. Use of a feminist theory lens to research history has promoted findings about nearly forgotten phenomena, such as women's writings during the American Revolutionary War (Botting, 2016), women's classical seventeenth-century poetry in England (Ray, 2016), and paintings of the comfort women of the Korean War (Kwon, 2017). Even though Ronneberger and Rühl (1992) posited that public communication is understood primarily as the establishing of a public sphere through the mass media, public relations research suggests that limiting the influence of women's work to the private sphere squelches important voices. In the case of the study reported in this book, feminist theory is used to expand community-building narratives by including pioneer women's early contributions to development of the field and to inspire a positive change to a broader definition of *public relations* going forward.

Whether or not consciously undergirding their work with feminist theory, some public relations researchers have critiqued public relations' "great man" history. In the U.S., Lamme (2015) argued for more attention to biography in public relations history and opined that perhaps one reason why figures like Lee and Bernays have been dually crowned as "fathers" of the field is that they were conscious of their legacy and quite skilled at shaping it. Rather than dethroning these figures, Lamme (2015) recommended using their example to "demonstrate the need for a more expansive and demanding analysis of [those] to whom we turn for precedents, inspiration and wisdom" (p. 52). Her critique is rooted in Gustavson's (1955) synopsis of a person's historical role according to either determinism (events would have occurred even without the *great person*) or "great man theory" (usually, the *great person* is a man who is uplifted to superhero status) – and the scholar's role is to untangle the two (p. 123). Unless we critique the words and context of a *great person*, we risk "institutionalizing those carefully crafted public personas as bona fide contributions to the historical record" (Lamme, 2015, p. 54).

In the organizational communication literature, Ashcraft and Mumby (2004) advanced *feminist communicology of organization* as a conceptual framework for considering organizations as gendered and as sites for the interplay of communication, power, resistance, and identity to fuel change. The goal of eradicating the treatment of women and ethnic minorities as second-class citizens by focusing on "gendered organizing" may be advanced by valuing diverse thinking and approaches (Ashcraft & Mumby, 2004, p. 114). Research targeted at considering the institutional barriers faced by women has also expanded the body of knowledge in public relations. Studies of the glass ceiling and the gendered salary gap (e.g., Aldoory, 2007; Toth, 2001) and home-work-life (im) balance are just a few symptoms of deeply rooted homophily among top-most organizational management wherein women engaged in paid work outside the home are also burdened with the majority of unpaid work at home (e.g., Yu, Jiang & Shen, 2016). Cabrera's (2009) leaky pipeline theory suggests that family-friendly policies that benefit female employees fail in organizations that lack full senior management support. More broadly, feminist communication theory, as advanced by British social anthropologist Ardener (1975) suggested that men's greater social power over women plays out in muting of women's voices and ultimately contributes to women's subordination.

Feminist Historical Geography: Feminist historical geography theory building is also useful when examining the phenomenon of Oregon Trail pioneer women's community-building work – as a means of exploring and illuminating events from a woman's perspective that may have been overlooked. Taking a feminist approach to history as an analytic method means broadly "understanding feminism as advocating equal rights" (Corn, 2014). Kay (1991) called for adding women's travel or pioneering narratives as correctives to gender-blind historical geographies. Failure to include feminist readings of a field's past marginalizes women's role in the recording of that past and the way students are taught history, propagating an "inaccurate understanding of the past" (Rose & Ogborn, 1988, p. 405). Kay (1991) and others have noted, however, that the struggle to overcome "male orientation and near-absence of material on women in North American regional historical geography" (p. 435) endures decades after scholarly work in women's history was introduced. Perhaps this trend persists because *gender* is conflated with *women* and "men who are not necessarily opposed to feminist historical geographies may be inclined to avoid feminism because it is seen as a 'women's issue'" (Morin & Berg, 1999, p. 312).

Shortcomings associated with *not* telling women's stories and illuminating their contribution to history impacts not only how students and practitioners learn about the roots of public relations, but how researchers build theory about it.

Hence, feminist historical geography offers a useful underpinning for critiquing gaps in the collective understanding of women's contributions to public relations history. Much recent work fueled by feminist historical geography examines the production of gender differences according to economic, political, cultural, and sexual social identity dimensions. Feminist historical geography brings both feminist and geographical sensitivities to bear on the study of past phenomena and involves destabilizing and rewriting historical geography through the cultural politics of space and place (Morin & Berg, 1999). As Rose (1995) noted, history and geographical knowledge are not neutral, but are infused with power relations that often erase *others* from the geography. Development of an explicitly feminist approach to historical geography involves "exploring in detail the processes and practices of patriarchy, often stressing resistance" (Rose & Ogborn, 1988). This is why multiple perspectives of events and issues are needed. Applying a feminist approach to historical geography is consistent with Hon's (1995) addition of feminist theory to explain public relations as a feminized field. Research findings reported in this book offer pioneer women's narratives as a corrective to gender-blind historical geographies and offer additional ways to look at history about the U.S. West. Simonsen (1996) wrote about social spatiality, where the practice or doing is seen as constituting space. As applied to the current study, recognizing the context of Oregon Trail pioneer women's societal role in the private sphere is central to understanding their first-person narratives and the ways they approached community-building tasks in the public sphere.

While feminist historical geographies subvert the erasure of women from the pages of history, recognizing Caucasian/White pioneer women's complicity in colonizing indigenous peoples' communities must be considered. Documenting the social construction of gendered selves is a political act "bound up with relations of power and oppression"(Morin & Berg, 1999, p. 325) and the process of writing women into the past involves negotiating a complex interplay of many intersections of social identity difference within particular spatial-historical contingencies (e.g. Johnson, 1995) and ways public space is created and accessed (e.g. Boyer, 1998). Taking direction from historical geographers who encourage investigations of the origins of gender differences in spatio-historical moments, the current study involved a careful reading of diaries, journals, and reminiscences of women who traveled the Oregon Trail and became homesteaders in Oregon's Willamette Valley and beyond – illuminating their contributions without celebrating their complicity in colonization's effects on the land and indigenous communities.

Network Theory: In addition to using feminist theory to understand community-building beyond formal organizational settings, this Oregon Trail pioneer women project demanded the utility of network theory. *Networks* are social structures shaped by communication among individuals (Stohl, 1995) which are instrumental and cultural, and constitute channels through which power and influence may be exerted (Littlejohn, 2002). Network theory is useful for integrating multiple perspectives and explains patterns and interactions across individuals at the level of input, processing, and output. In public relations research, network theory has helped researchers to better appreciate people's need and desire to communicate and to exchange information, which may lead to better relationships and more ethical decision-making with reduced conflict and greater harmony (Heath, 2013; Krippendorff, 1977). The concept of *openness* emerged as a key component of network theory when Fisher (1982) explained that permeable boundaries in a social system allow information exchange and support energy between actors and their environment. Communication between two people creates a *micronetwork* and a conjoining of micronetworks constitutes a *macronetwork* (a system or a suprasystem). Within a social network, individuals display degrees of inter-connectedness, forming a *cluster*, or a distinct, tightly knit set of people. Researchers have also investigated an individual's network role which connects groups in particular ways, such as actions of *bridgers* (people who have connections in multiple clusters) and *hubs* (influential people sought after by other members within a network (Carrington, Scott, & Wasserman, 2005).

So, when women on the Oregon Trail put their heads together to solve problems, they formed a series of informal micronetworks that collectively supported the macronetwork of the entire pioneer wagon train and developing communities of homesteading farmers. Individual stories with details of such events unfold in later chapters. Network theory is particularly useful in this project for investigating connections as people formed links (e.g., friendship, kinship) across a social network. Relationships may be either positive (alliance, friendship, love, partnership) or negative (anger, hatred, rivalry) (Saling, 2013). As people develop relationships with strangers over time, the quality of the relationship improves as they become more intimate, interdependence increases, and communication grows more effective (Gudykunst, Nishida, & Chua, 1987). Relationships with strangers also improve when uncertainty is reduced while interacting within one's own network. Faster familiarity with strangers happens when friends in common are shared (Gudykunst, Chua, & Gray, 1987). In public relations research, *trust* and *distrust* are both useful constructs for engaging with the public. The concept of *distrust* may inspire the public to take protective action to reduce vulnerability (Kang & Park, 2017) in support of community building.

Relatedly, we know that today's professional public relations practitioners serve as *boundary spanners* as part of their relationship building and information dissemination functions (Heath, 2013) across social networks. In formal settings, modern public relations practitioners both represent the interests of the organization to its stakeholders while also embedding themselves in the interests of stakeholders and then translating these back to the organization. Beyond brick and mortar organization contexts, however, Davidson (2016) applauded the boundary spanning function of public relations as a means of empowering socially disadvantaged groups. This framework serves as a useful tool for examining non-organizational contexts, historically, as when even the most financially comfortable pioneers faced reduced circumstances in the cross-continent journey and homesteading in Oregon.

Social Constructionism: While network theory is useful for explaining the ways people interact, it is useful to integrate feminist theory with the social constructionist paradigm to explore more fully the gap in public relations history created by a dearth of stories about women's contributions. Not unlike historical geography which narrates the past in order to understand the present (Gregson & Rose, 2013), a social constructionism lens promotes understanding of the ways gender roles and inequalities are socially constructed within a historical context rather than accepting them as occurring naturally or universally. Ultimately, understanding the social construction of gender inequalities can lead to change.

To begin, critique is not about placing blame, but rather about acknowledging the shortcomings associated with the writing of public relations history in order to do better. Combining the social construction tradition with a feminist approach to history facilitates the rediscovery of women's lived experiences for gender equity in narratives about how and why public relations developed. The roots of social constructionism may be traced to Kuhn's (1970) theory of scientific paradigm shifts and Berger and Luckmann's (1966) meta-theory about the ways *reality* is socially constructed. Overall, the social constructionist paradigm challenges assumptions about objectivity, neutrality, and truth – and considers the individual as a unit of analysis for knowledge generation (Weenink & Bridgman, 2017). Cultural theorist Raymond Williams (2001) wrote of a "cultural tradition" that invites constant comparison of phenomena to contemporary values and acknowledges infinite interpretations: "In a society as a whole, and in all its particular activities, the cultural tradition can be seen as a continual selection and re-selection of ancestors" (p. 69). According to Leeds-Hurwitz (2009), social constructionism focuses on artifacts created through social interactions and groups' shared assumptions. Focusing on gender as an ongoing social construction, Morrissey (1992) pondered "how cultural ideas about the social roles of men and women influenced western experiences" (p. 134). Simply put, social constructionism is a theoretical framework often used by communication scholars concerned about the ways people come to think of one another and make meaning of events. The social constructionist provides a useful tool for theorizing and for questioning "the taken-for-granted world" (Gergen, 1985, p. 267).

Social constructionist researchers invoke the concept of *dominant ideology* to explore meaning making and sets of beliefs situated in time that impose and reinforce understandings of the past and present as shaped by powerful elites (Althusser, 1971). Using social constructionism to underpin the research findings reported in this book supports the goal of filling a gap in the writing of public relations history. Carr (1961) recommended focusing on an individual's social context as part of historical enquiry since people are both products and agents of historical processes. Hence, thoroughly examining the societies in which individuals lived promotes a dialogue "between past and present societies" (Carr, 1961, p. 69). One important means to facilitate this work is to amplify Lamme's (2015) critique that "public relations history remains too neat, too packaged, too confined" (p. 64), as well as offering "scant mention of women in comparison to" men (p. 63). She also recommended researchers consider examining "other times" to discover additional lives, work, insights, and contributions (Lamme, 2015, p. 64). The interplay of knowledge and power, for Foucault (1980), shapes all political and social forms of thought. It wasn't until the 1980s that a campaign to pay attention to Western women as legitimate both inside and outside the academy was embraced (e.g., Jeffrey, 1979; Myres, 1982; Riley, 1977).

History's Sources for Women's Voices

Artifacts such as diaries, journals, and reminiscences offer important narratives when researching women's lived experiences of the past. Riley (1994) also supported the use of personal and household items that "speak of women's lives from the past" and offer "a kind of mute evidence … being rescued from libraries, attics, and other storage places" (pp. xii). As a *pioneer* herself in writing the history of women in the western U.S., Jeffrey (1998) explained that for many diarists, personal accounts of the Overland Trails were the only record of their own lives and the only historical record of the westward movement. Thirty-five years ago, the Coalition for Western Women's History was launched when a group of female historians met at a conference and vowed to organize and meet regularly thereafter to help people teach and write about Western women (Coalition for Western Women's History, n.d.), A "new Western history" emerged in the 1980s and many archivists collect women's source materials, books, and articles about Western women (Riley, 1994, p. xii) in support of sharing women's stories from the past. It is estimated that 1 out of every 250 Oregon Trail emigrants maintained a written record of the journey – and over 2,000 personal written documents are featured in special collections in archives, college/university libraries, historical societies, and public libraries across the U.S. (U.S. Department of the Interior – Bureau of Land Management, n.d.) The National Historic Oregon Trail Interpretive Center at Flagstaff Hill in Baker City, Oregon, also maintains a reference library and some pioneer descendants also treasure diaries of their ancient relatives.

Women's participation in the settlement of the West was once largely ignored, made invisible, or obscured in the scholarly literature by archetypes such as *pioneer in petticoats* and *Madonna of the prairie*; stereotypes largely based on what male writers and historians *thought* women represented in the West. Feminist historians of the West have interrogated such myths which diminished the seriousness of frontierswomen's contributions (Riley, 1994). Moreover, Vuolo (1975) posited that pioneer women's successes and struggles were "too long dismissed as trivial by our historians" (p. 36) and Riley (1994) opined that prior to the 1960s women's movement, women's lives generally were considered unworthy of serious study. Most emigrants set out from Independence, Missouri, as the main jumping off point to Oregon Country/Territory in the early 1800s (Butruille, 1993) (or Oregon upon statehood by 1959) – until the U.S. Bureau of the Census declared the frontier "closed" in 1890 (Riley, 2004, p. 7). Predominantly, these women were Caucasian/White and labored 14–16-hour days (Riley, 1994). Unfortunately, few sources reveal the thoughts and perspectives of Native Americans who encountered parties of Oregon Trail pioneers throughout Oregon Country/Territory: Arapaho, Bannock, Cayuse, Cheyenne, Comanche, Krikara, Nez Perce, Oto, Paiute, Pawnee, Shoshone, Sioux, Umatilla, Walla Walla, and Wasco (U.S. Department of the Interior – Bureau of Land Management, n.d.). Fortunately, most diaries, journals, and reminiscences examined for the current research project offer rich descriptions of Native American life and pioneer women's encounters with them. To date, the two best sources for Western women's daily lives are oral histories and private writings (Jameson, 1987).

Methodologically, the current study involves the use of a hermeneutic phenomenological theme analysis of pioneer women's diaries, journals, and reminiscences, a technique that is steeped in critically evaluating "lived experience" (Van Manen, 1990). Oregon Trail women's voices as confided to their diaries

Figure 1.2 Buffalo Bill Center of the West, Cody, Wyoming;
Source: Whitney Western Art Museum "Madonna of the Prairie" by WHD Koerner, 1921; 25.77.

and recalled years later in the form of reminiscences, often a response to insistent children and grandchildren, constitute the narratives explored in the current study. For frontierswomen, diaries and journals provided an outlet for their emotions which provide greater nuance in the face of early male-centric Western accounts that painted women as submissive, pure, and engaged in leisurely domesticity (Jameson, 1987). As part of a family's history, diaries and reminiscences passed on to new generations refute such images and have provided details about pioneer women's lived experiences which blended into twentieth-century family traditions (Norwood, 1988). History always is a "creative writing subject to the individual reading of data by the historical author" (L'Etang, 2014, p. xxv).

Summary

(Re)discovering the past for an understanding of public relations history today, as the title of this chapter suggests, is an invitation to join a journey of discovery in exploring pioneer women's voices, as shared in their diaries, journals, and reminiscences. Articulations of pioneer women's lived experiences, juxtaposed against contemporary professional public relations practice and research, means listening in a new way. The study findings unfolded in this book offer an alternative way of conceiving of community building during an important chapter of U.S. public relations history. Thinking about Oregon Trail women's diaries, journals, and reminiscences as evidence of their work performed in support of the new community in which they found themselves adds a new layer to public relations history. This, too, is a form of pioneering which responds to the challenge Jameson (1987) posed when she approached Western's women's history "through the experiences of the people who lived the history" (p. 161). This technique, comparable to Van Manen's (1990) lived experience framework, promotes asking new questions and discerning news ways to move forward by looking backward and expanding public relations history for greater inclusivity.

This chapter invited public relations students and researchers to begin considering an episode of U.S. history in a new way – not so much in terms of public relations as an occupational practice driving toward professionalization, but more as "a broader activity that includes the full and diverse range of public communication" (Fitch & L'Etang, 2017, p. 117) as it relates to community building. Like these public relations history scholars, I concur that historical work exceeds mere collection and interpretation of facts but opens new windows to theory building about "communicative action, change, and development in society" (Fitch & L'Etang, 2017, p. 117). For this current volume, the significance of findings includes new ways to consider the public relations profession and women's roles in today's feminized field globally.

Taking a critical feminist approach to history must be done carefully to avoid inspiring defensive reactions. Similarly, feminist historical research critique of institutionalized inattention to gender and intersectionalities with other social identity dimensions has been blamed for inspiring dissent. Among the public relations body of knowledge, L.A. Grunig (1988) called for a feminist research agenda and edited a *Public Relations Review* special issue on women. Hon's (1995) formal introduction of liberal feminist theory advocating for *feminist values* had a profound effect, inspiring a theoretical framework for exploring the feminization trend in U.S. public relations practice. In 2001, L. A. Grunig, Toth, and Hon carefully navigated ways to address the backlash when raising important gender issues among public relations practice and research. It is my hope that public relations history research that expands the timeframe beyond the twentieth century in order to include women's voices supports learning in our predominantly female-dominated classrooms without leaving male students with the impression that early men's contributions were any less significant.

Public relations feminist scholars have moved away from the 1980s decade's gender-specific "dichotomy of the dualist role schema" (Creedon, 1991, p. 78) which had characterized men as filling a public relations *manager* role while women filled a *technician* role (Dozier, 1988) – by instead focusing on practitioners' complex sets of contextualized relationships (Toth, 2001). This shift is consistent with Kruckeberg and Starck's (1988) focus on public relations as community building.

The focus of Chapter 2 is the lure of the West as this sets the stage for understanding how and why, doubts and hardships aside, women's optimistic mood "propelled the emigrants facing the unknown distance for the promised land of Oregon" (Butruille, 1993, p. 88) as they began community building.

References

Ahrne, G., & Brunsson, N. (2010). Organization outside organizations: The significance of partial organization. *Organization*, 18(1), 83–104.

Aldoory, L. (2007). Reconceiving gender for an excellent future in public relations scholarship. In E. L. Toth (ed.), *The future of excellence in public relations and communication management: Challenges for the next generation* (pp. 399–411). Mahwah, NJ: Lawrence Erlbaum Associates.

Althusser, L. (1971). *Lenin and philosophy*. London: New Left Books.

Ardener, E. (1975). Belief and the problem of women and the "problem" revisited. In S. Ardener (ed.), *Perceiving women* (pp. 1–27). London: Malaby.

Ashcraft, K. L., & Mumby, D. K. (2004). *Reworking gender: A feminist communicology of organization*. Thousand Oaks, CA: Sage.

Atwood, K., & Gray, D. J. (2003). *Claiming the land*. The Oregon History Project. Accessed February 17, 2020 from https://bit.ly/2HuSsBp.

U.S. Department of the Interior – Bureau of Land Management. (n.d.). Basic facts about the Oregon Trail. Accessed December 22, 2019 from www.blm.gov/sites/blm.gov/files/learn_interp_nhotic_faq.pdf.

Bentele, G. (2013). Public relations historiography: Perspectives of a functional-integrative stratification model. In K. Sriramesh, A. Zerfass, & J-N. Kim (eds), *Current trends and emerging topics in public relations and communication management*. New York: Routledge.

Bentele, G. (2015). Problems of public relations historiography and perspectives of a functional-integrative stratification model. In T. Watson (ed.), *Perspectives on public relations historiography and historical theorization: Other voices* (pp. 20–47). New York: Palgrave Macmillan.

Berger, P. L., & Luckmann, T. (1966). *The social construction of reality*. New York: Anchor Books Doubleday.

Botting, E. H. (2016). Women writing war: Mercy Otis Warren and Hannah Mather Crocker on the American Revolution. *Massachusetts Historical Review*, 18, 88–118.

Boyer, K. (1998). Place and the politics of virtue: Clerical work, corporate anxiety, and changing meanings of public womanhood in early twentieth-century Montreal. *Gender, Place and Culture*, 5, 261–276.

Brook, F., Ellenwood, D., & Lazzaro, A. E. (2016). In pursuit of antiracist social justice: Denaturalizing whiteness in the academic library. *Library Trends*, 64(2), 246–284.

Broom, G. M., & Sha, B-L. (2013). *Cutlip & Center's effective public relations* (11th edn). Upper Saddle River, NJ: Prentice-Hall.

Broughton, E. (2019). Belonging, intentionality, and study space for minoritized and privileged students. In D. M. Mueller (ed.), *ACRL 2019 Conference: Recasting the narrative* (pp. 1–11). Chicago, IL: Association of College and Research Libraries. Accessed December 22, 2019 from https://bit.ly/2PL7Q1E.

Brunner, B. (2017). Introduction. In B. Brunner (ed.), *The moral compass of public relations* (pp. 1–11). New York: Routledge.

Burns, T., & Stalker, G. M. (1961). *The management of innovation*. London: Tavistock.

Burt, E. (1998). Challenges in doing women's history. *Clio: Newsletter of the History Division of the Association for Education in Journalism and Mass Communication*, Fall, 31(1), 17–19.

Butruille, S. G. (1993). *Women's voices from the Oregon Trail: The times that tried women's souls and a guide to women's history along the Oregon Trail*. Boise, ID: Tamarack Books, Inc.

Byerly, C. (2018). Feminism, theory, and communication: Progress, debates, and challenges ahead. In D. Harp, J. Loke, and I. Bachmann (eds), *Feminist approaches to media theory and research* (pp. 19–35). London: Palgrave Macmillan.

Cabrera, E. (2009). Fixing the leaky pipeline: Five ways to retain female talent. *People and Strategy*, 32(1), 40–46.

Carr, E. H. (1961). *What is history?* New York: Vintage Books.

Carrington, P. J., Scott, J., & Wasserman, S. (eds) (2005). *Models and methods in social network analysis*. Cambridge: Cambridge University Press.

Coalition for Western Women's History (n.d.). About. Accessed August 15, 2019 from https://westernwomenshistory.org/about.

Commission on Public Relations Education (2018). Fast forward: Foundations and future state. Educators and practitioners: The Commission on Public Relations Education 2017 Report on Undergraduate Education. Accessed August 15, 2019 from www.commissionpred.org/wp-content/uploads/2018/04/report6-full.pdf.

Corn, G. (2014). Elementary feminisms: How useful is a feminist approach to history for historians? Accessed August 14, 2019 from https://thefeministwire.com/2014/10/useful-feminist-approach-history-historians.

Creedon, P. J. (1991). Public relations and "women's work:" Toward a feminist analysis of public relations roles. In L. A. Grunig & J. E. Grunig (eds), *Public relations research annual*, 3 (pp. 37–43). Hillsdale, NJ: Lawrence Erlbaum Associates.

Cutlip, S. M. (1995). *Public relations history: From the 17th to the 20th century. The antecedents.* Hillsdale, NJ: Lawrence Erlbaum Associates.
Davidson, S. (2016). Public relations theory: An agonistic critique of the turns to dialogue and symmetry. *Public Relations Inquiry*, 5(2), 145–167.
Delgado, R., & Stefancic, J. (2001). *Critical race theory: An introduction.* New York: New York University Press.
Dennis, M. (2014). Natives and pioneers: Death and the settling and unsettling of Oregon. *Oregon Historical Quarterly*, 115(3), 282–297.
DiStaso, M. (2019). Undergraduate public relations in the United States: The 2017 Commission on Public Relations Report. *Journal of Public Relations Education*, 5(3), 3–22.
Dozier, D. M. (1988). Breaking public relations' glass ceiling. *Public Relations Review*, 14(3), 6–14.
Ertem-Eray, T., & Pompper, D. (2020). Reconstructing the PR history time machine: Missing women and people of color in introductory textbooks. Paper presented at the Association for the Education in Journalism and Mass Communication Conference, San Francisco, CA, August 6–10, August 6.
Faragher, J., & Stansell, C. (1975). Women and their families on the Overland Trail to California and Oregon, 1842–1867. *Feminist Studies*, 2(2/3), 150–166.
Feltskog, E. N. (ed.) (1969). *The Oregon Trail.* Madison, WI: University of Wisconsin Press.
Ferree, M. M., & Hess, B. B. (2000). *Controversy and coalition: The new feminist movement across three decades of change.* New York: Routledge.
Fisher, B. A. (1982). The pragmatic perspective of human communication: A view from system theory. In F. E. X. Dance (ed.), *Human communication theory: Comparative essays* (pp. 192–219). New York: Harper & Row.
Fitch, K., & L'Etang, J. (2017). Other voices? The state of public relations history and historiography: Questions, challenges and limitations of "national" histories and historiographies. *Public Relations Inquiry*, 6(1) 115–136.
Freedman, R. (1983). *Children of the wild west.* New York: Clarion Books.
George, E. (2013). *In public relations: Why do women outnumber men?* March 12. Accessed August 16, 2019 from www.lovell.com/our-outlook/in-public-relations-why-do-women-outnumber-men.
Gergen, K. J. (1985). The social constructionist movement in modern psychology. *American Psychologist*, 40(3), 266–275.
Golombisky, K., & Holtzhausen, D. (2005). "Pioneering women" and "founding mothers": Women's history and projecting feminism onto the past. *Women and Language*, 28(2), 12–22.
Gower, K. K. (2006). Public relations at the crossroads. *Journal of Public Relations Research*, 18(2), 177–190.
Gregson, N., & Rose, G. (2013). Contested and negotiated histories of feminist geography. In G. Rose et al. (eds), *Feminist geographies: Explorations in diversity and difference* (pp. 13–48). New York: Taylor & Francis.
Grunig, J. E. (1992). What is excellence in management? In J. E. Grunig (ed.), *Excellence in public relations and communication management* (pp. 219–250). Hillsdale, NJ: Lawrence Erlbaum Associates.
Grunig, J. E. (1996). The history of an idea, unpublished paper, Washington, DC.
Grunig, J. E. (2006). Furnishing the edifice: Ongoing research on public relations as a strategic management function. *Public Relations Research*, 18(2), 151–176.

Grunig, J. E., & Hunt, T. (1984) *Managing public relations*. New York: Holt, Rinehart and Winston.

Grunig, J. E., & White, J. (1992) The effect of worldviews on public relations theory and practice. In J. E. Grunig (ed.), *Excellence in public relations and communication management* (pp. 31–64). Hillsdale, NJ: Lawrence Erlbaum Associates.

Grunig, L. A. (1988). A research agenda for women in public relations. *Public Relations Review*, 14, 48–57.

Grunig, L. A. (1992). How public relations/communication departments should adapt to the structure and environment of an organization ... and what they actually do. In J. E. Grunig (ed.), *Excellence in public relations and communication management* (pp. 467–481). Hillsdale, NJ: Lawrence Erlbaum Associates.

Grunig, L. A., Grunig, J. E., & Ehling, W. (1992). What is an effective organization? In J. E. Grunig (ed.), *Excellence in public relations and communication management* (pp. 65–90). Hillsdale, NJ: Lawrence Erlbaum Associates.

Grunig, L., Toth, E. L., & Hon, L. C. (2001). *Women in public relations: How gender influences practice*. New York: The Guilford Press.

Gudykunst, W. B. (1995). Anxiety/uncertainty management (AUM) theory: Current status. In R. L. Wiseman (ed.), *Intercultural communication theory* (pp. 8–58). Thousand Oaks, CA: Sage.

Gudykunst, W. B. (2005). *Theorizing about intercultural communication*. Thousand Oaks, CA: Sage.

Gudykunst, W. B., Chua, E., & Gray, A. J. (1987). Cultural dissimilarities and uncertainty reduction processes. In M. I. McLaughlin (ed.), *Communication yearbook*, 10 (pp. 456–469). Newbury Park, CA: Sage.

Gudykunst, W. B., Nishida, T., & Chua, E. (1987). Perceptions of social penetration in Japanese-North American dyads. *International Journal of Intercultural Relations*, 11, 171–189.

Gustavson, C. G. (1955). *A preface to history*. New York: McGraw-Hill.

Hall, S. (1969). The technics of persuasion. *New Society*, December, 948–949.

Heath, R. L. (2005). Milestones in the history of public relations. In *Encyclopedia of public relations* (1st edn) (pp. 915–918). Thousand Oaks, CA: Sage.

Heath, R. L. (2013). Network theory. In *Encyclopedia of public relations* (2nd edn) (pp. 603–605). Thousand Oaks, CA: Sage.

Hon, L. (1995). Toward a feminist theory of public relations. *Journal of Public Relations Research*, 7, 27–88.

Hon, L. C., & Grunig, J. E. (1999). *Guidelines for measuring relationships in public relations*. Gainesville, FL: The Institute for Public Relations, Commission on PR Measurement and Evaluation.

Huff, C. (1989). That profoundly female, and feminist genre: The diary as feminist practice. *Women's Studies Quarterly*, 17(3/4), 6–14.

Jameson, E. (1987). Women as workers, women as civilizers: True womanhood in the American West. In S. Armitage & E. Jameson (eds), *Writing the range: Race, class, and culture in the women's west* (pp. 145–164). Norman, OK: University of Oklahoma Press.

Jeffrey, J. R. (1979). *Frontier women: The trans-Mississippi West, 1840–1880*. New York: Hill & Wang.

Jeffrey, J. R. (1998). *Frontier women: Civilizing the west? 1840–1880*. New York: Hill & Wang.

Johnson, N. C. (1995). Cast in stone: Monuments, geography and nationalism. *Environment and Planning: Society and Space*, 13, 51–65.

Johnston, K. A., & Lane, A. B. (2019). An authenticity matrix for community engagement. *Journal of Public Relations Research*, 26(5), 436–454.

Kang, M., & Park, Y-E. (2017) Exploring trust and distrust as conceptually and empirically distinct constructs: Association with symmetrical communication and public engagement across four pairings of trust and distrust. *Journal of Public Relations Research*, 29(2–3), 114–135.

Kay, J. (1991). Landscapes of women and men: Rethinking the regional historical geography of the United States and Canada. *Journal of Historical Geography*, 17, 435–452.

Krippendorff, K. (1977). Information systems theory and research: An overview. In B. D. Ruben (ed.), *Communication yearbook*, 1 (pp. 149–171). New Brunswick, NJ: Transaction Books.

Kruckeberg, D., & Starck, K. (1988). *Public relations and community: A reconstructed theory*. New York: Praeger.

Kuhn, T. S. (1970). *The structure of scientific revolutions*. Chicago, IL: The University of Chicago Press.

Kwon, H. (2017). The paintings of Korean comfort woman Duk-kyung Kang: Postcolonial and decolonial aesthetics for colonized bodies. *Feminist Studies*, 43(3), 571–609.

LaLande, J. (2005). *Settling up the country. Americans return to the Oregon Country*. The Oregon History Project. Accessed February 17, 2020 from https://bit.ly/2vKevBO.

Lamme, M. O. (2015). Where the quiet work is done: Biography in public relations. In T. Watson (ed.) *Perspectives on public relations historiography and historical theorization: Other voices* (pp. 48–68). New York: Palgrave Macmillan.

Lamme, M. O., & Russell, K. M. (2010). Removing the spin: Toward a new theory of public relations history. *Journalism Monographs*, 11(4), 281–362.

Leeds-Hurwitz, W. (2009). Social construction of reality. In S. W. Littlejohn & K. A. Foss (eds), *Encyclopedia of communication theory* (pp. 892–895). Thousand Oaks, CA: Sage.

L'Etang, J. (2014). Writing PR history: Issues, methods and politics. In B. St. John III, M. O. Lamme, & J. L'Etang (eds), *Pathways to public relations: Histories of practice and Profession* (pp. xix–xxxviii). Abingdon: Routledge.

L'Etang, J. (2016). History as a source of critique: Historicity and knowledge, societal change, activism and movements. In J. L'Etang, D. McKie, N. Snow, & J. Xifra (eds), *The Routledge handbook of critical public relations* (pp. 28–40). New York: Routledge.

Littlejohn, S. W. (2002). *Theories of human communication* (7th edn). Belmont, CA: Wadsworth/Thomson Learning.

Logan, N. (2014). Corporate voice and ideology: An alternative approach to understanding public relations history. *Public Relations Review*, 40, 661–668.

Logan, N. (2016). The Starbucks race together initiative: Analyzing a public relations campaign with critical race theory. *Public Relations Inquiry*, 5(1), 93–113.

Maslow, A. H. (1970). *Motivation and personality*. New York: Harper & Row.

Matthews, J. (1986). Feminist history. *Labour History*, 50, 147–153.

Men, L. R., & Tsai, W. H. S. (2014). Perceptual, attitudinal, and behavioral outcomes of organization–public engagement on corporate social networking sites. *Journal of Public Relations Research*, 26 (5), 417–435.

Morin, K. M., & Berg, L. D. (1999). Emplacing current trends in feminist historical geography, gender, place and culture. *A Journal of Feminist Geography*, 6(4), 311–330.

Morrissey, K. G. (1992). Engendering the West. In W. Cronon, G. Miles, & J. Gitlin (eds), *Under an open sky: Rethinking America's western past* (pp. 132–144). New York: W. W. Norton & Company.

Myres, S. L. (1982). *Westering women and the frontier experience, 1800–1915*. Albuquerque, NM: University of New Mexico Press.

Neff, B. (2013). Community relations. In R. L. Heath (ed.), *Encyclopedia of public relations* (2nd edn) (pp. 169–172). Thousand Oaks, CA: Sage.

Ni, L., & Wang, Q. (2011). Anxiety and uncertainty management in an intercultural setting: The impact on organization–public relationships. *Journal of Public Relations Research*, 23, 269–301.

Norwood, V. (1988). Women's place: Continuity and change in response to Western landscapes. In L. Schlissel, V. L. Ruiz, & J. J. Monk (eds), *Western women: Their land, their lives* (pp. 155–181). Albuquerque, NM: University of New Mexico Press.

Pompper, D. (2005). "Difference" in public relations research: A case for introducing Critical Race Theory. *Journal of Public Relations Research*, 17(2), 139–169.

Prescott, C. C. (2012). The all-American eternal family: Sacred and secular values in Western pioneer monuments. In J. L. Meriwether & L. M. D'Amore (eds), *We are what we remember: The American past through commemoration* (pp. 334–358). Cambridge: Cambridge Scholars Publishing.

Public Relations Society of America (PRSA) (n.d.). PRSA code of ethics. Accessed January 1, 2020 from www.prsa.org/ethics/code-of-ethics.

Public Relations Society of America (PRSA) (2019). History of the profession presentation. Accessed October 27, 2019 from www.praccreditation.org.

Rawlins, B. (2009). Give the emperor a mirror: Toward developing a stakeholder measurement of organizational transparency. *Journal of Public Relations Research*, 21, 71–99.

Ray, M. E. (2016). John Taylor and the ghost of Long Meg of Westminster: Authorship and poetic authority in *The Women's Sharpe Revenge*. *Studies in Philology*, 113(4), 919–946.

Reinharz, S. (1992). *Feminist methods in social research*. Oxford: Oxford University Press.

Riley, G. (1977). Images of the frontierswoman: Iowa as a case study. *The Western Historical Quarterly*, 8(2), 189–202.

Riley, G. (1984). *Women and Indians on the frontier, 1825–1915*. Albuquerque, NM: University of New Mexico Press.

Riley, G. (1994). *Frontierswomen: The Iowa experience*. Ames, IA: Iowa State University Press.

Robbins, S. P. (1987). *Organization theory: Structure, design, and applications* (2nd edn). Englewood Cliffs, NJ: Prentice-Hall.

Robbins, W. B. (2002a). Resettlement and the new economy. A changing landscape and the beginnings of White settlement. Accessed February 17, 2020 from https://bit.ly/2uKwvff.

Robbins, W. G. (2002b). *A new legal landscape*. The Oregon History Project. Accessed February 17, 2020 from https://bit.ly/38BXIzi.

Ronneberger, F., & Rühl, M. (1992). *Theory of public relations. An outline*. Opladen: Westdeutscher Verlag.

Rose, G. (1995). Tradition and paternity: Same difference? *Transactions of the Institute of British Geographers*, 20, 414–416.

Rose, G., & Ogborn, M. (1988). Feminism and historical geography. *Journal of Historical Geography*, 14, 405–409.

Saling, K. (2013). Social network analysis. In R. L. Heath (ed.), *Handbook of public relations* (pp. 849–850). Thousand Oaks, CA: Sage.

Seltzer, T., Gardner, E., Bichard, S., & Callison, C. (2012). PR in the ER: Managing organization-public relationships in a hospital emergency department. *Public Relations Review*, 38, 128–136.

Sha, B-L. (2019). Editor's essay: Committing to community. *Journal of Public Relations Research*, 31(1–2), 1–4.

Simonsen, K. (1996). What kind of space in what kind of social theory? *Progress in Human Geography*, 20, 494–512.

Sriramesh, K., Kim, Y., & Takasaki, M. (1999). Public relations in three Asian cultures: An analysis. *Journal of Public Relations Research*, 11, 271–292.

Stafford, L., & Canary, D. J. (1991). Maintenance strategies and romantic relationship type, gender, and relational characteristics. *Journal of Social and Personal Relationships*, 8, 217–242.

Starck, K., & Kruckeberg, D. (2001). Public relations and community: A reconstructed theory revised. In R. L. Heath (ed.), *Handbook of public relations* (pp. 51–59). Thousand Oaks, CA: Sage.

Stohl, C. (1995). *Organizational communication: Connectedness in action*. Thousand Oaks, CA: Sage.

Tong, R. (2009). *Feminist thought: A more comprehensive introduction* (5th edn). Boulder, CO: Westview Press.

Toth, E. (2001). How feminist theory advanced the practice of public relations. In R. Heath & G. Vasquez (eds), *Handbook of public relations* (pp. 237–246). Newbury Park, CA: Sage.

U.S. Bureau of the Census (2010). Vintage 2019 population estimates. Accessed August 15, 2019 from https://bit.ly/2vULaVl.

U.S. Department of Education. (2018). National Center for Education Statistics, Integrated Postsecondary Education Data System (IPEDS). Accessed December 22, 2019 from https://nces.ed.gov/programs/digest/d18/tables/dt18_318.30.asp.

Van Manen, M. (1990). *Researching lived experience: Human science for an action sensitive pedagogy* (2nd edn). Albany, NY: State University of New York Press.

Vardeman, J., Kennedy, A., & Little, B. (2019). Intersectional activism, history and public relations: New understandings of women's communicative roles in anti-racist and anti-sexist work. In I. Somerville, L. Edwards, & Ø. Ihlen (eds), *Public relations, society, and the generative power of history* (pp. 96–112). Abingdon: Routledge.

Vasquez, G. M., & Taylor, M. (2001). Public relations: An emerging social science enters the new millennium. *Communication Yearbook*, 24, 319–342.

Vuolo, B. H. (1975). Pioneer diaries: The untold story of the West. *Ms.*, 3(11), 32–34.

Watson, T. (2013). Keynote speech to the International History of Public Relations Conference, Bournemouth University, June 24–25, June 24. Accessed October 27, 2019 from https://microsites.bournemouth. ac.uk/historyofpr/files/2010/11/Tom-Watson-IHPRC-2013-Keynote-Address4.pdf.

Waymer, D. (2012) (ed.) *Culture, social class, and race in public relations*. Lanham, MD: Lexington Books.

Webber, B. (1990). Introduction and contemporary comments. *The Oregon Trail diary of twin sisters Cecilia Adams and Parthenia Blank in 1852*. Medford, OR: Webb Research Group.

Weenink, E., & Bridgman, T. (2017). Taking subjectivity and reflexivity seriously: Implications of social constructionism for researching volunteer motivation. *Voluntas: International Journal of Voluntary and Nonprofit Organizations*, 28, 90–109.

Wilcox, D. L., Ault, P., & Agee, W. K. (2014). *Public relations: Strategies and tactics* (11th edn). New York: HarperCollins.

Williams, R. (2001). *The long revolution*. Cardigan: Parthian Books.
Yu, H., Jiang, A., & Shen, J. (2016). Prevalence and predictors of compassion fatigue, burnout and compassion satisfaction among oncology nurses: A cross-sectional survey. *International Journal of Nursing Studies*, 57(May), 28–38.

2 Re-examining the American West's Lure and Women's Role Representations

From feature films and television programs through staged re-enactments and public space monuments, the Oregon Trail westerly migration across the continent to the Pacific Coast has been captured in our collective memory as an enduring myth with traditional gender role representations. The U.S. West is a hyper-masculinized male space of valor, courage, and violence. Meanwhile, the female space is represented and remembered from history as a supporting role grounded in family and the domestic sphere. Because *collective memory* refers to "recollections that are instantiated beyond the individual by and for the collective" (Zelizer, 1995, p. 214), it is important to explore representations of women's role on the Oregon Trail and as essential members among Oregon settlers and homesteaders. Because "that which is not publicly known and spoken about will be socially forgotten," the study detailed in this book offers collective memory repair, or "work to prevent forgetting" (Irwin-Zarecka, 1994, p. 115) by offering a deeper examination of pioneer women's community-building role. Importantly, the traditional female gender role must be carefully considered to avoid incomplete interpretations that lead to limiting stereotypes. Re-examining the American West's lure, this chapter's theme means considering the West's appeal from the perspectives of the nineteenth-century women who emigrated via the Oregon Trail, as well as the ways representations of their role limit a fuller understanding of women's actual community-building work.

The sections for this chapter are: Oregon from Territory/Country, through Statehood, to the Homestead Act of 1862; Lure of the American West and Collective Memory; Gendering and Racing the West; Challenges of the Oregon Trail Journey Impacting Women's Perspectives; Collective Memory about Pioneer Women; Pioneer Women's Voices as Historians; and Summary.

Oregon from Territory/Country, through Statehood, to the Homestead Act of 1862

To understand the hugely impactful U.S. Homestead Act of 1862 as inspiring the building of new communities for Caucasians/Whites while destroying those of Native Americans, it is useful to step back in time for context. Many indigenous Native American people lived on Oregon land well before European traders, explorers, missionaries, and other early Caucasian/White settlers arrived. About 42 groups of indigenous communities included the Alsea, Bannock, Cayuse, Chinook, Clackamas, Clatsop, Coos, Coquille, Kalapuya, Modoc, Shasta, Tillamook, and Umpqua (Carey, 1922). Oregon Country/Territory was established in 1848 and became part of the U.S. as a result of the Oregon Treaty in 1846, including settlers of both the U.S. and Great Britain. Both nations settled on a boundary dividing the U.S. and Canada.

Commercial interests fueled by a nineteenth-century fashion trend for fur – especially beaver pelts for men's hats in the East – inspired the earliest travels West by Caucasian/White male trappers (Butruille, 1993). They became mountain men of legend. Robert Stuart, a Scottish-born Canadian and American fur trader, is believed to be the first Caucasian/White man to travel from Fort Astoria, on the coast of present-day Oregon, to St. Louis to develop the Pacific Fur Company, thus cutting an early 1800s trade route (Rollins, 1995). Fur trappers' stories about picturesque lands and opportunity in the West filtered back to the States.

In the mid-nineteenth century, back in Washington, D.C., Congress examined ways that the Louisiana Purchase lands could be settled "in a way that was fair to all" (Porterfield, 2004, p. 25). Congressman Galusha A. Grow sponsored the Homestead Act, just three years after Oregon officially was admitted into the Union as the thirty-third state in 1859. U.S. President Abraham Lincoln signed it into law and it became effective on January 1, 1863. The Homestead Act is one of the most important pieces of legislation in U.S. history, passing easily since 11 southern states had already seceded from the Union (Porterfield, 2004). By 1900, the legislation had led to the distribution of 160 million acres of "public land" according to the Library of Congress (Homestead Act, n.d.), meaning roughly 10% of the area of the U.S. was claimed and settled under the Homestead Act with vast displacement of Native American peoples (Gambino & Frail, 2012). The Homestead Act also supported railroad construction, remaining in effect in the U.S. until 1976, with homesteading ongoing in Alaska until 1986 (About the Homestead Act, n.d.). Between 1868 and 1955, the U.S. government distributed nearly 250 million acres to private individuals (Lindgren, 1991).

It was envisioned that the U.S. would be a nation of family farmers (Lindgren, 1991) and the Homestead Act of 1862 was designed to inspire Western migration by offering land for free to those who promised to live on it for five continuous years before receiving ownership of it (Porterfield, 2004). The Act was administered by the General Land Office within the Department of the Interior (Muhn, 1994) and applied to land west of the Mississippi River, so excluded the 13 original states and Hawaii, Kentucky, Maine, Tennessee, Texas, Vermont, and West Virginia. Emigrant colonizers, as settlers, miners, and ranchers, took what was considered to be empty, unclaimed lands – without the U.S. actually purchasing land rights from indigenous peoples (Lewis, 2014). To be eligible to become a *homesteader* an individual had to be a

Figure 2.1 Four-Cent U.S. Homestead Act Postage Stamp
Source: Donnalyn Pompper.

family head, at least 21 years old, and a U.S. citizen (or to have filed intentions to become a citizen, paying an $18 filing fee). When the bill became law, those interested in homesteading had to file their intentions at the nearest Land Office and pay a $10 temporary claim to the land with a $2 commission to the land agent. Once on the land, homesteaders had to build a home and farm the land (known as "proving up") for five years. With two neighbors or friends to vouch in tow, the homesteader proved the land's improvements, signed a document, paid a $6 fee, and got a deed-receipt signed by the U.S. president. Many new landowners displayed the receipt on their cabin wall as a badge of their achievement (About the Homestead Act, n.d.).

Single women and unwed mothers not yet 21 years of age could apply for land in the West under the Homestead Act because they qualified as family heads, as could women who were widowed, divorced, or deserted (Muhn, 1994) – but married women could not apply unless they were considered to be the household head. In other words, husbands of married women were deemed the household head by default under law. After the Civil War, many Union widows staked claims hoping to make a fresh start (Porterfield, 2004). It is estimated that women comprised 5% of the homesteaders in the early settlements and about 20% had established homesteads after 1900 (Roark, Johnson, Cohen, Stage, & Hartmann, 2016). Most homesteading women were young (at least 21), single, looking for adventure and the possibility of economic gain. Lindgren's (1991) research of the lived experiences among North Dakota's homesteading women found that they were the main characters in the settlement drama, shattering old stereotypes of women as reluctant pioneers or secondary helpmates. Some women eventually pursued careers as teachers, nurses, seamstresses, and domestic workers, as well as journalists and photographers, with many eventually marrying while some remained single and acquired additional land which they sold for a profit or as an investment (Lindgren, 1991). Under the Homestead Act of 1862, freed slaves were eligible to register a claim for a homestead and all African Americans were eligible to become homesteaders out West after they became citizens under the 14th Amendment in 1868, yet few applied due to rampant discrimination and systemic barriers (Merritt, 2016).

The mass media amplified the West as the *promised land* under the Homestead Act of 1862, as did touring lecturers paid by railroad companies who gave public talks. Guide books were sold as tools for mapping the journey for would-be settlers and popular novels about romance of the trek also were widely distributed. Copies of Fremont's Report on Lansford W. Hastings' *Emigrants' Guide to Oregon and California* helped emigrants to "puzzle out the deserts and mountains" from the pages (Feltskog, 1969, p. 24). Newspaper advertisements throughout the East "proclaimed the need for settlers" (Porterfield, 2004, p. 30). Ultimately, newspaper publisher Horace Greeley was one of the Homestead Act's leading advocates. However, newspapers' support and enthusiasm for the Homestead Act rarely factored in the financial cost of the journey West or anticipated just how unprepared many people were for the journey's terrain or a life of farming (Sloan, Stovall, & Startt, 1989).

Lure of the American West and Collective Memory

No piece of geography in the U.S. stands out in our collective memory quite like the West. As "a field of Americana," the West holds a "mystique" and "fascination" with the public as a "unique place" (Malone, 1991, p. 100). By the end of the Civil War when the nation was securely established on both coasts, the frontier no longer promised an "untouched garden in which the human community might still organize itself anew" (Kolodny, 1984, p. 199). This image of the West has endured in collective memory – as shaped by cowboys on horses with lassoes, "Indians," jagged rock formations and raging rivers, covered wagons, rattlesnakes, buffalo, coyotes, tumble weeds, and sage brush. Many of these symbols also fuel our folklore and the concept of *Americana*, a term for artifacts related to the history, geography, and cultural heritage of the U.S. (Sides, 2007). Riley (1994b) called settlement of the American frontier "one of the richest and most colourful themes in history of the United States" (p. xi).

A key player in supporting this imagery of the West was the U.S. railroad industry. As the first major industry of the U.S., railroads also played a significant role in the professionalization of public relations practice. Given the U.S. Homestead Act's promise of free land in the West with agricultural and industrial advantages, railroads hired lobbyists and publicists who wrote books and periodicals to sell the public and investors the virtues of Western living. In a chapter titled "Publicity Moves America West," Cutlip (1995) explained how railroad publicists defused skeptics who worried about safety, health, and eyesores by beginning to use romantic imagery to sell Mid-westerners and Easterners on the idea of westward emigration to California and Oregon. It was "one of the most effective promotional campaigns in history" (Billington, 1963, p. 6). Collectively, the transport, tourist, and information industries promoted "a new spirit of American nationalism" (Fifer, 1988, p. 2). Yet, publicists' writings were misleading in creating "a distorted canvas that plagues us to this day" (Cutlip, 1995, p. 141), misrepresenting actual development of farms and communities.

Today we acknowledge that idealized representations of the West offered a less than perfect picture. Our love of the American West must be balanced against the destructive effects of the westward migration on indigenous Native American populations, including displacement, murder, and death due to spread of diseases previously unknown to indigenous communities. Many in the U.S. still fail to acknowledge what Prescott (2019) called "the racial underpinnings of the national story of westward expansion" in ways that challenge Caucasian/Whites' enduring and widespread acceptance of "the notion of American manifest destiny" (p. 290). Moreover, the ecological balance of flora and fauna was disrupted across the land as a result of decades of migration and subsequent population growth. This less-than-rosy reality contrasts with "old" Western history that painted the West as a case study in "progress, development, and achievement" (Riley, 1994b, p. xii).

Gendering and Racing the West

Examining how narratives about the U.S. West have been gendered and raced promotes a better understanding of why our collective memory of the West is predominantly represented as masculine and Caucasian/White. The quintessential symbol of the Western frontier is the romantic hyper-masculine Caucasian/White cowboy of popular culture, privileging masculinity that for decades has limited our understanding and awareness of pioneer women's lived experiences. What we've learned about the U.S. West has been shaped by novels, big budget Hollywood films like *True Grit*, and television programs like *Gunsmoke, Bonanza, Little House on the Prairie*, and, more recently, *U.S. Marshall, Lonesome Dove*, and *Deadwood*. It was the cowboy story line that made Hollywood one of the largest industries in the U.S. (Kleinfeld & Kleinfeld, 2004). Decades later, *The Oregon Trail* computer game of the 1980s was designed to teach schoolchildren the realities of nineteenth-century pioneer life in an entertaining fashion. Players assume the role of a male leader guiding settlers in 1848 from Independence, Missouri, to Oregon's Willamette Valley. As of 2011, more than 65 million copies of *The Oregon Trail* game have been sold (Lussenhop, 2011). Players strategize about how to keep pioneers traveling westward despite the threat of overturned wagons, stolen cattle, and dysentery.

Sharply defined gender roles are fairly obvious when examining the language used to represent people and processes associated with nineteenth-century U.S. westward migration. Popular culture stories consistently celebrate images of "men's work" – the physical labor and bravery of Caucasian/White pioneers and cowboys busy "subduing Indians," building railroads, ranching, farming, logging, and establishing governments (Morrissey, 1992, p. 133) – while dutiful wives and mothers bear and raise children and perform domestic chores. For nearly 200 years, gendered metaphors that historians have used to describe westward expansionism include masculine "penetration" of the feminine "virgin wilderness" as a "fertile" land ripe for "rebirth and regeneration" (Kolodny, 1975 p. 136). Many historians have used the word *pioneer*, which means "a person who goes before, preparing the way for others, as an early settler … being one of the first of its kind, of or characteristic of the settlers of a new territory," according to *Webster's New World Dictionary* (Neufeldt & Guralnik, 1994). Feminist historians have created their own terms, such as *frontierswomen* (e.g., Riley, 1984), while some historians have avoided gender-specific labels by calling all Caucasian/White pioneers *emigrants* (e.g., Butruille, 1993).

Historian Frederick Jackson Turner (1894) advanced a frontier thesis expressing admiration for U.S. westward expansion as a redemptive and innovative environment; a myth that held sway until it began crumbling in the mid-1970s. Turner (1894) lamented that the frontier was closing; lands he celebrated as masculine. Oregon was considered an Edenic wilderness (Dennis, 2014). Male historians directed little attention to the female experience because they saw no need to do so (Pascoe, 1991). Hence, pioneer women and their participation in the settlement and development of the Western frontier constituted "one of the most neglected aspects of the story of American women" (Riley, 1994b, p. xiii). Pre-emigration West, the men had worked outside the home in the public sphere as clerks, shopkeepers, and farmers before outfitting for the five-to-six-month trip for about $200 plus about $25 for ammunitions – while the women had worked in the private sphere performing domestic labor. Families gathered in Independence, St. Louis, or Westport Landing along the Missouri River in late spring with a wagon, harnesses, and a team of oxen (Mattes, 1987). If mentioned at all by early historians, women on the Overland Trail trip were cast as "gentle tamers" or "exceptional women" who worked with "quiet force" to feminize the region (Brown, 1958, p. 136). In these accounts, women were "practical creatures," wives, and schoolmarms (Brown, 1958, p. 137). Historian Steven Ambrose said of Lewis and Clark's 1805 Corps of Discovery expedition that the Shoshone woman, Sacajawea, was highly regarded for bringing "a woman's touch," and with her baby, Jean Baptiste, inspired "cooperation and teamwork" by adding a dimension of "family" to the journey (Burns, Duncan, & Burns, 1997). Overall, pre-1970s historians retained a traditional framework of Western history as a male space (Morrissey, 1992, p. 134), generally without considering how women felt about the land (Schlissel, Ruiz, & Monk, 1988). As it turned out, pioneer women were highly complex people.

By the mid-1970s, new feminist historians considered the Turner frontier thesis and resulting conventional historical narratives too narrow and inadequate to explore women's actual lived experiences in the nineteenth-century

U.S. West. Influenced by new feminist scholarship in a variety of disciplines, including women's studies, they opted instead to write a new social history, revealing the influence of ideology upon historical representations. More work was needed beyond simply *adding* women to Western history. Posing complex questions about women's lived experience required detailed analysis to challenge the assumptions of Turner's male-centric frontier thesis (Armitage, 1985). Examining first-person accounts of community life, private and public sphere work, and the perceptions of Western landscapes from women's diaries, memoirs, and letters about moving to and living in the West revealed new findings about how women's and men's lives were fundamentally distinct. Taking inspiration from second wave feminism to validate women's history as a legitimate academic discipline, women historians such as Julie Roy Jeffrey, Sandra L. Myres, Glenda Riley, and Lilian Schlissel assumed the mantle of *pioneer* themselves. They dove into women's Kansas-to-Wyoming Overland Trail diaries and travel accounts to discover just how free from social constraints and liberating the trek West had been for pioneer women. Research findings suggested that pioneer women experienced *increased* domestic work and vulnerability to patriarchy (e.g., Jeffrey, 1979; Schlissel, 2004), dispelling earlier conclusions that the West was "somehow freer, more democratic, more individualistic, and more egalitarian than the East" (Pascoe, 1991, p. 41). In the process, these feminist historians also incorporated study of the natural environment by examining the physical landscape and ecological changes impacted by the Overland Trail pioneer movements.

As historians continue to challenge male-centric narratives of the Turner thesis era in order to include women by asking complex questions about their lived experiences, some scholars also have considered additional social identity dimensions and their intersections with female gender, such as ethnicity/race, for expanded inquiries. For example, Jameson (1988) problematized the term *Western women's history*, explaining "[w]hat Anglos called the 'West' was, after all, simply home for American Indians, the 'East' for Asians, the 'South' for Canadians, and 'El Norte' for northwestern Mexico for Mexicans and Spanish-Mexicans" (p. 761). Other historians of the West continue to explore social identity intersectionalities among gender, class, ethnicity/race, and sexuality as central to the U.S. West identity (e.g., Deutsch, 1987; Hurtado, 1999; Jameson & Armitage, 1997; Limerick, Milner, & Rankin, 1991; McManus, 2005; Pascoe, 1990; Riley, 1994a; Ruiz, 1987; Taylor & Moore, 2003; Warren, 2007; White, 1991), resolving that the West is less a frontier than a *multicultural space* where people of varied ideals and economies met – "a place of cultural contact and interaction between groups" (Jeffrey, 1998, p. 6, emphasis added).

Despite this critical turn or paradigm shift in the history discipline, the pervasive influence of the masculine image of the West endures, so that women have been represented in narratives primarily in juxtaposition to men. For example, *the saloon dance hall girl* with a heart of gold exists to please hard-drinking cowboys and the *sunbonneted pioneer wife* is subservient to the masculine fearless protector husband as she supports his labor in taming the frontier (Morrissey, 1992). As archetypes – either positive or neutral representations – these images offer pre-existing models from which future copies or examples are created. On the other hand, stereotypes are rarely neutral and almost always negative representations. Merskin (2004) defined *stereotype* as "over-generalized, reductionist beliefs, [that] are collections of traits or characteristics that present members of a group as being all the same" (p. 160). Overall, the way archetypal women in the U.S. West have been represented turns them into negative stereotypes characterizing women and their roles in an exceptionally limiting manner that contrasts with women's actual lived experiences.

Another widely promoted archetypal woman promoted by frontier historians and incorporated into popular culture narratives is *the female missionary* determined to proselytize the indigenous communities. Of course, religious fervor did inspire emigrants to establish missions and communities in the West to convert Native Americans to Christianity. As an archetype, *the female missionary* resonated with nineteenth-century notions of femininity as missionary women performed charitable work outside the home, including performing the role of a Sunday school teacher. Nineteenth-century mass media amplified this representation. During the 1830s and 1840s when opportunities to travel West became available, both single and married missionary women journeyed to take the gospel to "the heathen Indians" (Butruille, 1993, p. 17). For example, *Godey's Lady's Book* in 1860 noted that women should extend their efforts to help the "poor and ignorant" by carrying the message of Christianity throughout the world (Riley, 1984, p. 9). Oregon Country/Territory held a particular appeal for missionaries as a "definite land of supposed milk and honey" (Feltskog, 1969, p. 20). From 1829–1840, the American Society for Encouraging the Settlement of Oregon Territory registered 3,000 recruits in Boston who met up in St. Louis before setting out for Oregon Country/Territory.

Missionary wives were an eager subset of pioneers, yet the reality of filling the multiple roles of performing their own domestic work while recruiting converts, fundraising, and teaching for pay in a new land among unfamiliar cultures was a challenge for them (Jeffrey, 1998). After the Reverend Jason Lee founded the first mission and farming colony in Oregon Country/Territory's Willamette Valley in 1834, Narcissa Whitman and Elza Spalding (with their husbands) were among the first female missionaries to cross the Continental Divide in the Rocky Mountains (Riley, 2004). In 1837, the Whitmans settled in a part of Oregon Country/Territory that later was adjoined to the current state of Washington near Walla Walla. The Spaldings settled in present-day Idaho. Narcissa Whitman was the first Caucasian/White woman to give birth to a Caucasian/White baby on the frontier, according to history books (Gwartney, 2019). Such female missionaries saw themselves as part of a "national effort to save the West for Protestantism and civilization" (Jeffrey, 1998, p. 46) and generally believed in Caucasian/White superiority (Riley, 2004). The missionaries' stories about fertile land in Oregon Country/Territory further fanned support for "evangelical fervor" back East (Butruille, 1993, p. 17).

The Whitman Mission grew to become a major stopping point for other Oregon Trail émigrés. Many missionaries found co-existence between Native American and Caucasian/White communities to be an anomaly, however, with Native Americans reluctant to abandon their traditions and missionaries losing their enthusiasm to convert them. The Cayuse of today's Oregon and Washington states had first been exposed to the teaching of Christianity back when Lewis and Clark searched for an all-water route connecting the Atlantic and Pacific coasts of North America to Europe and the Far East back in the time of Columbus (Burns et al., 1997). The aggressive practices of Narcissa Prentiss Whitman, her husband, and the Spaldings involved insisting that the indigenous people recite scripture as the missionaries employed "hell intimidation tactics" (Gwartney, 2019, p. 95). Cayuse women were unwilling to adopt a Caucasian/White version of female domesticity and feared rising numbers of emigrants, while the Whitmans and other frustrated missionaries grew increasingly worried about "the contaminating influence of tribal culture" (Jeffrey, 1998, p. 66). A band of Cayuse and Umatilla peoples killed the Whitman family and about a dozen others at the Waiilatpu Mission in 1847, leaving Narcissa Whitman with a cracked skull and bare-backed whip wounds across her back before her body was rolled into an irrigation ditch and left for wolves or coyotes to dismember her limbs. This conflict altered the tone of westward settlement colonialism, with U.S. authorities taking a more adversarial role toward Native Americans in general and declaring war on the Cayuse in particular (Gwartney, 2019), while the media publicized sensationalist *massacre* stories. Beckham (1996) explained that until at least 1856, territory conflicts between homesteaders and indigenous communities spread throughout southwestern Oregon and northern California.

Rarely have popular culture American West folklore stories promoted horsewomen, female cattle wranglers, or cowgirls who broke gender role boundaries and worked in traditionally male jobs (McAndrews, 2006) – with one exception. As part of Buffalo Bill Cody's Wild West show, buckskin-and-boots-wearing frontier legend Annie Oakley displayed her sharpshooting talents during her peak career years, 1885–1913, developing into a businesswoman and public entertainer. Despite her talent, Oakley later was framed as an ugly duckling in the 1946 Broadway musical, *Annie Get Your Gun*; a Caucasian/White woman who had to emphasize her femininity with satin and lace before she could fulfill her female gender role, marry showman Frank Butler, and live happily ever after (Palmer, 1989). In reality, Oakley negotiated confronting the boundaries of female gender roles of the period while also reinforcing late-nineteenth-century notions of Victorian respectability (Riley, 2002). Oakley remained feminine but never wore pants, always rode sidesaddle, and wore her hair long. As a businesswoman, her salary in the Wild West Show exceeded that of male performers and she traveled extensively across the U.S. and Europe, following a fairly independent career (Riley, 2002). Yet, Oakley refused to support women's suffrage campaigns and eventually crafted a public persona as a married, modest, and domestic woman; a "civilizing force of the frontier" (Riley, 2002, p. 113).

Despite the new Western history and intersectional social identity research, popular culture creators today still prefer Turner's frontier thesis for stereotypes and fantasy drama. Turner (1894) posited that westward expansion and frontier settlement opened new opportunities for anyone willing to work hard. Ironically, it was Turner himself who posited that each generation interprets history anew to carve its own understanding rather than accepting written history as some static truth "set down once and for all" (Limerick, Milner, & Rankin, 1991, p. xii). Larry McMurtry, Pulitzer Prize winning author of the novel which served as the basis for the hit television mini-series, *Lonesome Dove*, tried to put an end to it in *The New Republic* (McMurtry, 1990), criticizing academic history departments for eschewing Old West fantasy. Frontier West historians' use of stereotypical images to represent women/femininity ignores the important research findings of feminist women historians since the mid-1970s. Popular culture creators who consult pioneer women's lived experiences as recorded in first-person diaries, journals, and reminiscences encounter more complete and authentic narratives.

Challenges of the Oregon Trail Journey Impacting Women's Perspectives

Once Oregon Fever broke out, waves of the Great Emigration used Independence, Missouri, as the main jumping off point for the Willamette Valley and beyond. About 400,000 Caucasian/White people emigrated West over about 40 years (Billock, 2016), with the mid-1830s seeing the first large wagon trains setting out for the fertile Willamette Valley (Chused, 1984). Oregon Trail migrations peaked in the 1850s, and blended with other Westward migrations by the 1860s (Butruille, 1993). The heaviest traffic westward to Oregon was between 1841 and 1867 as 350,000 traveled by wagon (Jeffrey, 1998) and later by transcontinental railroad, when it was completed in 1867, making travel West easier, safer, and more comfortable. "Civilization" lay to the east of Independence, and "wilderness" lay to the West through to Oregon City (Feltskog, 1969, p. 12). Located by a natural waterfall, Oregon City became a site for a town around 1842, providing "homeseekers from the States a center from which to spread" (Lavender, 1985, p. 384).

What else inspired westward emigration across the continent for Caucasian/White pioneers beyond the Homestead Act of 1862 incentive? Reasons ranged from economic, health, political, patriotic needs, to a desire to join family members who had relocated before them, as well as simply for adventure. Some pioneer women were motivated to emigrate West in pursuit of a more temperate climate for a loved one battling illness (Jeffrey, 1998; Riley, 1994b; Schlissel, 2004). Some went in search of a better life following the economic depression of the 1830s. The Donation Land Act of 1850 provided settlers with free land in Oregon. Men were the primary recipients of federal land before 1830, and even though the federal government preferred to delegate gendered land questions to states and territories because it was believed that women were "presumed to be incapable of buying land from the federal government," it increasingly recognized that men died or became incapacitated, necessitating the reality of female household heads (Chused, 1984, p. 53). After the turn of the century, the number of homesteading applicants who were women rose to more than one-third (Stuart, 1913).

Oregon Trail wagon trains were composed of people determined to endure a journey of roughly five-to-six months of westward travel into the unknown. Emigrants who gathered and outfitted along certain spots along the Missouri River formed "aggregates of nuclear families, loosely attached by kinship or friendship" (Faragher & Stansell, 1975, p. 151). It seems that "ignorance of the road" in the 1840s, cholera in the 1850s, and Civil War and "Indians" in the 1860s did not deter them (Schlissel, 2004, p. 130). Demographically, most of those who traveled the Oregon Trail were young and came from "the middle ranks of society" (Jeffrey, 1998, p. 39), or property-owning people (Butruille, 1993), as opposed to those who could not afford to finance a trip to the West. According to guide books of the day, the cost of the Oregon Trail trip for a family of four was at least $600, possibly offset by selling any surviving cattle or wagons upon arrival in Oregon. Over the years, travel costs increased due to entrepreneurs setting up ferry tolls for the river crossings. In the 1840–1850s, most women who traveled the Oregon Trail were rural family people emigrating from Indiana, Illinois, Iowa, Ohio, Kentucky, Missouri, or Tennessee. It was predominantly *single* men who set out for California for the Gold Rush of 1849 as "renegades and adventurers" (Butruille, 1993, p. 15). In 1841, it was mostly single men on the Oregon Trail, too, as Lavender (1985) offered in this example: among the Bidwell-Bartelson party of about 50 people, only 5 were women (3 were wives) and 10 were children. Soon, Oregon Trail emigrations were "essentially a family phenomenon" (Faragher & Stansell, 1975, p. 150; Schlissel, 2004) as greater numbers of women and children joined Oregon Trail migration waves from the 1840s onwards (Mattes, 1987). Moving was not a completely new experience for pioneer women, as many had moved several times from the East when they were children. Women may have been somewhat prepared to care for their family and others since they already had been accustomed to producing whatever their family needed and bartering for the rest.

Emigrants' letters mailed home and sensational media accounts in the form of news, editorials, and advertisements, promoted nineteenth-century migration to the West. Conflict women experienced in setting out for the unknown, pulling up their roots, and leaving behind family and friends has been described as "Janus-faced;" simultaneously looking forward and back (Butruille, 1993, p. 83). Some emigrants were motivated to join family members who had already relocated to Oregon and were inspired by letters written home telling of fertile land and beautiful vistas there. Once settled in their new home in the West, women wrote letters begging sisters to join them. A sister's "letter of entreaty" was too much to ignore (Cowles, 1929, p. 86), as she described "wondrous tales of rich Western lands" (Butruille, 1993, p. 17) and a mild climate (Schlissel, 2004, p. 36). Some letters were published in local newspapers. For single women, potential marriage in the West was another incentive. The June 24, 1837 issue of *Iowa News* declared that "every respectable young woman who goes to the west, is almost sure of an advantageous marriage." *The Wisconsin Herald* campaigned to bring "virtuous and refined" women from the East (Riley, 1984, p. 13). The long-held assumption was that single women moved West to marry a single man already settled in a new land, but despite the stereotype of nineteenth-century women as weak and dependent, Riley (1994b) found that many ambitious single women traveled the Overland Trail to work as missionaries, teachers, and laborers. Also, Europeans learned about the mass migrations West from the news coverage, so chose to make the trek themselves for "another new beginning" (Riley, 1994b, p. 9).

Among the pioneers who had left their farms and homes in the Midwest and East to join family members who had already emigrated to Oregon Country/Territory were 23-year-old twin sisters Cecilia E. Adams and Parthenia Blank – along with their husbands, parents, and three siblings. The twins wrote in a shared diary about walking most of the plains and mountains of the 2,200-mile trek from Missouri to Oregon City in 1852 to join older brother, James H. McMillan, who had emigrated seven years earlier in 1845. Several of the twin sisters' diary entries during the final weeks of the journey mention encounters with Oregon Country/Territory people who knew or had met McMillan, offering reassurance that the long and demanding journey to join an older brother would be worth the risk. For example, on October 14, Cecilia E. Adams wrote that she met William S. Torrence, an "Indian Agent" traveling to Milwaukie in Oregon who was "well acquainted" with her brother. The husband of Cecilia E. Adams had been invited to join the McMillan family on the westward journey in 1852 shortly after he had finished medical school in Ohio: "When, after three years, she asked me to come with her to Oregon, I had to come … into the land of Oregon we came …" (Webber, 1990, pp. 10–11).

In caravan formation, the Overland Trail emigrants embarked West together making only about 15–20 miles per day up to the Platte River Valley through current-day Kansas and Nebraska, converging near Fort Kearney, then crossing the Rocky Mountains at South Pass in current-day southwestern Wyoming by mid-summer (Faragher & Stansell, 1975). Travel over the plains and prairies between the Mississippi River and the Pacific Ocean was dangerous (stampedes were common), slow, and filled with uncertainty about food and disease. As they crossed the Continental Divide at South Pass, a junction now known as "Parting of the Ways" as marked by a tall monument, several pioneer women noted the landmarks and wrote about rivers' flow direction change. Fort Laramie and Fort Bridger saw more than 2,700 emigrants pause and pass on to Oregon and California (Feltskog, 1969). Idaho was the halfway point of the journey as the trails to California and Oregon diverged. While families tended to head toward Oregon for homesteading of rich farmland, single men advanced to California in search of adventure and gold. Furthermore, Butruille (1993) noted:

> To this day in Oregon, the story goes that at a branch on the trail, a pile of gold quartz marked the way to California, with a signed lettered 'to Oregon' directed the travelers north. Those who could read turn north.
>
> (pp. 15–16)

The second half of the trip offered the more dangerous terrain with rugged mountains, scorching deserts, and boggy salt flats (Mattes, 1987). Emigrants generally reached their final destinations by late fall or early winter. According to the U.S. Bureau of Land Management, conservative estimates are that about as many as 20,000–30,000 (10%) of the approximately 300,000 pioneers who traveled the Oregon Trail died on the way (Basic facts about the Oregon Trail, n.d.)

Wagon wheel ruts carved shoulder-deep paths that eventually served as a literal road map for subsequent travelers, with many ruts carved in rocks that still exist today, up to five feet deep in Guernsey, Wyoming – as well as in Kansas, Nebraska, and Idaho (Billock, 2016). So many wagons and people passed over the Oregon Trail in present-day Wyoming that the sage brush does not grow in the ruts (Webber, 1990). Jeffrey (1998) explained that the wagon traffic was so heavy that parts of the trail resemble a several-miles-wide highway. It was men, predominantly, who repaired broken wagons and often they didn't have to wait long for another wagon to pass with help (Webber, 1990). Less enduring over the passage of time were ruts cut across the prairie where

Figure 2.2 Parting of the Ways
Source: Randy Brown, www.wyohistory.org.

Figure 2.3 Oregon Trail Wagon Ruts
Source: Deposit Photos.

the wagon trains fanned out over up to five miles due to dust and then the parties rejoined one another in tighter clusters at night, to cross rivers, or at narrow mountain crossings (Butruille, 1993).

Figure 2.4 Oregon Trail Ruts State Historic Site
Source: Deposit Photos.

Collective Memory about Pioneer Women

How we remember, forget, and reconstruct the past over time shapes how we act in the present and anticipate the future. This process is referred to as social, public, cultural, or collective memory. This kind of memory is not merely a retrieval of stored information, but use of shared cultural understanding (Bartlett, 1932). In his study of public memory, commemoration, and patriotism, Bodnar (1992) wrote that pioneer remembrances across the Midwest routinely refer to pioneers as "courageous;" they were honored as part of the centennial celebrations for their cooperative spirit, with women "especially lauded for overcoming adversity" (p. 34).

Commemorations create new historical narratives that enable people to engage with the past in personal ways, with attention to the social identity dimensions of class, gender, ethnicity/race, religion/faith, and sexuality changing as social values change (Meriwether & D'Amore, 2012). As part of these celebrations, praising pioneer women's success in dealing with adversity on the Trail has been linked to the traditional female gender role as keeper of the domestic realm in terms of cooking and cleaning – rather than independence from these tasks. Domesticity was one way that women of the past fulfilled their civic duty in the nineteenth century, and through the mid-twentieth century it served as convenient framing in support of national patriotism in response to a perceived Communist threat (Bodnar, 1992). Memorializing pioneers was exceptionally popular in late-nineteenth-century Oregon with parades, dances, banquets, and speeches in response to uncertainties associated with realities such as an 1895 worldwide economic depression negatively impacting Oregon wheat farmers and a rearrangement of time-honored gender roles as more women joined the workforce (Boag, 2014). The memorialization of pioneers as heroes of the past became the obsession of organizations such as the Oregon Pioneer Association formed in 1873, the incorporation of the Oregon Historical Society in 1898, and the formation of the Oregon Native Sons and Oregon Native Daughters organizations in 1899. Virtues of morality, courage, perseverance, vigor, and intelligence were ascribed to pioneers for overcoming adversity associated with plains crossing, illness and death, and worry about indigenous peoples. Post-World War II urbanization and industrialization inspired nostalgia for the ebbing family farming frontier and some of the earliest tributes to Western settlers in the form of monuments were installed in Oregon (Prescott, 2012). Lewis (2014) opined that Caucasian/White Oregonians' attachment to nostalgia enabled them to "feel better about themselves as a blameless, feeling people" since indigenous peoples by then were "safely dead or removed" (p. 286).

Remembering is broader than simply recalling or reminiscing and we use objects such as monuments to help us to remember. Over the past 125 years, "pioneer mother" statues have been erected across the Midwest through to Oregon. Stott (1996) speculated that these appeared throughout the West from the Missouri River to the Pacific Ocean in response to women's transition to work in the public sphere. By the 1920s, the "Pioneer Mother Movement" as maternalist rhetoric in the form of pioneer family images captured the attention of sculptor Avard T. Fairbanks, perhaps in response to "questions about women's proper roles in society" and changing morality as evidenced by the "shocking image of the 'flapper'" (Prescott, 2012, p. 338). Images of "courageous men joined [by] their nurturing wives and tender children in keeping with changing family norms" appealed to Fairbanks as he created commemorative bronzes during the Great Depression and World War II (Prescott, 2012, pp. 349–350). Some 185 public monuments erected since 1890 pay homage to the pioneers and contribute greatly to heritage tourism (Prescott, 2019). Artifacts on display in museums and monuments offer a "sense of the past" through socially constructed understandings of history. Because interpretations of the past are subjective, the narratives propagated may not serve every person the same way due to varying reactions to and sensibilities toward them (Radley, 1997). It is the diversity of impressions that makes the understanding of remembering so important. Images of "saintly mothers," "sturdy white men," and "wholesome pioneer families" offer a window on gender identity and a complex history of remembering, forgetting, and rediscovering pioneers (Prescott, 2019).

Pioneer monuments anchored in public spaces offer gendered narratives that helped to build and reproduce modern views of women's role and the ideal U.S. family. Pioneer Mother monuments reinforce traditional female gender values, as evidenced by "remarkably similar" statues of Caucasian/White

Figure 2.5 Pioneer Mother Statue
Source: University of Oregon.

women in sunbonnets. In the 1920s, Caucasian/White Americans may have been blasé about the displacement of indigenous people, but they were unwilling to accept changes in gender role norms (Prescott, 2019, p. 4). Pioneer mother monuments connect historical knowledge and public mythology about public historical monuments (Prescott, 2019) and tend to cement traditional women's private sphere gender role norms as part of "an impulse to mould history into its rightful pattern" explained art historian Kirk Savage (1997, p. 4).

On the University of Oregon's Eugene campus, a large pair of bronze statues sculpted by Canadian artist Alexander Phimister Proctor – a Pioneer Mother and a Pioneer Father –commemorated the Willamette Valley's pioneer past. Both monuments, considered "symbols of racism and oppression," were torn off their pedestal by protesters on June 13, 2020 and University of Oregon President Michael H. Schill reported in an email message to the university community that neither would be re-installed (A message, June 15, 2020). The Pioneer Mother, fondly referred to as "Elvira," sits slumped forward in a chair with a book in her lap, peacefully resting after her struggles or "passively and contemplatively in old age" signifying a conservative vision of womanhood (Dennis, 2014, p. 297). Prescott (2012) described the Pioneer Mother statue as "combination of Oregon Trail Madonna and domestic pioneer mother" (p. 338). Donated in 1932 by the University of Oregon's Vice President, Burt Brown Baker, in loving memory of his mother (University of Oregon Libraries, 2019), the Pioneer Mother sat atop a granite base in the middle of "Women's Quadrangle," near Gerlinger Hall and Hendricks and Susan Campbell Dormitories. This area is behind Johnson Hall, the university's main administration building which houses the offices of the university president and provost. Meanwhile, the Pioneer Father, sculpted earlier in 1918, was positioned in front of Johnson Hall. He boldly strides forward carrying a whip and firearm. Those who escort students, families, and prospective employees on campus tours romantically commented on how – with a little imagination – one could see the statues gazing at one another through two Johnson Hall glass doors on opposite ends of the building. Dennis (2014) opined that such monuments become "second nature simply part of the landscape," giving passers-by permission to forget because they "do not teach us about or connect us with the actual historical actors in Oregon's pioneer era" (p. 291). Similarly, Weaver-Hightower (n.d.) characterized Pacific Northwest pioneer monuments as "a defense mechanism" in response to guilt. Prescott (2019) called it resolving tension between indigenous dispossession and conquering heroes' success "in dominating wild lands rather than wild peoples" (p. 43).

Twentieth-century historians and celebration commemorators largely remembered women for their support function in a private sphere domesticity context. Casting women from the past this way is consistent with a national nostalgia steeped in gender role stereotypes – women of emphasized femininity contrasted with hyper-masculinized men. Sociologist Maurice Halbwachs (1992) first described the collective memory concept, positing that a society can have a large-group memory of individuals and events of the past, so that a group memory exists wherein any one person's understanding of the past is based on a group consciousness. As a society we remember events and individuals based on "a reconstruction of the past achieved with data borrowed from the present" (Halbwachs, 1992, p. 69). Findings of the study reported in this book offer evidence that nineteenth-century pioneer women played active community-building roles on a par in importance with achievements attributed to male pioneers.

Examining processes associated with remembering the past as a re-affirmation of tradition also helps us to better understand the power of nostalgia. Nostalgia is a social experience, "a form of recollection based on shared ideas about the past and present and on cultural definitions of better and worse" (Kitch, 2005, p. 133) This yearning for the past is rooted in a belief that social life in the past was preferable to that of the present (Lash & Urry, 1994). All cultures experience memory gaps between the real and some ideal, projecting the fictionalized ideal to a time when social life is imagined to have conformed to that ideal (McCracken, 1988). For example, *Reminisce* and *Good Old Days* magazines publish reader-supplied content that uses healthy doses of nostalgia to "paint a past that was a simpler and better time and place than the present, even if life was harder" and relies on aspects of memory revision as an "identity-affirmation and survival strategy" for older female audiences, in particular (Kitch, 2005, p. 11). In both magazines, Kitch (2005) found that stereotypical gender roles are frequent and that women are celebrated as a family's strength during hard times, such as the Great Depression. This is the same theme used at pioneer commemorations.

Collective memory of the Western frontier is rooted in episodes of trauma and tragedy, offering historians opportunities to examine how this memory is used in national identity formation. Anwarfield (2014) posited that by linking Halbwachs' (1992) ideas about collective memory and national identity with Turner's (1894) frontier thesis about the West being a redemptive and innovative environment enables us to sharpen focus on why certain realities associated with Western emigration became mythologized. In addition to pioneer women's lived experiences being neglected early on, those of indigenous peoples were also limited. For example, Custer's Last Stand has become a metaphor for justifying subjugation of Native Americans in the cause of the rising U.S. power and wealth (Slotkin, 1998). More broadly, the archetypical frontiersman/Indian hunter myth promoted a hyper-masculine Caucasian/White male ideal exerting power over the wilderness and indigenous people in a conquest of the West that reflected the interests of post-Civil War industrialized capitalism (Slotkin, 1996).

Pioneer Women's Voices as Historians

Through their diary and journal writings, nineteenth-century Oregon Trail pioneer women were among the first historians of the Western experience.

When a complete picture of women's lives is "hidden from history" (Rowbotham, 1974), a limited brand of the female gender role is emphasized that occludes broader views on women's lived experiences. Foss (1996) defined rhetoric as "the process by which our world comes into being" (p. 6). Narratives that amplify archetypes, stereotypes, and myths steeped exclusively in women's domestic roles maintains an *emphasized femininity* to the exclusion of women's other contributions to society. Connell's (1987) critique of gender and power called for a reassertion and recovery of marginalized forms of femininity in the experiences of spinsters, lesbians, unionists, prostitutes, madwomen, rebels, maiden aunts, manual workers, midwives, and witches. Examining the lived experiences of Oregon Trail pioneer women as community builders is a response to this charge and a means for expanding public relations history.

Literate Caucasian/White pioneer women of the nineteenth century regarded diaries and journals on the Oregon Trail as a means of making a cathartic recording of their personal thoughts and experiences, perhaps to share with family "back East" or in Europe (Riley, 2004, p. 2), as well as a place to release tension and to list grievances (Jeffrey, 1998). Recording in their diaries and journals was for women a way – not of pleasing others, as we may do today in a context of social media exchanges – but of connecting with their own thoughts. Most women on the Oregon Trail and while homesteading in Oregon were too busy to write a lot and women may have considered their notes inconsequential for any audience. Although surviving original source material is slim, pioneer women's diaries and journals have significantly contributed to the historical record of the westward movement (Jeffrey, 1998) and in many cases offer the only record of women's lives. In a comparison of Overland Trail diary styles across gender, Faragher (1979) found that women wrote of concerns with "family and relational values" in contemplative ways rather than in degrees of success as men did in describing "fight, conflict and competition and … hunting" (p. 14). Most women who journeyed the 2,000+ miles from the Midwest to Oregon were of childbearing years, an age period often referred to as "vulnerable" (Butruille, 1993, p. 6). These women had much to say, but few (if any) friends to converse with since they had left them behind. Paradoxically, Oregon Trail women had feelings of melancholia as well as feelings of anticipation about starting a new life west of the Mississippi River. So, it would seem logical for Oregon Trail women to confide feelings of melancholia alongside those of anticipation about starting a new life west of the Mississippi River. Yet, we are left to ponder just how free each woman felt to express herself authentically and what restrictions might have shaped her private writing. Certainly, the limits of her education and experience might have impacted the ways she expressed herself. Norwood (1988) opined that what women wrote in diaries and journals was probably a mixture of what they thought they *should say* as much as what they *actually* thought. We also know that the oral culture of the migration West was rooted in women's campfire conversations, gossip, storytelling, and singing where women made their own gendered space which was marginalized from male-dominated spaces (Faragher & Stansell, 1975). Kolodny (1980) wrote about *languagescape* to explain how women dealt with what they saw by linking observations and experiences to the domestic sphere they knew best. It has been speculated that the eighteenth-century woman was "trapped in others' expectations – her mother's and later her husband's, and also her time's and her church's," (Gwartney, 2019, p. 12). Even though homesteading women wrote about what they regarded as their sphere – private, domestic environments – the covered wagon caravans that headed for Oregon added new context to women's lived experiences so that their observations were not limited exclusively to domestic tasks. No longer considered "trivial" by historians, such testaments to pioneer women's contributions are rife for exploration and "we owe it to ourselves and our children to retrieve our own history" (Vuolo, 1975, p. 36).

Summary

Re-examining the lure of the American West and ways women's role has been represented contributes to the foundation for an investigation of nineteenth-century Oregon Trail pioneer women's lived experiences as community builders in early public relations. By contextualizing the appeal of the American West and critiquing limitations of the Turner frontier thesis, traditional archetypes, and stereotypes in historical narratives and popular culture representations of women and femininity, this chapter offers further support for adding the nineteenth-century Oregon Trail phenomenon to early public relations history for women's community-building role. When exploring the beginnings of Oregon Country/Territory settlement through statehood in 1859, it is clear that the Homestead Act of 1862 inspired much westward wagon train emigration traffic. Because pioneer women's words were mostly shaped by prevailing ideas of the period about women's domestic work, examining gender roles and migration challenges sets the tone for understanding the ways necessity required women to break out of a prescribed domestic existence and to adapt to a new role. Finally, this chapter concluded with critique of the ways memory about pioneer women's contributions to the American West story have also challenged us to fully consider nineteenth-century pioneer women's community-building role.

Without doubt, the past remains susceptible to reconstruction and rewriting "to accord with present views" (Schudson, 1992, p. 205) and to enrich the present (Lowenthal, 1985). The voices of Oregon Trail women, as presented in this book's findings in subsequent chapters, respond to what Thelen (1989) considered society's "changing needs" (p. 1123). In this case, the need is to expand public relations history beyond the framework of industry, organizations, mass media, and men only. L'Etang's (2014) critique inspired the current inquiry when she wrote: "rigid frameworks, which apparently inhibit alternative explanations, are dangerous in any field" (p. xxxii). Yet, from anthropological, sociological, and psychological standpoints, history writing about the past can be highly resistant to additional perspectives. Examinations of the past can be motivated by a "search for guidance" and to learn lessons and "problemistically to resolve, calm, guide, instruct" (Schudson, 1992, p. 213). Zelizer (1995) underscored how "incomplete" our understanding of memory is – notably, "the omissions, rearrangements, [and] strategic moments of forgetting" (p. 214) – by bearing in mind that remembering is steeped in identity formation, power, and authority. Building upon a foundation that acknowledges that there is an integrity to the past that deserves respect, there also is an imperative to "study the past, to think and rethink it, to debate it" (Schudson, 1992, p. 221). Monuments in public spaces endure in ways perhaps unintended by artists who created them to become "evidence on which other interpretations of the past can be reconstructed" (Radley, 1997, p. 58).

Indeed, collective memory research positions social phenomena as reconstructions of the past through shared consciousness with others (Halbwachs, 1992), involves revealing the influences of power and authority (Zelizer, 1995), and examines beliefs, values, and rituals (Huyssen, 1995). As such, collective memories are changeable over time, contextual, and impressionable; no less stable than personal memories, which may also be forgotten or repressed. We know that historical events change from one generation to the next according to contemporary frames (Schwartz, 1982). There is an ongoing necessity to discover more about "strategic moments of forgetting" (Zelizer, 1995, p. 214), especially as it relates to an ongoing celebration of hyper-masculinity as the enduring primary lure of the American West. In Oregon, the pioneers retain their mythical status as an icon of state tourism, inspiration for the NBA franchise of the Portland Trail Blazers, street names, and small business names (e.g., Pioneer Pizza).

To do women's history justice when recalling the Oregon Trail means tempering the nostalgia and enthusiasm with the negative such as recognizing the nineteenth-century context and ultimate harm done to indigenous peoples, wildlife, and the land. So, what pioneer women confided to their diaries, journals, and recalled later in life as reminiscences is examined for the research project reported in this book to build a new chapter in public relations history's attention to community building. The next part transitions to examining early pre-professional public relations work as community building by (un)gendering and expanding roles with an interrogation of pioneer women's role as caretaker/advocate in Chapter 3.

References

About the Homestead Act (n.d.). Accessed August 28, 2019 from www.nps.gov/home/learn/historyculture/abouthomesteadactlaw.htm.

Anwarfield (2014). Collective memory of the frontier. Accessed August 31, 2019 from http://courses.shroutdocs.org/his458-spring2014/2014/03/10/collective-memory-of-the-frontier.

Armitage, S. (1985). Women and men in Western history: A stereotypical vision. *The Western Historical Quarterly*, 16(4), 381–395.

Bartlett, F. C. (1932). *Remembering: A study in experimental and social psychology*. Cambridge: Cambridge University Press.

Basic facts about the Oregon Trail (n.d.). U.S. Department of the Interior – Bureau of Land Management. Accessed December 22, 2019 from www.blm.gov/sites/blm.gov/files/learn_interp_nhotic_faq.pdf.

Beckham, S. D. (1996). *Requiem for a people: The Rogue Indians and the frontiersmen*. Corvallis, OR: Oregon State University Press.

Billington, R. A. (1963). *Words that won the West*. New York: Foundation for Public Relations Research and Education.

Billock, J. (2016). Nine places where you can still see wheel tracks from the Oregon Trail. Accessed August 25, 2019 from www.smithsonianmag.com/travel/follow-relics-oregon-trail-180960589.

Boag, P. (2014). Death and Oregon's settler generation: Connecting parricide, agricultural decline, and dying pioneers at the turn of the twentieth century. *Oregon Historical Quarterly*, 115(3), 344–379.

Bodnar, J. (1992). *Remaking America: Public memory, commemoration, and patriotism in the twentieth century*. Princeton, NJ: Princeton University Press.

Brown, D. (1958). *The gentle tamers: Women of the old wild West*. Lincoln, NE: University of Nebraska Press.

Burns, K. (Writer), Duncan, D. (Writer), & Burns, K. (Director) (1997). *Lewis & Clark: The journey of the Corps of Discovery*. Washington, DC: Public Broadcasting Service.

Butruille, S. G. (1993). *Women's voices from the Oregon Trail: The times that tried women's souls and a guide to women's history along the Oregon Trail*. Boise, ID: Tamarack Books, Inc.

Carey, C. H. (1922). *History of Oregon*. Chicago, IL: Pioneer Historical Publishing Company.

Chused, R. H. (1984). The Oregon Donation Act of 1850 and nineteenth century federal married women's property law. *Law and History Review*, 2(1), 44–78.

Connell, R. W. (1987). *Gender and power*. Stanford, CA: Stanford University Press.

Cowles, F. C. (1929). *Early Algona: The story of our pioneers, 1834–1874*. Des Moines, IA: Register and Tribune.

Cutlip, S. M. (1995). *Public relations history: From the 17th to the twentieth century. The antecedents*. Hillsdale, NJ: Lawrence Erlbaum Associates.

Dennis, M. (2014). Natives and pioneers: Death and the settling and unsettling of Oregon. *Oregon Historical Quarterly*, 115(3), 282–297.

Deutsch, S. (1987). *No separate refuge: Culture, class, and gender on an Anglo-Hispanic frontier in the American Southwest, 1880–1940*. New York: Oxford University Press.

Faragher, J. (1979). *Women and men on the Overland Trail*. New Haven, CT: Yale University Press.

Faragher, J., & Stansell, C. (1975). Women and their families on the Overland Trail to California and Oregon, 1842–1867. *Feminist Studies*, 2(2/3), 150–166.

Feltskog, E. N. (ed.) (1969). *The Oregon Trail*. Madison, WI: University of Wisconsin Press.

Fifer, J. V. (1988). *American progress: The growth of the transport, tourist and information industries in the nineteenth-century West*. Chester, CT: Globe Pequot Press.

Foss, S. K. (1996). *Rhetorical criticism: Exploration & practice*. Prospect Heights, IL: Waveland Press.

Gambino, M., & Frail, T. A. (2012). *Document deep dive: How the Homestead Act transformed America*. Accessed August 28, 2019 from www.smithsonianmag.com/history/document-deep-dive-how-the-homestead-act-transformed-america-60005030.

Gwartney, D. A. (2019). *I am a stranger here myself*. Albuquerque, NM: University of New Mexico Press.

Halbwachs, M. (1992). *On collective memory*. Chicago, IL: The University of Chicago Press.

Homestead Act. (n.d.). Accessed August 28, 2019 from www.loc.gov/rr/program/bib/ourdocs/homestead.html.

Hurtado, A. (1999). *Intimate frontiers: Sex, gender, and culture in old California*. Albuquerque, NM: University of New Mexico Press.

Huyssen, A. (1995). *Twilight memories: Marking time in a culture of amnesia*. New York: Routledge.

Irwin-Zarecka, I. (1994). *Frames of remembrance: The dynamics of collective memory*. New Brunswick, NJ: Transaction Publishers.

Jameson, E. (1988). Toward a multicultural history of women in the Western United States. *Signs*, 13(4), 761–791.

Jameson, E., & Armitage, S. (eds) (1997). *Writing the range: Race, class, and culture in the women's West*. Norman, OK: University of Oklahoma Press.

Jeffrey, J. R. (1979). *Frontier women: The trans-Mississippi West, 1840–1880*. New York: Hill & Wang.

Jeffrey, J. R. (1998). *Frontier women: Civilizing the west? 1840–1880*. New York: Hill & Wang.

Kitch, C. (2005). *Pages from the past: History and memory in American magazines*. Chapel Hill, NC: University of North Carolina Press.

Kleinfeld, J., & Kleinfeld, A. (2004). Cowboy nation and American character. *Society*, 41(3), 43–50.

Kolodny, A. (1975). *The lay of the land: Metaphor as experience and history in American life and letters*. Chapel Hill, NC: University of North Carolina Press.

Kolodny, A. (1980). Honing a habitable languagescape: Women's images for the New World frontiers. In S. McConnell-Ginet, R. Borker, & N. Furman (eds), *Women and language in literature and society* (pp. 188–204). New York: Praeger.

Kolodny, A. (1984). *The land before her: Fantasy and experience of the American frontier, 1630–1860*. Chapel Hill, NC: The University of North Carolina Press.

Lash, S., & Urry, J. (1994). *Economies of signs and space*. London: Sage.

Lavender, D. (1985). *Westward vision: The story of the Oregon Trail*. Lincoln, NE: University of Nebraska Press.

L'Etang, J. (2014). Writing PR history: Issues, methods and politics. In B. St. John III, M. O. Lamme, & J. L'Etang (eds), *Pathways to public relations: Histories of practice and profession* (pp. xix–xxxviii). Abingdon: Routledge.

Lewis, D. G. (2014). Four deaths: The near destruction of Western Oregon tribes and native lifeways, removal to the reservation, and erasure from history. *Oregon Historical Quarterly*, 115(3), 414–437.

Limerick, P. N., Milner, C. A., & Rankin, C. E. (eds) (1991). Preface. In P. N. Limerick, C. A. Milner, & C. E. Rankin, *Trails: Toward a new Western history* (pp. ix–xv). Lawrence, KS: University Press of Kansas.

Lindgren, H. E. (1991). *Land in her own name*. Norman, OK: University of Oklahoma Press.

Lowenthal, D. (1985). *The past is a foreign country*. Cambridge: Cambridge University Press.

Lussenhop, J. (2011). *Oregon Trail: How three Minnesotans forged its path*. Accessed August 30, 2019 from https://web.archive.org/web/20110123012937/http://www.citypages.com/content/printVersion/1740595.

Malone, M. P. (1991). The new Western history: An assessment. In P. N. Limerick, C. A. Milner, & C. E. Rankin (eds), *Trails: Toward a new Western history* (pp. 97–102). Lawrence, KS: University Press of Kansas.

Mattes, M. J. (1987). *The Great Platte River Road: The covered wagon mainline via Fort Kearny to Fort Laramie*. Lincoln, NE: University of Nebraska Press.

McAndrews, K. M. (2006). *Wrangling women: Humor and gender in the American West*. Reno, NV: University of Nevada Press.

McCracken, G. (1988). *Culture and consumption: New approaches to the symbolic character of consumer goods and activities*. Bloomington, IN: Indiana University Press.

McManus, S. (2005). *The line which separates: Race, gender, and the making of the Alberta-Montana borderlands*. Lincoln, NE: University of Nebraska Press.

McMurtry, L. (1990). How the West was won or lost. *The New Republic*, October 22, 32–38.

Meriwether, J. L., & D'Amore, L. M. (2012). *We are what we remember: The American past through commemoration*. Newcastle upon Tyne: Cambridge Scholars Publishing.

Merritt, K. L. (2016). Race, reconstruction, and reparations. Black perspectives. Accessed August 28, 2019 from www.aaihs.org/race-reconstruction.

Merskin, D. (2004). The construction of Arabs as enemies. *Mass Communication & Society*, 7(2), 157–175.

Morrissey, K. G. (1992). Engendering the West. In W. Cronon, G. Miles, & J. Gitlin (eds), *Under an open sky: Rethinking America's Western past* (pp. 132–144). New York: W. W. Norton & Company.

Muhn, J. (1994). Women and the Homestead Act: Land department administration of a legal imbroglio, 1863–1934. *Western Legal History*, 7(2), 283–307.

Neufeldt, V., & Guralnik, D. B. (1994). *Webster's New World Dictionary of American English* (3rd College edn). New York: Prentice Hall.

Norwood, V. (1988). Women's place: Continuity and change in response to Western landscapes. In L. Schlissel, V. L. Ruiz, & J. J. Monk (eds), *Western women: Their land, their lives* (pp. 155–181). Albuquerque, NM: University of New Mexico Press.

Palmer, P. (1989). *Domesticity and dirt: Housewives and domestic servants in the United States, 1920–1945*. Philadelphia, PA: Temple University Press.

Pascoe, P. (1990). *Relations of rescue: The search for female moral authority in the American West, 1874–1939*. New York: Oxford University Press.

Pascoe, P. (1991). Western women at the cultural crossroads. In P. N. Limerick, C. A. Milner, & C. E. Rankin (eds), *Trails: Toward a new Western history* (pp. 40–58). Lawrence, KS: University Press of Kansas.

Porterfield, J. (2004). *The Homestead Act of 1862: A primary source history of the settlement of the American heartland in the late nineteenth century*. New York: Rosen Publishing Group.

Prescott, C. C. (2012). The all-American eternal family: Sacred and secular values in Western pioneer monuments. In J. L. Meriwether & L. M. D'Amore (eds), *We are what we remember: The American past through commemoration* (pp. 334–358). Cambridge: Cambridge Scholars Publishing.

Prescott, C. C. (2019). *Pioneer mother monuments: Constructing cultural memory*. Norman, OK: University of Oklahoma Press.

Radley, A. (1997). Artefacts, memory and a sense of the past. In D. Middleton & D. Edwards (eds), *Collective remembering* (pp. 46–59). Thousand Oaks, CA: Sage.
Riley, G. (1984). *Women and Indians on the frontier, 1825–1915*. Albuquerque, NM: University of New Mexico Press.
Riley, G. (1994a). *Building and breaking families in the American west*. Albuquerque, NM: University of New Mexico Press.
Riley, G. (1994b). *Frontierswomen: The Iowa experience*. Ames, IA: Iowa State University Press.
Riley, G. (2002). *The life and legacy of Annie Oakley*. Norman, OK: University of Oklahoma Press.
Riley, G. (2004). *Confronting race: Women and Indians on the frontier, 1825–1915*. Albuquerque, NM: University of New Mexico Press.
Roark, J. L., Johnson, M. P., Cohen, P. C., Stage, S., & Hartmann, S. M. (2016). *The American promise: A history of the United States* (7th edn). Boston, MA: Bedford St. Martin's.
Rollins, P. A. (ed.) (1995). *The discovery of the Oregon Trail: Robert Stuart's narratives of his overland trip eastward from Astoria in 1812–13*. Lincoln NE: University of Nebraska Press.
Rowbotham, S. (1974). *Hidden from history* (2nd edn). London: Pluto Press.
Ruiz, V. (1987). *Cannery women, cannery lives: Mexican women, unionization, and the California food processing industry, 1930–1950*. Albuquerque, NM: University of New Mexico Press.
Savage, K. (1997). *Standing soldiers, kneeling slaves: Race, war, and monument in nineteenth century America*. Princeton, NJ: Princeton University Press.
Schlissel, L. (2004). *Women's diaries of the westward journey*. New York: Schocken Books.
Schlissel, L., Ruiz, V. L., & Monk, J. (eds) (1988). *Western women: Their land, their lives*. Albuquerque, NM: University of New Mexico Press.
Schudson, M. (1992). *Watergate in American memory: How we remember, forget, and reconstruct the past*. New York: Basic Books.
Schwartz, B. (1982). The social context of commemoration: A study in collective memory. *Social Forces*, 61(2), 374–402.
Sides, H. (2007). *Americana: Dispatches from the new frontier*. New York: Anchor Books.
Sloan, W. D., Stovall, J. G., & Startt, J. D. (1989). *The media in America: A history*. Worthington, OH: Publishing Horizons, Inc.
Slotkin, R. (1996). *Regeneration through violence: The mythology of the American Frontier, 1600–1860*. New York: Perennial.
Slotkin, R. (1998). *The fatal environment: The myth of the frontier in the age of industrialization, 1800–1890*. Norman, OK: University of Oklahoma Press.
Stott, A. (1996). Pioneer women and Prairie Madonnas: Images of emigrant women in the art of the old West. *Prospects*, 21, 299–325.
Stuart, M. L. (1913). The lady honyocker: How girls take up claims and make their own homes on the prairie. *Independent*, 75, 133–137.
Taylor, Q., & Moore, S. A. W. (eds) (2003). *African American women confront the West, 1600–2000*. Norman, OK: University of Oklahoma Press.
Thelen, D. (1989). Memory and American history. *Journal of American History*, 75(4), 1117–1129.
University of Oregon Libraries (2019). Accessed November 1, 2019, from https://library.uoregon.edu/architecture/oregon/xpioneermother.
Vuolo, B. H. (1975). Pioneer diaries: The untold story of the West. *Ms.*, 3(11), 32–34.
Warren, K. (2007). Gender, race, culture, and the mythic American frontier. *Journal of Women's History*, 19(1), 234–241.

Weaver-Hightower, R. (n.d.). Frontier fictions: Settler stories and the origins of white guilt (unpublished manuscript). In possession of Weaver-Hightower.

Webber, B. (1990). Introduction and contemporary comments. *The Oregon Trail diary of twin sisters Cecilia Adams and Parthenia Blank in 1852* (pp. 9–14). Medford, OR: Webb Research Group.

White, R. (1991). *The middle ground: Indians, empires, and republics in the Great Lakes region, 1615–1815*. Cambridge, MA: Cambridge University Press.

Zelizer, B. (1995). Reading the past against the grain: The shape of memory studies. *Critical Studies in Mass Communication*, 12(2), 214–239.

Part II
Gendering and Expanding Roles as Early Public Relations Work

3 Interrogating Pioneer Women's Role as *Caretaker/Advocate*

The concept of *community* has long provided the foundation for developing public relations theory and practice (Hallahan, 2004) – and taking care of and advocating for community is central to relationship building. At the most fundamental level, public relations is "best defined and practiced as the active attempt to restore and maintain a sense of community" (Kruckeberg & Starck, 2004, p. 136). In the U.S. in the nineteenth century, women who traveled the Oregon Trail and ultimately settled in Oregon quickly learned the importance of community beyond the traditional private, domestic sphere they had been socialized to embrace.

In addition to sharing similar ethno-socioeconomic profiles, emigrating families were a heterogeneous group of strangers. Pioneer women performed a critical role as boundary spanners as they cared for one another and advocated for others. Families pulled up roots primarily from farms and shops in the Midwest, upper South, and small Midwestern towns, as well as some Northeastern states. Fewer women from the northeastern middle classes hit the Oregon Trail than from other regions (Faragher & Stansell, 1975). Butruille (1993) characterized most pioneers as property owners who knew how to grow their own food and to barter for whatever else they needed. Collectively, they were committed to the 2,000+-mile journey and weren't impoverished, but they were far from wealthy. Kinship and friend groups outfitted and set out from the Missouri River in Independence, St. Louis, and Westport Landing each spring in groups of ten to several hundred wagons in several waves throughout the mid-to-late nineteenth century. The Oregon Trail experience shook up traditional gender role traditions. Women initially considered the journey to pursuing better economic opportunity as a male-managed enterprise since breadwinning was traditionally a masculine concern among all but the lowest socioeconomic strata in the U.S in the nineteenth century. While women generally embraced the traditional female gender roles of childrearing, household economy, and moral and religious life, the spring-through-summer Oregon Trail journey period also included a new-found autonomy amidst the disintegration of work roles along gender lines. Indeed, women increasingly took on what commonly had been considered men's work. The reverse was less true, but occasionally men cooked for themselves. Jeffrey (1998) wrote that men taking on women's tasks was considered doing them a *favor*, while women performing men's tasks was considered *necessary*.

This chapter examines an important theme that emerged in the diaries, journals, and reminiscences of women who journeyed the Oregon Trail in the nineteenth century – pioneer women's role as *Caretaker*, which led to a closely aligned role as *Advocate*. This chapter offers evidence of pioneer women's key roles with regard to helping and advocating for others and these findings parallel what we now consider an advocacy role in professional public relations practice (e.g., Brunner, 2017). The context for considering multiple ways women's gender identity and labor played out over the course of their Oregon Trail journey and homesteading experience is examined next with subsections of: 1) Gender Roles in the U.S. in the Nineteenth Century and the Civil War; 2) Blurred and Broken Lines of Gendered Division of Labor; 3) Oregon Trail Women's *Caretaker/Advocate* Role; and 4) Summary.

Gender Roles in the U.S. in the Nineteenth Century and the Civil War

Historians and other scholars offer varied opinions about exactly when a public-private sphere gender divide emerged in the U.S. Some suggest that it was during Andrew Jackson's (1829–1837) presidency that a "woman's place" was articulated, relegating women to the private sphere while men acted in the public sphere (Faragher & Stansell, 1975). This coincided with what came to be known as a *cult of true womanhood*, or women's "piety, purity, submissiveness, and domesticity" (Welter, 1966, p. 59) which Coontz (1993) suggested adds up to the roles of mother, daughter, sister, and wife in the domestic sphere. By the mid-nineteenth century, women's virtues positioned them as morally superior to men, albeit ornamental, emotional, delicate, evangelic, and physically inferior (Hogeland, 1976). Feminist scholars have long critiqued division of labor according to gender and the use of labor as a basis for defining femininity. Girls and women are socialized to internalize subordination in a social order based on a male worldview (e.g., Tong, 2009). Expecting women to adopt these qualities has a way of turning in upon girls and women in a patriarchal culture that binds them to a life of servitude for the benefit of everyone but themselves.

Even though Oregon Trail pioneer women were moving west of the direct Civil War combat, they nonetheless experienced an important outcome of the period – women shifting from the exclusively private sphere roles of wife and mother and blending into the public sphere. Leonard (1994) chronicled ways that the gender-appropriate behavior expected of women in the restrictive Victorian age began crumbling as women pushed through barriers. While nineteenth-century pioneer women journeyed to Oregon with their family for a fresh start, others hit the Oregon Trail accompanying a male family member pursuing free land under the Homestead Act of 1862 (with some dodging the Civil War combat), or to escape economic liability. Meanwhile, women back in the States were patriotically contributing to the war effort, serving in the field as soldiers, couriers, spies, nurses, cooks, and laundresses – and at home, maintaining family businesses and filling jobs vacated by enlisted men (Schultz, 1994). Aid societies and church clubs organized war efforts and Southern women staged the 1861–1863 Bread Riots to protest against inflated bread prices, pillaging bakeries to feed starving children (McPherson, 1988). These women's lives were much more complex than a *cult of true womanhood* might suggest.

The onset of the Civil War conflict, confusing hometown community dynamics, and uncertain federal government support inspired 18-year-old Arvazna A. Spillman Cooper and her extended family to start for Oregon on April 7, 1863. In 1901, she recorded her journey in a reminiscences document. It begins with a reflection on "the great Rebellion," concerns about an ill-equipped homeland of "Enrolled Militia," and lack of faith that it would protect her family from "rebels" whom she wrote treated all Northerners as abolitionists and routinely dispatched "bushwackers" at the state border:

> It seemed to us that we were left without a status in our beloved Government ... it seemed we were doing no good toward aiding in suppressing the Rebellion, so we longed exceedingly to get away ... I felt I would venture anything, to live where law and order reigned again and was eager to make the attempt.

Spillman Cooper's perceptions are consistent with Chudacoff's (1981) characterization of the war as *intruding upon* Northern communities. Westward emigration numbers dipped during the Civil War years of 1861–1865 (Schlissel, 2004) when able-bodied men volunteered or were conscripted to fight. The Coopers' April 8, 1863 Oregon Trail departure slightly preceded unrest in the North during the "bloodiest" (Werstein, 1957, p. 13) civil demonstration in American history when Caucasian/Whites murdered African American men – not yet considered citizens – in conjunction with a July 1863 conscription lottery drawing in New York City. Congress had passed the Conscription Act when, after two years of fighting, the Union Army needed reinforcement and too few volunteers were forthcoming. Spillman Cooper wrote that her family outfitted for the westward journey within three weeks but had difficulty provisioning for the trip given the reduced availability of dried fruit, beans, and tin cups and plates during wartime. As part of her reminiscences document, Spillman Cooper added that "canned goods were unknown at the time."

Many Oregon Trail pioneer women's diaries began with words about happiness and enthusiasm, tinged with a good measure of uncertainty and anxiety about what lay ahead. One week into the journey after leaving Monroe County, Iowa, Amelia Stewart Knight began writing on April 14, 1853 with jaunty prose: "Hurrah boys, all ready, we will be the first to cross the creek this morning ... away we go the sun just rising." Yet, her happy tone disintegrated two days later as details about spring rains, mud, and sickness dominated her diary entry: "Husband is scolding and hurrying all hands (and the cook) and Almira says she wished she was home, and I say ditto. 'Home Sweet Home'." Domestic duties filled Knight's routine as she wrote a few days later on April 22: "I have been busy cooking roasting coffee, etc. today, and have come into the wagon to write this and make our bed." Writing in a diary or journal can prove comforting and cathartic for capturing "the little experiences of everyday life that fills most of our working time and occup[ies] the vast majority of our conscious attention," with psychological and physiological benefits gained from managing stress in challenging times (Wheeler & Reis, 1991, p. 340).

Blurred and Broken Lines of Gendered Division of Labor

Physically, most pioneer men were in their prime and most pioneer women were in their childbearing years. This made women's health especially vulnerable to the elements and other rigors of the journey, with as many as 20% of Oregon Trail women being pregnant (Jeffrey, 1998). However, very few women mentioned their physical condition in diaries or journals, and this included pregnancy. For example, among the first-person documents examined for the study reported in this book, Keturah Belknap, who

Figure 3.1 Amelia Stewart Knight
Source: Public Domain.

traveled the Oregon Trail in 1848 from Iowa, revealed at no point in her diary that she was pregnant.

The harsh elements and wagon travel demands transformed family household norms. Socially acceptable behavior was soon abandoned as women assumed roles traditionally fulfilled by men. Pioneer women discovered early in the journey that they had to perform more physical labor than usual just to prepare family meals and take care of children; much of it considered to be *unladylike*. Lines demarcating the traditional gender role division of labor became blurred or were broken completely as the trip westward to the Pacific coast wore on and pioneers succumbed to bare necessity and survival so that women's work came to be "no less indispensable than men's" (Faragher & Stansell, 1975, p. 151). For example, 23-year-old twins Cecilia E. Adams and Parthenia Blank wrote during their Missouri-to-Oregon journey on July 14–16, 1852 that they spent their time "washing, repairing the wagons and making a new tent" while "our boys killed an antelope which we all relish very much." The twins also gave details in several late-August/early September 1852 diary entries of "large salmon jumping out of the water, but can't catch them."

Harriet A. Loughary and her family started their journey from Burlington, Iowa, to Oregon's Willamette Valley on March 30, arriving on September 1, 1864. Loughary's journal described equitable labor division among her family. By June 24, she took over driving the wagon team in present-day Wyoming and Idaho after the family's hired hand deserted the wagon train for a gold prospecting career:

> The 'Wind River' range are white with snow and of course quite cold at night and morning, but our camp life is such a busy one that we have no time to consider the weather. Since leaving the Bannock Road, where our hired man left us for the gold region, my work has been greatly increased. In addition to preparing food and beds for eight in family, I am compelled to harness and drive a four horse team while my husband and our thirteen year old son looked after feed and water and loose stock. My husband yoked and drove the ox team and with the aid of the small children got the wood, water and all manner of camp work.

Keturah Belknap also wrote in her diary of driving the family wagon in 1848 when her family, journeying from Iowa, stopped in Illinois, expecting to winter there before heading on to Oregon:

> The second day we had to cross an eighteen mile prairie and in the afternoon it turned cold and the wind from the Northwest struck us square in the face and we had bought some cows at Rushville, had some boys driving them, and they would not face the storm so I had to take the lines and drive the team while my husband helped with the stock. I thought my hands and nose would freeze; when I got to the fire it made me so sick I almost fainted.

Everyone labored on the five-to-six-month Oregon Trail journey and women found little downtime, working day and night. Men used brute strength driving livestock and pulling wagons out of mud, over rocky terrain, and on/off ferries, repairing wagons and harnesses, hunting, ferrying cattle and wagons across rivers, and standing guard at night. Women continually cooked, cleaned, and attended to children – labor that may have required less strength than men exerted, but women's tasks lasted longer and required stamina and patience. The gendered division of labor meant women's daily routine involved working together with other women, "existing primarily in the presence of other women" (Schlissel, 2004, p. 77). All this made for never-ending labor for women, as even when families observed the Sunday Sabbath without forward travel, women worked preparing meals, unloading wagons and drying out the contents to avoid rot – after heavy rains, at river crossings, and when wagons got stuck in the mud.

The blurred and broken lines of gendered division of labor opened new possibilities. Neither men nor women of the period "seemed concerned with defining what women were or what their unique contribution to society should be" (Gordon, Buhle, & Schrom, 1971, p. 22). Moreover, most women did not frame the Oregon Trail journey this way in their personal writings. Rather, they noted yearning for home and stressed over loss of control over their work more than they realized any liberating possibilities associated with out-in-the-open displays of their labor. Expanded work roles for women provided them with "socially essential work" (Faragher & Stansell, 1975, p. 161) that contributed to degrees of female-male gender equality, both physically and emotionally.

Oregon Trail Women's *Caretaker/Advocate* Role

Pioneer women's lived experiences offer historical evidence that they served as active community-building agents working to create and maintain a new way of life. Their community-building work paralleled at least one of the eight ways that today's professional public relations practitioners support stakeholders by helping people to "find security and protection through the association with others" (Kruckeberg & Starck, 2004, p. 141). The *Caretaker/Advocate* role performed by Oregon Trail pioneer women inspires further reflection on the concept of *community*. Based on the Chicago School's usage of *community*, Kruckeberg and Starck (1988) identified six essential elements. One of those – "[t]he individual participates in the common life of the community, is aware of and interested in common ends, and regulates activity in view of those ends" through communication (p. 56) – resonates with Oregon Trail women's community-building work as it played out in exploring and finding new ways to give care and to advocate for others amidst unfamiliar landscapes and rough conditions.

The remainder of this chapter outlines subthemes characterizing pioneer women's *Caretaker/Advocate* role, offering specific evidence of the ways they performed community building as part of the Oregon Trail journey and beyond as Oregon homesteaders and settlers – a) Cook/Cleaner, b) Livestock Caretaker, c) Apothecary, d) Nurse/Midwife/Undertaker, e) Conflict Intermediary, and f) Ambassador/Liaison.

Cook/Cleaner

As meal preparation and cleaning constituted the bulk of pioneer women's domestic work during the Oregon Trail journey together with being homesteaders and settlers, they predominantly were responsible for gathering water and campfire burning materials. Transitioning to life amidst the elements and finding ways to perform domestic tasks in new environments involved negotiating bumpy wagon travel and walking in all kinds of weather through present-day Kansas and Nebraska along the Platte River Valley and then crossing the Rockies in present-day southern Wyoming at South Pass by mid-summer. Perhaps the most basic expansion of female labor on the Oregon Trail – a necessary adjunct to meal preparation responsibilities – was the gathering of buffalo dung (also called buffalo muffins) and weeds for fuel, as actual firewood was scarce for much of the plains-area journey marked by a terrain lacking in trees but plentiful in dust, rocks, mud, grass, raging rivers, and glare. Webber (1990) characterized these housekeeping-related tasks as "allied chores" (p. vii). Also, as the century wore on, teams of wagon train pioneers had already used whatever fire fuel was available for easy gathering. Nearly every woman's diary, journal, and reminiscences examined for this study mentioned labor associated with supplying the campfire fuel required for making coffee, boiling beans, baking biscuits and bread, and cooking whatever animals could be caught, trapped, or shot (e.g., rabbits), as well as washing and cleaning.

Arvazna A. Spillman Cooper and her husband and grandfather traveled to Oregon in 1863 by ox-drawn wagons during the second year of their marriage shortly before she became pregnant with her second child while on the Oregon Trail. She wrote in reminiscences in 1901: "The ubiquitous buffalo chips were our only fuel for many days, and were much more satisfactory, than any one would suppose who had never tried them." About three weeks into the journey begun May 5, 1851 from Illinois to Umpqua Valley, Oregon, 26-year-old Amelia A. Hammond Hadley also noted the virtues of buffalo chips as campfire fuel in her diary: "Camped on the river had to cook with buffalo chips for the first time. It makes verrry good fuel when dry, and is more prefforable than wood for the verry good reason, (can't get it.)."

As a young bride, Amelia A. Hammond Hadley chronicled her family's trek, which began only four days after she and Samuel B. Hadley married. The Cecilia E. Adams/Parthenia Blank 1852 diary also noted using wood from abandoned wagons and burning sage for fuel.

The first three months of the journey along the Platte River route seemes to have been fairly straightforward for the West-bound emigrants. The tone of diaries and journals shifted as the novelty and adventure of the

Figure 3.2 Ada McColl Collecting Buffalo Dung
Source: Kansas Historical Society.

five-to-six-month journey tended to wear off. By midpoint on the Oregon Trail in present-day Idaho, where travelers forked off for either a California or an Oregon destination, women's caretaking by foraging for and preparing meals and carrying potable water for consumption and cleaning was further challenged by scorching deserts, deep rivers, boggy salt flats, downpours, and rugged mountains. Seventeen-year-old Jane (Jennie) Paul Eakin Hanna chronicled her extended family's four-month journey from Bloom, Illinois (now Chicago Heights) to join two aunts and uncles already settled in Oregon's Willamette Valley in 1866. She wrote of the difficulties in drawing water from rivers and streams for cooking, washing, and storage in wooden kegs to help her mother and grandmother. Jane (Jennie) Paul Eakin Hanna also offered detailed descriptions of the weather, road conditions, and work doing sewing, washing, and meal preparation. On June 15, 1866 Jane (Jennie) Paul Eakin Hanna wrote: "We joined the Oregon train this noon. Corralled with them tonight. Camped very late. I do hate the company we are in. The women are all rough, course and ugly and the men all swear." But by the next day, June 16, 1866, she added: "Camped about a mile from the river and had to carry water that far," noting optimistically how she enjoyed meeting "four young ladies" of other trains: "A lot of women and girls come over to our camp all the time." By journey's midpoint on July 30, 1866, however, the tone of Jane (Jennie) Paul Eakin Hanna's diary entries shifted to "How I long for a home again" as she punctuated her writing with multiple lamentations of "rough, rocky," "dreadful," "terrible dusty," "awful steep," and "roughest, steepest, highest mountain roads ever seen or imagined."

Beyond the physical demands of walking and lifting, gathering fire wood and water on the Oregon Trail was not as straightforward for pioneer women as we might think today. The natural environment, impacted by wagon trails marking the route after several years' worth of wagon traffic and livestock hoof tracks, had carved the land with deep ruts. Emigrants spread out across the prairie sometimes four-to-five miles wide to minimize inhaling each other's dust and then rejoined at night forming camps. Traffic increasingly diminished food supplies for people and livestock, as well as depleted fire making materials used for cooking, heating water for sanitation, and warmth at night. These complications made the last months of the journey even more difficult. The Oregon Trail followed the North Platte River out of present-day Nebraska and past Fort Laramie to the Sweetwater River, which leads west toward South Pass and over the Rockies. Amelia A. Hammond Hadley commented in her daily diary on June 15, 1851 on the worn-out conditions along the Sweetwater River due to so many pioneer trains:

> This river is 8 rods wide 2 ft deep swift current good water as soft as snow water which it is coming from melted snow from the mountains. This water tastes like sap which gave it this name. I always had a curiosity to taste of it. Have to cross the river for grass, so many have camped here that they have eat it all up on this side.

Amelia A. Hammond Hadley's diary noted that this spot was about 200 miles from the popular stopping point of Fort Laramie. It was a fur trade post

Figure 3.3 Jane (Jennie) Paul Eakin Hanna's Headstone, Pioneer Cemetery, Eugene, Oregon
Source: Donnalyn Pompper.

founded in 1835 which ultimately became an important stop on the Oregon, Mormon, and California Trails, as well as a strategic military location often used for treaty signings.

While men tended to socialize around campfires after dinner, women's cooking/cleaning work on the Oregon Trail never ended, given a litany of meal preparation details. For while men performed most of the heavy lifting (e.g., pulling wagons across rivers and through mud up slopes and long grades), they did have periods of rest and relaxation at the day's end. Women, on the other hand, enjoyed very little respite throughout their waking hours because there always something that needed washing or cooking. Many women on the Oregon Trail journey concluded "that the journey had reduced them to work that was only fit for hired hands" (Schlissel, 2004, p. 36). Jane (Jennie) Paul Eakin Hanna wrote in her 1866 diary that bouts with heavy rains meant a continual need to "air everything that was in the wagon" and communal washing when "we women all came over in one wagon" and "some of the women in the train made it a wash day," which required water collection and campfire fuel gathering. These dynamics required great stamina and hardiness.

Livestock Caretaker

The Oregon Trail pioneers' survival depended on women's vigilant care of livestock (cows, horses, oxen) – not just to provide milk and to pull wagons, but to serve as a commodity for sale once emigrants arrived in Oregon. By

Figure 3.4 Independence Rock
Source: Deposit Photos.

Oregon Trail journey midpoint, women began to be responsible for driving cattle, steering wagons, the feeding and caretaking of livestock, as well as repairing wagons and rafts (Barnett, 1928) when a non-gender-specific all-hands-on-deck response became necessary as men had died due to sickness and accidents. Schlissel (2004) concluded that as the Overland Trail experience progressed, more and more women assumed physically demanding tasks that earlier had been associated only with men, such as yoking cattle, pitching tents, packing, and unpacking. The three basic concerns of daily life involved in emigrants' travel with domesticated animals were feeding the stock, crossing rivers, and replacing animals. Emigrants formed "partnerships" with animals on the Overland Trail journey (Ahmad, 2012, p. 178), and often it was the women who provided the compassion and caretaking of them. Amelia A. Hammond Hadley noted in her diary the poor quality and insufficient quantity of grass for the horses used in her family's train, as well as the frequently poor quality of water (muddy, alkaline) which was critical for everyone's survival. Her caregiving to all beings on the journey suggested Amelia A. Hammond Hadley's willingness to expand her caring role beyond the needs of her immediate family or wagon train neighbors. However, after about a month, Amelia A. Hammond Hadley's patience with living off the land with little variety in meal cooking options as part of her caregiving duties began to wear thin. On June 9, 1851 she wrote:

> [C]amp on the river plenty of wood, grass & water, had some antelop to night see some hens called sage hens, I have heard say that they were good to eat, some of our company killed some, and I think a skunk, prefarable, their meat tastes of this abominable mountain sage, which I have got so tired of that I can't bear to smell it, they live wholly upon it and it scents their flesh.

Elizabeth Julia Ellison Goltra maintained a journal in 1853 while journeying from Missouri to Oregon Country/Territory with her husband whom she had married two years previously. She paused on July 4 to write about her workload uninterrupted by the Independence Day holiday:

> This is indeed a beautiful morning to celebrate the anniversary of our Independence but to us it is like all other days, the same work to do, drove 12 miles today and have not much grass for our cattle to-night, passed Ice-springs at the right of the road, it is said ice can be found here at any season of the year by digging 2 or 3 feet deep, we saw some of it near the top of the ground.

Just three weeks shy of arrival at the home of her Oregon-settled family on August 25, 1866, Jane (Jennie) Paul Eakin Hanna wrote in her diary on August 2: "Did not travel this afternoon because the stock has not had good feed lately." She was not alone in her notations about livestock care. Amelia Stewart

Knight's diary entries routinely mentioned that she was tasked with feeding livestock by mixing flour with meal for their food when rocky terrain yielded no grass. Amelia Stewart Knight also wrote of weeping for livestock that fell sick, lame, and died. On June 14, 1853 Amelia Stewart Knight told of the risks "poison or alkali water posed to livestock. It is almost sure to kill man or beast who drink it" and then in subsequent days made notes about dying and dead cows. By late July through mid-August 1853, Amelia Stewart Knight noted cows dying of poisoned water or weeds in present-day Idaho:

> Left our poor cow for the wolves … another fine cow died this afternoon… our best milk cows died. Cattle are dying off very fast all along this road. We are hardly ever out of sight of dead cattle, on this side of Snake River. This cow was well and fat an hour before she died … Lost some of our oxen … continually driving around the dead cattle, and shame on the man who has no pity for the poor dumb brutes that have to travel and toil month after month on this desolate road. (I could hardly help shedding tears, when we drove around this poor ox who had helped us along thus far, and has given us his very last step.

Apothecary

Oregon Trail women also administered medical treatment, especially when no doctor was among the wagon train, and acted as apothecaries gathering wild herbs, berries, and roots. Cecilia E. Adams' husband, William, had recently completed medical studies at Oberlin College in Ohio before they – with twin sister Parthenia Blank – set out for Oregon City with other family members from the Gentryville, Missouri, area in 1852. Several members of their party also benefitted during the six-month journey from the sisters' travel preparations of "medicines and notes on when and how to use them" as advised by a guide book that also included information about distances between stops, warnings about "Indian trouble," advice to bring wood, and notations about the locations of watering holes and grass for livestock. Historians of the westward emigration have widely noted the value women placed on sharing household remedies for a variety of injuries, rashes, and insect bites (Feltskog, 1969). In the summer heat of June 1852, Cecilia E. Adams and Parthenia Blank noted in their diary that they lost their guide book "which caused us to go much farther today than we expected."

Nurse, Midwife, Undertaker

Amongst the Oregon Trail journey challenges, dealing with illness, birth, death, and burial was designated as women's work. When pioneer women weren't writing in their diaries and journals about food preparation and cleaning, they were detailing childcare responsibilities and nursing for those who were injured or ill. Women were considered a natural for tending to pregnant women, delivering babies, caring for children, as well as nursing and visiting the injured, sick, dying, and burying the dead (Jeffrey, 1998). Older family members usually rode inside wagons and those who were sick were made as comfortable as possible.

Without doubt, keeping an eye on children was a challenge. Only 18 years old herself, Arvazna A. Spillman Cooper wrote in 1901 about camping outside for the first time in 1863 – and with her toddler:

> I was very inexperienced in every way, especially was it so about camping out, and the first night was a very trying one. I was morbidly shy as a strange man was travelling with us, and too, my little baby Belle was just learning to walk, and would cling to my skirts, or if left to herself would get into things. Her favorite pursuit was washing the dishrag in the water bucket, which proved rather a serious matter, when we got farther on to where water was a very scarce article.

Arvazna A. Spillman Cooper reminisced about how daughter, Belle, repeatedly got into mischief:

> There were already some wagons waiting there and belonging to one was a woman with a very sick baby. Grandma and I went to see it, leaving Belle with the children at our wagons, but by this time she had concluded that every outfit on the plains belonged to her, or she to them, she was treated with such consideration by every one that it was no small matter to keep track of her. So while we were sitting in the tent where the sick child was, the woman's children came and whispered something to her, and they all seemed embarrassed. I was wondering what was the matter, when I hear rattling among the pots and pans outside, and went out to investigate. There sat Belle by a pot of beans, from which she had removed the cover, helping herself with her hands. She did not stop when I came but looked up and said 'Belle likum beans'. I tried to impress it on her mind that she must wait to be invited but she was only 17 months old, and she soon forgot the lesson.

Nursing the sick was difficult on the move along the Oregon Trail trek. Travel in rain, cold, wind, and snow/ice with poor nutrition and food poisoning, insufficient clothing and shelter, accidents including drowning, childbirth, as well as encounters with new people who carried diseases contributed to many deaths. Large-scale cholera epidemics (1849, 1850, 1852), measles, typhoid, tuberculosis, malaria, dysentery, pneumonia, smallpox, yellow fever, and mountain fever (tick fever) translated to women learning on the fly how to care for physical and emotional illnesses and injuries. Poor sanitation on the Oregon Trail, with common drinking cups and food preparation processes mixing with human and animal waste all complicated by dust and weather, made for breeding grounds for infectious diseases. Jane (Jennie) Paul Eakin

Hanna noted in 1866 that her grandmother fell from a wagon injuring her face and wrist, a male family member fell and broke a hip, and her grandfather fell sick. She also expressed concern for her 42-year-old mother whom she described on July 2, 1866 shortly after a June 14 birthday: "Mother not very well. This trip is hard on her."

Women were believed to have an inherent wisdom and softness lacking in men (Riley, 1994), which made them ideal caretakers. Seventeen-year-old Jane (Jennie) Paul Eakin, who journeyed from Illinois to Oregon's Willamette Valley in 1866, wrote extensively in her diary about caring for the sick and injured. The 1852 diary of twins Cecilia E. Adams/Parthenia Blank featured an entry about their daily chores and a harrowing description of childbirth in their wagon train party. The delivery had stopped the caravan after half a day's travel with only one day layover since the team has moving through an area considered unsafe with "Indians … not friendly" … "the child was doubled up in the womb, making it a serious and strenuous birth."

Some women's diaries suggested that they provided mental care, too – maintaining high spirits – despite periods of low morale. On the other hand, Cecilia E. Adams showed a sense of humor when she wrote on June 6, 1852 about the loss of a dress on the day following a stampede in her camp: "Last night my clothes got out of the wagon and the oxen ate them up and I consider I have met with a great loss as it was my woollen dress." While Oregon Trail pioneer women wrote extensively about caring for others in the first-person documents examined for this study, seldom did they write about caring for their own needs. Buss (1996) also noted that references to pregnancy, birthing, lactation, and other bodily functions are seldom found in settler women's memoirs. Self-censorship took the form of women writing about how they "feel sick and then suddenly a baby will appear" (Butruille, 1993, p. 113). Some historians have noted that conservative family members who sometimes typed original diary pages may have censored out childbirth and any allusions to sex to avoid any family embarrassment. Keturah Belknap, who traveled the Oregon Trail in 1848, never once mentioned in her diary she was expecting a child. Thirty-six-year-old Amelia Stewart Knight was in the first trimester of pregnancy when she traveled the Oregon Trail in 1853, setting out from Monroe County Iowa on April 9 and arriving in Oregon mid-September. Knowing this fact in retrospect lends context to her diary mentions of nausea linked to certain smells (e.g., dead oxen along the road) and diary recordings about children and men gathering water daily for cooking rather than doing it herself. Butruille (1993) wrote of documented odors associated with the last leg of the Oregon Trail journey: "Some said you could smell your way to Oregon from the stench of dead oxen and find your way by the litter and the graves" (p. 96). Amelia Stewart Knight's last diary entry on September 17, 1853 finally mentioned that she had given birth:

> A few days later my eighth child was born. After this we picked up and ferried across the Columbia River, utilizing skiff, canoes and flatboat to get

across, taking three days to complete. Here husband traded two yoke of oxen for a half section of land with one-half acre planted to potatoes and a small log cabin and lean-to with no windows. This is the journey's end.

Livestock deaths were not the only casualties lamented on the pages of women's Oregon Trail diaries, journals, and reminiscences. It is estimated that perhaps 10% of the people making the trip died before reaching their Oregon destination – about 20,000–30,000 pioneers across age groups (Basic facts about the Oregon Trail, n.d.) Just as pioneer women were responsible for gathering wood for the camp's cooking, cleaning, and warmth, they also scoured the terrain for wood to fashion a homemade casket to bury the dead. Yet, because wood was scarce, many dead bodies were simply wrapped in blanket, quilt, or old clothes (Basic facts about the Oregon Trail, n.d.) These conditions made scavenging of corpses by coyotes and other wildlife commonplace. Lydia Allen Rudd's 1852 diary mentioned illness, dying, death, and graves in nearly every entry chronicling her six-month journey. Julia Thomas's reminiscences, dated July 28, 1907, detailed her crisis responses in caretaking for the sick, comforting survivors, and burying the dead. Together with her husband and four children she set out for Oregon in 1859 with two wagons, a yoke of oxen, and four cows when she was age 23. Julia Thomas experienced the death of her baby, the incapacitation of her husband, and abandonment by hired help and others in their wagon train. Perhaps what stood out most in her recollection nearly 50 years later was the frequency with which death struck and she buried people, noting many gravesites marking the Oregon Trail path as she sat:

> In the night and listen to the howl of the cayotte and remember the graves that but yesterday we had passed where the cayotte had more than once unearthed those that had been or at least should have been laid to rest and just to think of it who would not try to forget.

Oregon Trail commemorations have been celebrated by historical societies in several U.S. states over the years, such as a convention of the Oregon-California Trails Association. Members visited the grave of cholera victim, Rebecca Burdick Winters, on August 15, 1852. Webber (1990) wrote that the Burlington Railroad changed its route after a survey in order to preserve the "lonely little grave on the plains" that features a carved granite monument and is fenced in with iron pipe. Folklore holds that engineers on passing trains blow whistle salutes "She came first in this desert wide; Rebecca … holds the right of way" (Webber, 1990, p. 48). Webber (1990) noted in the editorial portions of the publication of the Cecilia E. Adams/Parthenia Blank 1852 diary that "every grave along the Oregon Trail is important because in it are remains of someone who was loved" (p. 48).

Conflict Intermediary

Public relations scholars have researched ways that professional public relations practice often involves problem solving to navigate friction between organizations and stakeholders (e.g., Plowman, 2005, 2013). A continuum ranging from pure advocacy to pure accommodation has provided public relations researchers with a heuristic for assessing the contingency model of conflict (e.g., Christen & Lovaas, 2010). Back on the Oregon Trail, tempers often flared up along the route in conjunction with chore/task assignments, replete with grumbling, objections, and quarrels that sometimes turned physical (Butruille, 1993, p. 15).

A key portion of Arvazna A. Spillman Cooper's reminiscence about the westward trip explained how she and other pioneer women worked to resolve conflict. Arvazna A. Spillman Cooper recounted in reminiscences that "complaints and dissentions waxed hotter" among parties who made up the train in which her family traveled to Oregon when a family group's children (Johnsons) came down with whooping cough. Collectively, mothers responded to their fears of contagion with a strategic health decision: "[W]e had the foresight to stipulate that they [Johnsons] should form on one side of the corral, and we on the other, and each keep our children on their own side."

Ambassador/Liaison

Other periods of gender labor divide included pioneer women's encounters with Native Americans that may be considered on a parallel with today's professional public relations advocacy work. On the Oregon Trail, adults undertook strategic defense measures and some women served as Ambassador/Liaison among indigenous peoples in order to learn more about their way of life and to maximize bartering opportunities. Pioneer women historian Riley (2004) has noted that as Caucasian/White women discovered how strong and courageous they could be, they "were able to view Indians not just as dangerous enemies, but as real human beings" (p. 2). Pioneer women had no vested interest to promote, or to influence public opinion, but rather their words serve as a record of attitudes toward indigenous peoples as wagon trains journeyed westward (Riley, 2004). Arvazna A. Spillman Cooper's 1901 reminiscences chronicled multiple encounters with Native Americans along her wagon train's six-month journey from Kansas to Polk County in Oregon's Willamette Valley. Several pages noted some boredom linked to the unchanging plains and tedium of dusty travel. Yet, the detail with which she described "Indians," their homes, and family life pays testament to her respect in seeking knowledge – with caution and with caring – throughout her family's journey. For example, Arvazna A. Spillman Cooper recounted toll ferrying across a river, a money-making venture run by a group of Cherokee men. As the century unfolded, the Oregon Trail itself gradually developed as a commercial road with supply stations, guides, ferry operators, trappers, and other provisioners providing services. Arvazna A. Spillman Cooper and some other pioneer women used river travel time to commune with and engage in relationship building with Cherokee women who "came down to the river and politely invited" the Caucasian/White women to visit their homes. Arvazna A. Spillman Cooper recollected in her reminiscences:

> I found them well fixed with household affairs, and very sociable. One woman had a young babe, and had a handy contrivance she called an Indian cradle. It is what we call a hammock now, adapted to the size of an infant and hung between two bedposts. I thought it ingenious … very convenient.

Amelia A. Hammond Hadley was not altogether open-minded about Native Americans in her 1851 diary, even though several diary entries characterized information and cultural exchanges that may be interpreted as a form of relationship building:

> [S]cenery delightful, find some of the most beautiful flowers none that we see in the states except wild roses, I love to walk along and gather them, came to an Indian camp about noon where they had quite a little village of wigwams & a great many poneys. They are the tribe of Soos. They are kind and hospitable and are the most polite and cleanest tribe on the road. They are whiter, to than any that we have seen. They are well dressed and make a fine appearance, went in one of their houses made of dressed skins sewed to gether and verry large. They are all busy some of them jerking Buffalo, some painting skins for boxes which looked vey nice. The old chief came out shook hands with me invited me in, and seemed almost tickled to death to see a white woman, quite a curiosity.

As *Ambassadors* for their respective wagon trains, Amelia A. Hammond Hadley and Arvazna A. Spillman Cooper were inspired to experience Sioux and Cherokee culture; receptive to learning about and from those who invited them into their private spaces. In an earlier gender comparison of Overland Trail diaries, Faragher (1979) also noted that women described "Indians" as helpful guides and purveyors of services rather than as enemies. Unruh (1979) speculated that often female pioneers simply wrote of daily exchanges with "Indians" as part of life on the road while male pioneers perhaps responded with more bravado consistent with traditional masculinity and male gender roles. As for the writings examined for this current research study of Oregon Trail women en route to Oregon's Willamette Valley, outcomes of encounters with Native Americans were often filled with cautious curiosity and conflict avoidance. Despite long-standing mythology and popular culture narrative treatment of savage, uncivilized, or violent Native Americans, most encounters between them and the pioneers were mutually beneficial and peaceful (Basic facts about the Oregon Trail, n.d.) Some Caucasian/White pioneers overreacted to "Indians" who desired nothing more than clothing, firearms, metal tools or cutlery in exchange for labor herding livestock, acting as guides, or assisting with river crossings (Basic facts about the Oregon Trail, n.d.) Unruh (1979) estimated that 362 emigrants and 426 Indians were killed as a result of conflict on the Oregon Trail between 1840 and 1860, mostly due to small skirmishes linked to paranoia, retaliation, or theft.

Most of the pioneer women's diaries examined for the research project reported in this book mention indigenous peoples. In 1852, Lydia Allen Rudd bartered with Native Americans several times, according to multiple entries in her diary. Perhaps due to several delays linked to bouts of illness among the men in their wagon train party, the Rudds' six-month journey from May 6 to October 27 meant encountering slippery, windy, snowy, and freezing conditions toward the end of their journey over the Cascade mountain range and down the Columbia River en route to Oregon City. In July, Rudd traded her "hard bread" for "good berries" from the Snake Indians and an apron for a pair of moccasins from other "Indians." She also traded "an old shirt some bread and a sewing needle" for a "salmon fish" of "seven or eight pound[s]." By late September and October, dangerous travel through the Blue Mountains in northeast Oregon and down the Deschutes River among Oregon's Cascades range and Columbia River encouraged her to engage passage with "Indians" as guides with canoes to transport her family for parts of the last leg of their Oregon Trail journey. Amelia Stewart Knight also used her diary to record exchanges with Cayuse peoples as barter partner-provisioners and guides, especially once her wagon train had crossed into Oregon Country/Territory in August 1853:

> After looking in vain for water, we were about to give up as it was near night when husband came across a company of friendly Cayuse Indians about to camp, who showed him where to find water ... I am waiting for water to get supper. This forenoon we bought a few potatoes from an Indian, which will be a treat for our supper.

Then on September 1, 1853, Amelia Stewart Knight noted:

> we have camped not far from the Columbia River. Made a nice dinner of fried salmon. Quite a number of Indians were camped around us, for the purpose of selling salmon to the emigrants.
>
> Twins Cecilia E. Adams and Parthenia Blank also included in their diary several stories about bartering with indigenous peoples. On September 4, 1852, they wrote toward the end of their westward journey: Here we find some Indians with some very nice salmon for sale and we all got a good supply. They will trade them for powder, lead, caps, bread, beads, brass nails, old shirts, or almost anything you have ...

In fall or early winter, the emigrants arrived in Oregon and set about the work of homesteading. Some noted the land's bounty and the neighborly community-building attitude of residents. For example, Jane (Jennie) Paul Eakin Hanna's diary entry for August 23, 1866 happily told of free apples and potatoes for meals and grazing pastures for livestock: "Farmers are generous in Oregon." Oregon City in present day Clackamas County, is considered the Oregon Trail's terminus, with the nickname "End of the Oregon Trail" and the city motto "First and mothertown of our state" (Oregon City, n.d.) By the 1840s, Oregon City had become the destination for homesteaders who sought to file land claims after traveling the Oregon Trail (Oregon City, n.d.) However, some wagon trains of pioneers concluded their journey in eastern Oregon when they found promising locations, while others pushed past Oregon City to join family or friends who had already settled.

That pioneer women recognized and nurtured relationship building opportunities with Native Americans – as *Ambassador* – is in keeping with advocacy skills developed among contemporary professional public relations practitioners. Such outreach is consistent with the Public Relations Society of America definition of *public relations*: "a strategic communication process that builds mutually beneficial relationships between organizations and their publics" (PRSA, n.d.). Granted, large organizations wouldn't emerge in the U.S. until the twentieth century, which is when PRSA dates the beginning of formal professional public relations practice (PRSA, n.d.). However, it must be noted that community-building Oregon Trail pioneer women respectfully used interpersonal skills for advocacy and caretaking among diverse individuals and groups earlier – in the nineteenth century.

Summary

Interrogating pioneer women's role as *Caretaker/Advocate* underscores women's lived experiences as they transitioned from a stationary bricks/sticks home to a mobile one out of doors, responding to the need to build a new kind of community amidst uncertainty and meager resources. Pioneer women welcomed the magnitude of scenery change early on, according to their first-person accounts. As the reality of the six-month journey settled in, however, women quickly discovered important ways they needed to expand their traditional work roles. A significant theme across the writings examined for this research project was the emergence of a *Caretaker/Advocate* role which has great similarity with aspects of what we today consider to be public relations work. While traveling along the approximately 2,000-mile Oregon Trail, emigrant women who ultimately settled in Oregon served as active community-building agents building relationships through dialogue and deeds performed as *Caretaker/Advocate* in many small and large ways as Cook/Cleaner, Livestock Caretaker, Apothecary, Nurse/Midwife/Undertaker, Conflict Intermediary, and Ambassador/Liaison.

As Oregon Trail women worked to preserve tradition while building and maintaining new ways of doing things, they experienced an expanded female gender role. Of necessity, women underwent a metamorphosis, taking what they knew from the private sphere work of childbearing and raising, cooking, washing, and cleaning – and building upon these tasks for survival as *Caretaker/Advocate*. We know that professional public relations today supports society's democratic elements (Yang & Taylor, 2013) and this chapter offers evidence of pioneer women's key roles in caretaking and advocating which supported democratic operations on the Oregon Trail. Pioneer women summoned up strength to support others in the face of danger since many people engaged in conflict and sometimes crossed one another while crossing the plains, climbing mountains, forging rivers, tending livestock, battling weather, and engaging with indigenous communities. The relationship building that took place as pioneer women interacted with other émigrés across wagon trains and moved into indigenous communities is testament to their *Caretaker/Advocate* skills. In particular, pioneer women's outreach with Native Americans out of curiosity and willingness to learn about new cultures and to barter with them for survival and mutual benefit does credit to their strong character and commitment to the common good, or "moral life as a whole" (Christians, 2008, p. 3). It also reflects positively on the way women embraced the responsibility of serving the public interest through collaboration and developing mutual understanding – which resonates with public relations' core professional values of collectivism and collaboration (J. E. Grunig, 2000). The *public interest* is the welfare or well-being of the general public, or society. Lippmann (1955) offered that "the public interest may be presumed to be what men [sic] would choose if they saw clearly, thought rationally, acted disinterestedly and benevolently" (p. 42).

Clearly, all men and women who made it safely across the Oregon Trail to arrive in Oregon had worked hard and suffered greatly. That a pregnant 36-year-old Amelia Stewart Knight made such careful diary notes while acting as *Caretaker/Advocate* to many underscores a commitment to the enterprise and support for achieving this fresh start. On June 1, 1853, a day of rain, Amelia Stewart Knight optimistically wrote:

> The men and boys are all soaking wet and look sad and comfortless. The little ones and myself are shut up in the wagons from the rain. Still it will find its way in and many thigs are wet; and take us all together we are a poor looking set, and all this for Oregon. I am thinking while I write, 'Oh, Oregon, you must be a wonderful country'.

This chapter has addressed ways in which the Oregon Trail trek laid a foundation for Oregon settlement and expanded community-building roles for women, further problematizing the traditional nineteenth-century female gender role. Morrissey (1992) noted that masculine images such as the cowboy, soldier, gold miner, and fur trader shaped the stereotypical male American identity as they conquered a virgin land (Smith, 1950) and contributed to a "cultural myth of the West" (pp. 133–134). Accepting popular culture narratives about Oregon Trail pioneer women offers a limited perspective on wife and motherhood, domesticity, home, and family. That suggests only part of the picture, while Oregon Trail pioneer women's first-person narratives reveal a much more complex and active role. The findings of this study suggest an amended record of what we now consider as early public relations practice in terms of community building through a *Caretaker/Advocate* role. Rarely has public relations history represented women as such active agents. Similarly, feminist historians identified women's perspectives as distinct from men's (e.g., Schlissel, Ruiz, & Monk, 1988), with Riley (1988) arguing that patterns among pioneer women's words necessitate a reconsideration of female gender roles. I posit that the public relations history chapter could benefit from similar thinking. Women's early community-building role must be added to public relations history rather than enabling frameworks of organizations, industry, and mass media to occlude understandings of fundamental relationship building function of public relations early on.

The lived experiences of pioneer women included in this chapter ranged in age and marital status – Arvazna A. Spillman Cooper, Amelia A. Hammond Hadley, Jane (Jennie) Paul Eakin Hanna, Amelia Stewart Knight, Lydia Allen Rudd, and Julia Thomas – but the ties that bind their stories include their important work as *Caretaker/Advocate* as they traveled to Oregon in the nineteenth century. The constellation of relationships that emerged across these spaces have much to teach us about early relationship building. As feminist historical geographer Philo (1994) referenced the past so that we may affect positive change in the present, I also hope that pioneer women's narratives earn space on public relations history's pages for today's students to explore. Gregson and Rose (2013) opined that histories are almost always present-ist because they narrate the past to offer greater understanding of the present.

In Chapter 4, a care perspective is thematically extended to explore pioneer women's role as *Community Builder of Meeting Houses and Schools*.

References

Ahmad, D. L. (2012). "I fear the consequences to our animals" emigrants and their livestock. *Great Plains Quarterly*, 32(3), 165–182.

Barnett, J. (1928). *Long trip in a prairie schooner.* Whittier, CA: Western Stationery Co.

Basic facts about the Oregon Trail (n.d.). U.S. Department of the Interior – Bureau of Land Management. Accessed December 22, 2019 from www.blm.gov/sites/blm.gov/files/learn_interp_nhotic_faq.pdf.

Brunner, B. (2017). Introduction. In B. Brunner (ed.), *The moral compass of public relations* (pp. 1–11). New York: Routledge.

Buss, H. (1996). Listening to the "ground noise" of Canadian women settlers' memoirs: A maternal intercourse of discourses. *Essays on Canadian Writing*, 60, 199–214.

Butruille, S. G. (1993). *Women's voices from the Oregon Trail: The times that tried women's souls and a guide to women's history along the Oregon Trail.* Boise, ID: Tamarack Books, Inc.

Christen, C. T., & Lovaas, S. (2010). The dual-continuum approach: An extension of the contingency theory of conflict management. Unpublished paper presented at the Public Relations Division of the Annual Conference of the Association for Journalism and Education in Mass Communication, Denver, CO, August 4–7, August 5.

Christians, C. G. (2008). Media ethics on a higher order of magnitude. *Journal of Mass Media Ethics*, 23, 3–14.

Chudacoff, H. P. (1981). *The evolution of American urban society* (2nd edn). Englewood Cliffs, NJ: Prentice-Hall, Inc.

Coontz, S. (1993). *The way we never were: American families and the nostalgia trap.* New York: Basic Books.

Faragher, J. (1979). *Women and men on the Overland Trail.* New Haven, CT: Yale University Press.

Faragher, J., & Stansell, C. (1975). Women and their families on the Overland Trail to California and Oregon, 1842–1867. *Feminist Studies,* 2(2/3), 150–166.

Feltskog, E. N. (ed.) (1969). *The Oregon Trail.* Madison, WI: University of Wisconsin Press.

Gordon, N. S., Buhle, M. J., & Schrom, N. E. (1971). *Women in American society.* Somerville, MA: New England Free Press.

Gregson, N., & Rose, G. (2013). Contested and negotiated histories of feminist geography. In G. Rose et al. (eds), *Feminist geographies: Explorations in diversity and difference* (pp. 13–48). New York: Taylor & Francis.

Grunig, J. E. (2000). Collectivism, collaboration, and societal corporatism as core professional values in public relations. *Journal Public Relations Research,* 21(1), 23–48.

Hallahan, K. (2004). "Community" as a foundation for public relations theory and practice. *Communication Yearbook,* 28, 233–279.

Hogeland, R. W. (1976). The female appendage: Feminine life-styles in America, 1820–1860. In J. E. Friedman and W. G. Shade (eds), *Our American sisters: Women in American life and thought* (2nd edn) (pp. 133–148). Boston, MA: Allyn and Bacon, Inc.

Jeffrey, J. R. (1998). *Frontier women: Civilizing the West? 1840–1880.* New York: Hill & Wang.

Kruckeberg, D., & Starck, K. (1988). *Public relations and community: A reconstructed theory.* New York: Praeger.

Kruckeberg, D., & Starck, K. (2004). The role and ethics of community building for consumer products and services. In M-L. Galician (ed.), *Handbook of product placement in the mass media: New strategies in marketing theory, practice, trends, and ethics* (pp. 133–146). New York: Best Business Books.

Leonard, E. D. (1994). *Yankee women: Gender battles in the Civil War.* New York: W. W. Norton and Company.

Lippmann, W. (1955). *The public philosophy.* Boston, MA: Little, Brown.

McPherson, J. M. (1988). *Battle cry of freedom: The Civil War era.* New York: Random House Publishing Inc.

Morrissey, K. G. (1992). Engendering the West. In W. Cronon, G. Miles, & J. Gitlin (eds), *Under an open sky: Rethinking America's Western past* (pp. 132–144). New York: W. W. Norton & Company.

Oregon City (n.d.). The Oregon Trail. Accessed December 23, 2019 from https://bit.ly/2SlI8lR.

Philo, C. (1994). History, geography and the "still greater mystery" of historical geography. In D. Gregory, R. Martin, & G. Smith (eds), *Human geography: Society, space and social science* (pp. 252–281). Minneapolis, MN: University of Minnesota Press.

Plowman, K. (2005). Strategic management, conflict, and public relations. *Public Relations Review,* 31, 131–138.

Plowman, K. (2013). Conflict resolution. In R. L. Heath, *Encyclopedia of public relations* (2nd edn) (pp. 176–180). Thousand Oaks, CA: Sage.

Public Relations Society of America (PRSA) (n.d.), About PRSA. Accessed August 15, 2019 from www.prsa.org/about/all-about-pr.

Riley, G. (1988). *The female frontier: A comparative view of women on the prairie and the plains.* Lawrence, KS: University Press of Kansas.

Riley, G. (1994). *Frontierswomen: The Iowa experience*. Ames, IA: Iowa State University Press.

Riley, G. (2004). *Confronting race: Women and Indians on the frontier, 1825–1915*. Albuquerque, NM: University of New Mexico Press.

Schlissel, L. (2004). *Women's diaries of the westward journey*. New York: Schocken Books.

Schlissel, L., Ruiz, V. L., & Monk, J. (eds) (1988). *Western women: Their land, their lives*. Albuquerque, NM: University of New Mexico Press.

Schultz, J. E. (1994). Race, gender, and bureaucracy: Civil War army nurses and the pension bureau. *Journal of Women's History*, 6(2), 45–69.

Smith, H. N. (1950). *Virgin land: The American West as symbol and myth*. Cambridge, MA: Harvard University Press.

Tong, R. (2009). *Feminist thought: A more comprehensive introduction* (5th edn). Boulder, CO: Westview Press.

Unruh, J. D. (1979). *The plains across: The overland emigrants and the trans-Mississippi west, 1840–1860*. Chicago, IL: University of Illinois Press.

Webber, B. (1990). Introduction and contemporary comments. *The Oregon Trail diary of twin sisters Cecilia Adams and Parthenia Blank in 1852*. Medford, OR: Webb Research Group.

Welter, B. (1966). The cult of true womanhood, 1820–1860. *American Quarterly*, 18, 152–174.

Werstein, I. (1957). *July, 1863*. New York: Julian Messner, Inc.

Wheeler, L., & Reis, H. T. (1991). Self-recording of everyday life events: Origins, types and uses. *Journal of Personality*, 59, 339–354.

Yang, A., & Taylor, M. (2013). The relationship between the professionalism of public relations, societal social capital and democracy: Evidence from a cross-national study. *Public Relations Review*, 39, 257–270.

4 Exploring Public Relations from the Care Perspective
Pioneer Women's Role as *Community Builder of Meeting Houses and Schools*

Introduction

Some pioneer women's *Caretaking/Advocacy* role which they developed or honed while traveling the Oregon Trail translated into a deeper community-building role once they settled in the Willamette Valley and beyond in Oregon. This geographic region is about 675 square miles, extends nearly the length of the Willamette River, and consists of the present-day Oregon counties of: Benton, Clackamas, Lane, Linn, Polk, Marion, Multnomah, Yamhill, and Washington. Oregon Trail women's diaries, journals, and reminiscences offer evidence of a more richly textured understanding of an early form of public relations, historically, in terms of the ways pioneer women employed community-building techniques to establish a new way of life on the West coast. Oregon Trail pioneer women's work has not made it into the history chapter of public relations which has long been dominated in the U.S. by Progressive Era foci on twentieth-century industrial and commercial development/expansion with the rise of formal organizations in a capitalist economy. This too was a period of mass media expansion, including muckraking journalists who exposed the abuse of power and the negative social impact of wealthy Caucasian/White men and their organizations. The current study was designed to supplement the public relations history chapter with community-building contributions made by Oregon Trail women during the nineteenth century without romanticizing the colonialist impact of the emigration on indigenous communities and the geographic physical environment.

In both practice and theory building, the ideal social role of public relations involves facilitating dialogue that is beneficial to society (Grunig & White, 1992). This social role also applies in a historical context to the community building of nineteenth-century Oregon Trail pioneer women. The social role principle inspired Kruckeberg and Starck (1988) to advocate for public relations as a means of emphasizing commonalities while communicating across differences and of focusing on the *community-building* role of public relations: "Our theory is that public relations is better defined and practiced as the active attempt to restore and maintain a sense of community" (p. xi). The Chicago School of thought (e.g., John Dewey, Harold A. Innis, Daniel J. Boorstin, and

James W. Carey) provided Kruckeberg and Starck (1988) with a solid foundation upon which to consider "the Great Community" (p. xiii) in conjunction with the responsibility of public relations to serve society at large. The Chicago School saw relationships between community and communication as "necessary to a healthy social structure" (Kruckeberg & Starck, 1988, p. 70; Starck & Kruckeberg, 2001). *Community relations*, in all its various activities for relationship building, is among the most important and characteristic in the application of public relations skills (Kruckeberg & Starck, 1988, p. 23). However, our understanding to date of conceptualizing public relations in terms of social and historical elements in community relations remains underdeveloped.

While in modern professional public relations practice, *community* is qualified according to locality where specific organizations are physically built, the specific literature of *community relations* "is grossly deficient and inappropriate" (Kruckeberg & Starck, 1988, p. 25) and ripe for update. Perhaps L'Etang (2014) had this in mind when she wrote that *public relations history* could benefit from "a broader view" (p. xxix) and a distinction being made between "history of the term [public relations] and history of the activity" (p. xxx). *Community* is conceptualized as "a group of people who share a common experience, identity, or interest and who are joined together through their interaction or communication" (Hallahan, 2013b). Those who practice public relations often frame *community relations* in terms of stakeholders who have a direct financial interest in an organization (Kruckeberg & Starck, 1988). In relation to Oregon Trail émigrés, *community* refers to all who traveled westward as part of wagon trains, indigenous peoples they met along the way – as well as localities once the émigrés settled in the Willamette Valley and across other parts of Oregon Country/Territory that has been recognized as a U.S. state since 1859. In the nineteenth century, once Oregon Trail émigrés had settled, informal *community-relations* and *community-building* activities may be considered to be the pioneers' "planned, active, and continuing participation with and within a community to maintain and enhance its environment" to the benefit of all – a definition comparable to Peak's (1983, p. 70) without framing *community* in terms of institutions. I also borrow from Kruckeberg and Starck's (1988) framing of *community relations* as a positive outcome for assuring "survival and prosperity" as part of community maintenance (p. 25). These senior scholars rued the loss of *community* as an outcome of modern communication and transportation tools and advanced a *communitarian approach* by encouraging other public relations researchers to view public relations from a deeper philosophical base. The current study's interpretation of the lived experience of Oregon Trail pioneer women working to adjust to their challenging new environment has been influenced by these senior scholars' invitation.

The following sections build a foundation for examining the Oregon Trail pioneer women's role as *Community Builder of Meeting Houses and Schools* while settling in Oregon's Willamette Valley and beyond: 1) Adopting a Care Perspective, 2) Transitioning from Oregon Trail to Settlement, 3) Spanning Boundaries, 4) Becoming Organizers and Community Planners, 5) Discovering the Community Project Manager Role, 6) Laying Community Foundation with Meeting Houses and Schools, 7) Settling in and Setting up as Entrepreneurs in Search of Commercial Enterprise, and 8) Summary.

Adopting a Care Perspective

The *Caretaker/Advocate* role introduced in the previous chapter is expanded upon in this chapter by incorporating the care perspective concept to explain pioneer women's role as *Community Builder of Meeting Houses and Schools*. Once pioneers arrived in and established communities in Oregon as homesteaders and settlers, women's caretaking assumed additional new dimensions. To help explore the breadth of their contributions, care scholarship is borrowed from the feminist theory building literature. The care perspective concept was introduced in the late 1970s and early 1980s by feminist scholars working in education, philosophy, political science, social work, and women's studies. It is *feminist* because the care perspective seeks to challenge and reverse gender inequalities embedded in historic and current care practices so that care work may be "accomplished without reproducing and perpetuating gender inequality" (Baines, Evans, & Neysmith, 1998, p. 13). A high quality of care in community service is fundamental to "good government and meaningful citizenship" (Butruille, 1993, p. 529). Unfortunately, women's lived experiences have not figured prominently in explanations of American public organizational life (Burnier, 2003) – and even though public relations has made significant contributions to the study of organizational management (Pearson, 1992), women's lived experiences have not been recorded equitably in public relations history narratives. This chapter argues that care drives community building so that telling stories about "how care [has been] valued and practiced by people at all levels" (Mackay, 2001, p. 155) expands public relations history research discourse. Recognizing that public relations is an "active attempt to restore and maintain a sense of community" (Kruckeberg & Starck, 1988, p. 21) opens wide the opportunity to incorporate women's voices in ways that other frameworks for interpretation may not have fully supported.

Care is an important human value and practice that was central to the émigrés' survival, helping them transition to their new life homesteading and settling in Oregon. Drawing upon Kant's (1997) and Heidegger's (1927) understandings of *care*, Hummel and Stivers (1998) advanced the care perspective as "a way of approaching life that shapes and is shaped by experience" (p. 37). Gilligan's (1982) moral orientation research findings suggested that men are no less moral by nature, but that women's voice is rooted in a commitment to doing no harm, making connections, supporting interdependence, and building relationships. Women are perhaps more likely to speak in an ethical, care-focused voice given their "experiences as primary child rearers and care givers within the family and community" (Burnier, 2003, p. 532). The care perspective consists of four distinct phases and draws parallels with public relations community building. The phases are: 1) *caring about* (recognizing that care is required in the first place), 2) *taking care of* (having recognized a need, somebody must be willing to be responsible for meeting another's needs), 3) *care giving* (concrete activities associated with care), and 4) *care receiving* (person receiving care responds to care givers) Tronto (1993). Ideally the four phases are integrated, Tronto (1993) explained, adding that there may be conflict in the form of disagreements about defining *good care* and *who* will address it– as well as disagreement about recognizing, defining, and assessing needs. The care perspective shares much in common with public relations community building since specific skills associated with human society organization include persuasion, conflict resolution, and relationship building wherein decision-making for the greater good is heavily dependent upon people's ability to build community (Kruckeberg & Stark, 1988).

Transitioning from the Oregon Trail to Settlement

By the time women had journeyed for roughly 2,000 miles and reached Oregon, many of them were transformed by the experience and soon discovered new avenues for their caretaking and advocacy work. In 1903, a young woman named Margaret Bannard solicited stories about early Oregon pioneer life as part of a research project either at the University of Oregon in Eugene or for a heritage organization such as pioneer women's clubs (Collection of Oregon Pioneer Letters, 1903). A letter by J. W. Miller in Margaret Bannard's file described the Willamette Valley area as "prairie lands" where emigrants pitched tents near plentiful water and firewood so they could measure and mark their homestead land claims. Temporary houses constructed of fir, cedar, and pine, with earthen floors were assembled without nails, rather with an auger and wood pegs. Tick beds were filled with straw, corn husks, or "Oregon feathers" (dried grass). The same letter described the pioneers' priority of establishing school programs for educating children in their new home. Many homesteaders found themselves starting from scratch in Oregon since they either lost or abandoned heavy household items like stoves to lighten the load of weary animals pulling wagons. An 1840s female homesteader who set up housekeeping with a new husband wrote of having one stew kettle which she used for multiple purposes (making coffee, baking bread, cooking meat) over an open fire as she tried to make the best of her situation because "there was no returning home" (Jeffrey, 1998, p. 70).

For Oregon Trail women who emigrated to Oregon, the urge to reinstate a culture of domesticity in their new settlements was strong but their experiences of expanding upon the traditional female gender role bound up in a cult of womanhood standards (Schlissel, 2004) fostered a complex dynamic. In reality, boundaries separating women's and men's work had blended. So, setting up house in Oregon was different from what these Caucasian/White women had experienced back East where they were expected mostly to remain in the domestic private sphere most of the time raising children, while husbands moved about in an "external world of male commerce" (Norwood, 1988, p. 155).

Demographically, the gender ratio in Oregon Country/Territory towns varied. The Willamette Valley was settled by Caucasian/Whites who originally were Southerners with pro-slavery attitudes (Riley, 2003). In more populated areas like Portland, homesteaders were predominantly poor Caucasians/Whites and at least half the women were under 30, married, with 20–30% parenting one or two children (Jeffrey, 1998). In Oregon's larger populated areas like Portland and mining and cattle communities, women outnumbered men by three to one (Jeffrey, 1998). Some young married women who opted to live in hotels and boarding houses had often had their fill of domestic labor on the westward journey (Jeffrey, 1998).

Oregon Trail women had endured trial by fire and learned how to perform well under pressure, proving their flexibility. In many cases when husbands and fathers became sick or died, women took control of the family's westward journey (Jeffrey, 1998). These women soon realized that the ideals and female behavior norms that they had been socialized to internalize and routinize must make way for new skills required for the westward journey. Women had to build upon these new skills as residents of a new land where culture often conflicted with environment. This chapter posits that the Oregon Trail journey ultimately served as a boot camp experience, preparing women for community service and relationship building across Oregon as part of homesteading and settlement life.

Care ethics are embedded in particular historical contexts, considering individuals relationally as interdependent with others across webs of social, personal, and familial relations (Held, n.d.). These dynamics are consistent with the International Public Relations Association's definition of *public relations* as being "tasked with building relationships and interests between organizations and their publics based on the delivery of information through trusted and ethical communication methods" (International Public Relations Association, 2019, para. 2). Analyses of Oregon Trail pioneer women's first-person accounts in diaries, journals, and reminiscences offer evidence that community-building work exists beyond formal organizations and supports an argument for updating public relations history pages to include women's informal early community-building work in the nineteenth century. Doing so will advance a revised framework that supports a broader interpretation of public relations history beyond important contributions of nineteenth-century Caucasian/White men. Women settling into the Willamette Valley and beyond in Oregon were also well positioned to build upon a *Caretaking/Advocacy* role as community builder with indigenous peoples. Bartering exchanges and home visits to indigenous communities to learn new cultures provided the first steps for ambassadorship and building important relationships. Yet, images and myths perpetuated by nineteenth-century media prevented "generations of observers" in the twentieth century from discovering authentic exchanges in favor of prejudice and discriminatory treatment of both women and Native Americans (Riley, 1984, p. 252).

Analyses of the Oregon Trail pioneer women's diaries, journals, and reminiscences for the study reported here suggest that at least some of the women were surprised by the challenging experience of transitioning back to a stationary home base. Feminist historians have concluded that the dominant perspectives about female gender and ideas about women's work have resulted in much similarity across historical narratives about women (Riley, 1988). For example, 26-year-old Amelia A. Hammond Hadley, who left her Galesburg, Illinois, home with husband Samuel B. Hadley on May 5, 1851 and arrived in Oregon Country/Territory in late August, stopped to camp at a farm owned by a man named Foster who had emigrated from Maine years before. Whereas Amelia A. Hammond Hadley only had just sketched a prairie landscape that spring, collected buffalo chips for campfires, and visited a Cherokee family home, she finally found herself en route to Portland and quickly had to re-acclimate to domestic life indoors: "I could not walk strait after not being in a house for so long when I got up to go across the floor I was like an old sailor that had not been on land for a long time." According to Holmes (1996), the Hadleys took up their land claim on December 1, 1851 a little further south in the Umpqua Valley near what would become Roseburg where timber "was to be the main center of their activities for the rest of their lives" (p. 55). Another example of a culture shock transition following months on the Oregon Trail is evidenced in the diary of Jane (Jennie) Paul Eakin Hanna, 17, who had lived on the Trail the spring–summer of 1866 before settling in Oregon's Willamette Valley. She wrote:

> Crossed the Willamette River on a ferry boat. We are at the end of our long journey at last where Uncle Andrew and Aunt Maria (McCornack) and Uncle Robert Pattison and Aunt Isabel live. Took tea with Aunt Isabel tonight.

Taking tea was not an activity Jane (Jennie) Paul Eakin Hanna had written about in her diary recorded along the Oregon Trail over several months and the stories she and her aunt must have exchanged are left to our imagination.

Spanning Boundaries

Bonding experiences that women shared as part of their Oregon Trail journey provided linkages for building community as homesteaders and settlers in Oregon. Expanding early public relations history by adding nineteenth-century Oregon Trail pioneer women's lived experiences means considering community building as early public relations work prior to the emergence of large industrial organizations and global mass media in the twentieth century. Themes that emerge from pioneer women's diaries, journals, and reminiscences suggest that they developed a means to span boundaries as they built communities and put these skills to work in adjusting to and establishing new permanent homes in Oregon. As émigrés began thinking about how to fit in and adapt to their new surroundings, a dominant goal was the setting up of infrastructures mirroring those they had left behind. This caretaking attitude was gendered, with women using diaries to think through what they could do and the roles they might play. From studies of early-nineteenth-century city life, public administration researchers revealed that female reformers were concerned with helping citizens receive improved living conditions through water, health, and recreation (Stivers, 2000). Private sphere operations served as the model for these turn-of-the-century women reformers back East who sought to help people in cities through caring relationships based on a desire to "cultivate mutuality and connection" (Burnier, 2003, p. 537; McGurty, 1998; Pickles, 1998). From feminist historical geographers we know that there exist gendered differences in the way one uses public space (e.g., Boyer, 1998), enacts citizenship (e.g., Cope, 1998), participates in nation building (e.g., Johnson, 1995), and adapts private sphere space (e.g., Blunt, 1994).

Pioneer women had learned new ways to multitask on the fly as they developed a new set of skills while balancing an already-heavy domestic workload. Oregon Trail pioneer women had discovered how to be even more resourceful caretakers and advocates as they rode and walked westward gathering weeds for livestock to eat, buffalo chips and anything that would burn for warmth and cooking fires, as well as roots, weeds, berries, and herbs for apothecary and wagon train meals (e.g., strawberries, gooseberries, currants). Women discovered new ways to be resourceful in a new climate that both physically and emotionally challenged them. Oregon Trail pioneer women proved that they were not fragile creatures whose gender required complete dependence upon men for survival (if ever they were). They had challenged prevailing nineteenth-century cultural norms that women are subservient, delicate creatures. Despite the trials the frontier presented them with, many emigrant women continued to see themselves within the mainstream of nineteenth-century culture, with their first-person diary and journal accounts offering up evidence that women expected to "work hard and long to achieve their goals" (Jeffrey, 1998, pp. 95–96). Even though it was men in new Oregon Country/Territory settlements who primarily performed the most physically demanding tasks, this does not mean that women were only passive spectators. Jeffrey (1998) argued that the women's style was to influence and even argue such that their participation in decision-making *should* "pass into Western folklore" (p. 41). For example, by the end of a May–October 1852 journey, Lydia Allen Rudd proved that she was not so weak in mind or body that she could not survive her baby's death, her own bout of cholera, as well as her husband's infirmity for much of the trip. She had learned how to barter with Native Americans, trading an apron for a pair of moccasins and an old shirt and some needles for salmon. So, perhaps it was exhaustion or low spirits talking when she concluded her overland journey diary with these words on October 26, 1852:

> Our men have been looking around for a house and employment and have been successful, for which I feel very thankful. Harry has gone into co-partnership with Mr. Donnal in the mercantile business and we are to

live in the back part of the store for this winter. Henry and Mary are going into Mr. D's house on his farm for the winter, one mile from here. Mr. D. will also find him employment if he wants. I expect that we shall not make a claim after all our trouble in getting her on purpose for one. I shall have to be poor and dependent on a man my life time.

Schlissel (2004) wrote of Lydia Allen Rudd that after arriving in Oregon she and "other wives in the Oregon frontier" (p. 197) sought land in their own name under provisions of the Donation Land Act which reduced the size of a land claim from 640 to 320 free acres.

Becoming Organizers and Community Planners

Oregon Trail women participated in organizing processes during the westward journey, so were not shy about extending such skills to organizing and community planning in Oregon as it grew and was granted 33rd statehood on February 14, 1859. For example, Arvazna A. Spillman-Cooper told of an 1863 incident that supported her community organizing and coalition building education:

> We began selecting our crowd, by consulting with those we liked best among the only outfits we had become acquainted with ... There were 14 wagons of us now, and we got along so pleasantly, we did not like to enlarge our party, so we journeyed along till we came to the place to turn off to Oregon.

Back East, many women reformers got to work using communication tactics as leaders advocating for public opinion support and influencing policy in conjunction with Progressive Era movements by using public relations tactics like media relations and relationship building to support charitable institutions (Gower, 2007). In Oregon, Arvazna A. Spillman-Cooper became instrumental in founding the Children's Farm Home School in Corvallis, Oregon; a home for orphans and neglected children. She was described by Mrs. F. W. Bayley (Collection of Arvazna A. Cooper Papers, 1845–1900):

> Grandchildren meant much to her, she helped bring some of them into the world. Fortunately her own, later babies came in between helping with the grandchildren. In fact you might say children were her hobby. She helped build the Farm Home for them, at Corvallis, causing us to call her, eventually, mother of all the orphans of Oregon.

Twins Cecilia E. Adams and Parthenia Blank arrived at The Dalles in Oregon Country/Territory on October 5, 1852 and took a boat ride to where their brother James H. McMillan met them and escorted the families to his Washington County farm, near the village of Reedville between present-day

Beaverton and Hillsboro, Oregon. Ultimately settling in the Portland area, the McMillan, Adams, and Blank families all supported Pacific University and Tualatin Academy, a congregational educational institution, with Parthenia Blank regularly entertaining students in her home (Robertson, 1905). Dr. George Adams, husband of Cecilia, wrote to the Oregon Pioneer Association on June 1, 1905 that his wife had taught at a district school when they met three years before they wed and their extended family emigrated to Oregon Country/Territory:

> I was poor and in debt, and in no circumstances to keep a wife just then; and I told her so; but she said I wouldn't have to keep her. She would help me more than she would hinder me, even in my practice and so she did.
>
> (Webber, 1990)

Discovering the Community Project Manager Role

Because senior public relations scholars have long urged researchers and practitioners to "approach communication as a complex, multiflow process having

Figure 4.1 Cecilia Adams
Source: Public Domain.

the potential to help create a sense of community" (p. xiii), interpreting an Oregon Trail pioneer woman's work in settling the Willamette Valley and other areas of Oregon as *Community Builder of Meeting Houses and Schools* offers a new perspective on her community project manager role. Once they arrived in Oregon, women got busy organizing and building their new community's social life through shared meeting spaces to support those recovering from physical and emotional wounds inflicted by accidents, death, disease, and sickness. In addition to managing their own families and households, women were responsible for preserving and recording family histories, as well as perpetuating ethnic traditions and cultural institutions while attending to the "reweaving of families separated and broken by the migration" (Norwood, 1988, p. 155). While men tended livestock and plowed/planted crops, women raised and preserved vegetables and tended poultry and milked cows. Women also continued to care for the sick and to raise children, prepare meals, and clean. Jameson (1987) concluded that pioneer family survival depended on "flexibility and interdependence in work roles" (p. 150) of women. Riley (1988) also argued that women stoked the home fires while husbands, fathers, and brothers participated in military expeditions that pushed into other new frontier lands. Juggling all of these tasks required expert time management and organization.

Laying a Community's Foundation with Meeting Houses and Schools

Homesteading women were determined to carve settlements out of the Oregon wilderness and one means to accomplish this end was to build meeting houses, schools, and a formal education system. Women schooled children over the course of the westward journey as best they could as part of their caretaking role, but mobile outdoor-living challenges in conjunction with unpredictable weather and time limitations left several women feeling unsatisfied with the quality of children's schooling on the prairie and over the mountains. A letter in Margaret Bannard's collection of Oregon pioneer letters by J. W. Miller (Collection of Oregon Pioneer Letters, 1903) described the Willamette Valley area pioneers' priority of establishing school programs. The first building to be erected in any new community was nearly always a school, with the lag time between settlement and schoolhouse construction depending on homesteaders' needs in a given geographic area and their financial resources (Harris, 1987). Schlissel (2004) saw pioneer women's use of school building and curriculum development as an effort to re-establish familiar frameworks and stability as soon as possible in their new Oregon home. Women's work in the "reweaving of families separated and broken by the migration" made them culture carriers and community organizers establishing a fabric of social life (Norwood, 1988, p. 155), providing comfort for other women and a sense of stability after five–six months of *in*stability and uncertainty on the Oregon Trail. Dewey's (1927) advancement of communitarianism as a member of The Chicago School of Social Thought included reverence for the public school as an instrument for creating a sense of community, which he considered a requirement for a healthy social structure. Like Dewey (1916/2018), pioneer women regarded the local school as an "embryonic community" built through personal contact and cooperative work that also served as a community center unifying a neighborhood. Eventually, community meeting center buildings served multiple functions for schooling and as places of worship (Riley, 1988). The schoolhouse, post office, or mercantile became the hub for social, commercial, and religious/faith activities in developing settlements (Jeffrey, 1998). Prior to emigration West, most of the Oregon Trail women were considered "middle-class women … home-based, living in gentle domesticity, responsible for the acculturation of future generations, sheltered from the strife and competition of the external world of male commerce" (Norwood, 1988, p. 144), but upon reaching Oregon, women had survived the perils of the journey and were well prepared to begin a new life outside the bonds of traditional female roles.

Female gender was a key factor in determining pioneer women's duties and interests in the new Oregon settlements. In every "frontier setting," Riley (1988) found "striking similarity" (p. 10) across Oregon areas where the Caucasian/Whites' new settlements sprang up. Regardless of economic base or predominant occupations, women were charged with starting the formal education process and as communities continued to build, it was women who staffed the schools. Jeffrey (1998) estimated that as many as one-fifth to one-quarter of women taught at some point in their lives. Educating children was perceived as a natural extension of women's mothering skills. Yet, for women who depended on an income, teaching jobs offered little security especially when schools were never built or lost community support (Jeffrey, 1998).

When women joined together to establish meeting houses and schools, they formally entered public life to accomplish goals connected to family needs, which was a role considered appropriate for women (Jameson, 1987, p. 160). East coast educator and philosopher, Catharine Beecher (1829) advocated for women to work as teachers as a "road to honorable independence and extensive usefulness where she need not out step the prescribed boundaries of feminine modesty" (p. 84). Beecher saw the mid-nineteenth-century emphasis on family as "a means of elevating the status of women rather than confirming traditional patriarchy" (Sklar, 1973, p. 84) and believed that women filled a subordinate position in American society in order to promote the general good of society as a whole (Riley, 1984). Teaching provided women with a respectable alternative to marriage. According to Riley (1984), it was frontier women who set up schools and taught spring sessions, while men taught winter school session and got paid more for it. With frontier community growth, men found better paying jobs and teaching became known as younger women's work – until women married. Back East, Beecher criticized women's "unjustly denied equal compensation" for equal work and advocated for making room for women in filling civil service and professional positions (Sklar, 1973, p. 268).

The path to gender equity for women was complicated by a reality that women's roles in new Oregon settlements were often steeped in tradition.

Jeffrey (1998) explained that early on, men in the new Western settlements worked as teachers in winter and by 1854 as communities matured, women became the community teachers because they would work for half of what men required and men could find higher wages elsewhere. For married pioneer women, teaching was considered a natural extension of motherhood and held to be a respectable occupation even though stereotypes of women as "weak in body and intellect" (Jeffrey, 1998, p. 235) endured despite women showing their mettle on the Oregon Trail. Jeffrey (1998) also found that early on no women were listed on school boards or boards of trustees in the West, even though women played influential roles in starting the educational process, establishing and servicing schools, and teaching in the schools as public education became a reality on the frontier (Jeffrey, 1998). Oregon women were highly committed to education in life and in death. For example, Tabatha Brown, founder of Pacific University, a private school in Forest Grove, Oregon (Oregon, 2010), stood up to boards of trustees opposing motions to discontinue schools in states of disrepair. When she died in 1857, Brown had donated her land, house, bell, and $550 of her earnings.

While pondering the phenomenon of Oregon Trail women fulfilling early public relations-like roles in building community, one's thoughts could stray to the related question of why women's contributions in the nineteenth century have failed to gain access to the history pages of public relations. Popular culture's representation may have something to do with it. Consider that intersecting the social identity dimensions of age (youth), female gender, and single marital status meant that women working outside the home for pay were sometimes marginalized in Hollywood's stories about frontier life. Riley (1988) has hypothesized that stereotypical representations of Western women, so deeply entrenched as subservient, for decades prevented pioneer women's actual lived experience from coming to light. Riley (1984) persuasively argued that nineteenth-century contemporaries seemed unable to ignore their "prejudicial images of women and American Indians to pursue a more accurate portrayal of them as rational, capable beings" (p. 251) and it's little wonder that primarily male writers and publishers largely ignored women or promoted positive images of indigenous peoples in their interviews, sketches, and essays about the American West. Unmarried teachers, working either formally or at home have been caricatured across popular culture as *schoolmarms*. According to Pascoe (1991), examples include Molly Wood in *The Virginian* or the pioneer spinster or wife in any television Western, such as Miss Beadle in *Little House on the Prairie*. This stereotype has been slow to dissipate, but images of women's participation in the westward movement are becoming increasingly complex in popular culture representations (Riley, 1988). North of Hollywood, California, in the Willamette Valley's city of Eugene, Oregon, the University of Oregon offered a coeducational campus early on but still considered women as lesser teachers when male college graduates replaced them (Jeffrey, 1998).

Settling in and Setting up as Entrepreneurs in Search of Commercial Enterprise

Finally, a common theme that emerged across Oregon Trail women's diaries, journals, and reminiscences is attention to financial costs – a useful skill that ultimately would serve women who developed commercial enterprises in the public sphere and for household maintenance in the private sphere – all part of women's settlement in Oregon Country/Territory. Balancing expenses against income and budgeting are fundamental skills in communication management and, more specifically, central to writing and implementing public relations campaigns. A *budget* is a spending plan required to allocate resources toward communication objectives, to assess outcomes against objectives to measure return on investment, and to monitor financial activities to avoid overruns (Hallahan, 2013a). The results of being savvy about financial matters include possessing several related qualities, such as being analytical, strategic, responsible, results-oriented, and persuasive. For example, public relations practitioners must be skilled at negotiating with purse string holders to acquire the resources necessary to navigate public relations activities (Heath & McKinney, 2013). Today, whether working in a for-profit or nonprofit arena, navigating arenas of *investor relations* or *financial public relations* involves in-depth knowledge of finance, accounting, and law (U.S. Securities and Exchange Commission's integrated disclosure system) (Petersen & Martin, 1996).

The economic management of family finances was an important task of several nineteenth-century Oregon Trail pioneer women who recorded their experiences in diaries and journals, and reflected in reminiscences on the cost of food and supplies for themselves, the livestock required for the journey at the outset, travel across the continent, and once they began homesteading in Oregon. Carter (1999) wrote about ways nineteenth-century women created a hybridized space with their diary as an account book for recording on the pages or in the back household expenses like prices paid for tea, how much their family was owed and owed itself, and how many hours paid domestic help worked. Some nineteenth-century manufacturers of diaries marketed them as account books with places too for recording births, deaths, holidays, and visits (Carter, 1999). Before leaving their Midwest or East coast home, many women who lived on farms had earned money by selling milk, cheese, and eggs or performing sewing tasks for pay, called "women's cheese and eggs money," which they managed and kept track of in journals (Butruille, 1993, p. 27). This made women central to the family and the economy. Furthermore, pioneer women were no stranger to bartering, a skill they further honed on the Oregon Trail among Caucasian/ White and Native American provisioners. Many women's diary entries from May through September on the Oregon Trail addressed budgeting and paying for provisions and ferry crossings. Amelia Stewart Knight filled her diary with details and concerns about money. About a month into the journey, on May 12, 1853, Amelia Stewart Knight wrote about paying to cross one of the largest Platte River tributaries in present-day Nebraska:

Beautiful weather, but very dusty. We are camped on the bank of Loup Fork, awaiting our turn to cross. There are two ferry boats running, and a number of wagons ahead of us, all waiting to cross. Have to pay three dollars a wagon for three wagons and swim the stock. Traveled 12 miles today. We hear there are 700 teams on the road ahead of us. Wash and cook this afternoon.

Harriet A. Loughary traveled with her family from Burlington, Iowa, to the Willamette Valley in 1864 and noted details in her journal about the cost of ferry crossings and provisions. On April 16, 1864, she recorded:

Traveled all day over an uninhabited country, reaching a small village at night and camped. Here we found grain, paying 50¢ per bushel, in 'greenbacks', worth in exchange only 40¢ to the dollar. We met here the first emigrant teams going to Oregon waiting for grass and rest.

Whether or not Oregon Trail pioneer women carried the actual family purse on the wagon train is unclear, but it is certain that they understood the importance of knowing the cost of specific goods and their value, and could negotiate for what they needed. At the conclusion of a long Oregon Trail journey on September 13, 1853, Amelia Stewart Knight and her party stopped at the first farm they saw that morning to buy feed for their stock and themselves. She wrote:

1.50 per hundred for hay. Price of fresh beef 16 and 18 cts. Per pound, butter ditto 1 dollar, eggs 1 dollar a dozen, onion 4 and 5 dollars per bushel, all too dear for poor folks, so we have treated ourselves to some small turnips at the rate of 25 cents per dozen.

Undoubtedly, Amelia Stewart Knight's monitoring of expenses throughout the long spring and summer reflected her perspective of the family's socioeconomic status as new Oregon Country/Territory homesteaders.

Settling in Oregon's Willamette Valley after an arduous five-to-six-month journey, most émigrés arrived during the autumn season and farmers among them found the Willamette Valley to offer fertile, high-quality soil. A letter by J. W. Miller in Margaret Bannard's file (Collection of Oregon Pioneer Letters, 1903) described the Willamette Valley area as attractive to those who planned to pursue "stock raising" and farming. On August 31, 1864, Harriet A. Loughary boasted in her journal of replenishing the family provision chest with "luscious fruit in the market ... large apples of all varieties, pears, peaches, and plums." Harriet A. Loughary wrote on August 30, 1864 about accommodations:

Nature has done nobly in the site of this pretty place. A little farther down and we reach the Willamette River, one of the largest tributaries of the lower Columbia River. We turn into it and go twelve miles and reach

> Portland. There is but little in this place yet, but in anticipation … busy hands are felling these great trees, hauling and burning bush, trees and stumps … It was with some difficulty that we found a smooth place among the stumps and fallen trees to drive our wagon and pitch our tent …

As she reflected in her reminiscences document of 1901, Arvazna A. Spillman-Cooper told of a happy ending in 1863 when her family's wagon train anticipated Oregon's Willamette Valley:

> By this time we met droves of people going to the mines about Boise, who told us about the wonderful red apples, and all manner of good things in the Willamette Valley. As we were not gold crazy, we went on to this goodly land as fast as possible.

Arvazna A. Spillman-Cooper also wrote in a 1901 reminiscences document about how smart investment in livestock helped her family to set up farming in the Willamette Valley:

> In our place in Polk County we had 200 acres, for which we paid five dollars an acre in livestock, which consisted of a Jack which we had taken at three hundred dollars in Missouri, as part payment of our land in that state. Besides the land we got a cow, fifty bushels of wheat, and all the farm implements and apples we wanted, for this one animal.

It is evident from pioneer women's personal writings that they also continued filling their *Caretaker/Advocacy* role by finding ways to provide community-building services to their wagon train community and new settlement in Oregon Country/Territory. Eventually, many women pursued money-making opportunities in the public sphere in addition to their unpaid labor at home in the private sphere. Some women capitalized on skills they had been performing for many years, such as sewing and tending house. Others branched out to launch their own boarding house.

Feminist historians have noted that frontierswomen gained self-sufficiency and self-confidence on the overland trails. Some women translated this into marketable skills such as developing their own commercial interests for paid work outside the home (e.g., milliner, dressmaker, dry goods clerk, boarding-house keeper, teacher, housekeeper, prostitute, tavern keeper, clerk in an Indian Agent office), paid work inside their home, as homesteader-farmers, or by selling land from which they benefited financially under the Homestead Act (e.g., Riley, 2003). Working more often as a "helper rather than the boss," often pursuing occupations shaped by economic pursuits of their fathers, brothers, and husbands, pioneer women cared for farm animals, helped with planting and harvesting, cooked meals for hired hands and customers, cleaned business places, stocked goods, and engaged in customer relations (Riley, 1988).

As for unmarried women, they were still expected to contribute to the domestic care of the household wherever they lived (Jeffrey, 1998). According to the 1850 census of Oregon Country/Territory, at least 40% of the households listed featured kinship ties with one or more other household (Jeffrey, 1998).

Some Caucasian/White female settlers found that they could satisfy a need, make a reasonable wage, and have steady work (Exley, 1985). Women who took up land as an investment often used their earnings to pay for their own or others' education and/or to support their family after divorce, desertion, or a spouse's death (Riley, 2003). Women who worked doing housework made about $2 per week in the 1890s, while teaching could pay up to three times more (Harris, 1987).

Traditionally considered "a twentieth century phenomenon" (Kruckeberg & Starck, 1988, p. 6), the beginnings of formal public relations have been oversimplified and somewhat limited by Grunig and Hunt's (1984) impactful typology of four evolutionary models chronicling the history of public relations. The first model in the longitudinal typology, press agentry/publicity, has been pegged as evolving from 1850 to 1900 and described in terms of "public relations-like activities" (Kruckeberg & Starck, 1988, p. 8), particularly in terms of *promotion*. Unfortunately, this framework is oversimplified, incomplete, and has facilitated the exclusion of women's contributions to the history of public relations. The study reported in this book seeks to add Oregon Trail women's lived experiences and their informal public relations work to our history chapter in ways that have almost nothing to do with mass media use or promotion.

Summary

Introducing the care perspective to public relations history writing opens the viewfinder to incorporating nineteenth-century women's lived experiences. Pre-twentieth-century traditional gender roles excluded women from much public sphere participation, and it may be logical that women were overlooked in public relations history writing because the effects of women's work in the home was were less visible. In the nineteenth century, however, pioneer women were literally out of the house, expanding domestic responsibilities by building community through schools. Considering the contributions of Oregon Trail pioneer women in a context of informal public relations-like work in the nineteenth century before the modern public relations profession was officially named in the twentieth century responds to the critique that public relations history telling has been limited by categorization according to an "evolutionary template" (St. John III, Lamme, & L'Etang, 2014, p. 3). Rather, incorporating Grunig and White's (1992) focus on the development of public relations as a social role promotes a broader (and more useful!) framework for considering social improvement, reform, and change. However, while these senior scholars considered such a worldview to be "radical" (p. 52), I consider it to be an authentic demonstration of social responsibility to those studying public relations so that they have a more nuanced understanding of their chosen profession's history.

Public relations is an important component when facilitating social change, but comparatively little public relations research and theory building is recognized in social change literature (Martinelli, 2014). Considering nineteenth-century Oregon Trail women as social change agents in performing a community-building role in Oregon's Willamette Valley and beyond lends nuance to the history chapter of U.S. public relations. This chapter weaves together the first-person narratives of women who worked as social change agents even though that may not have been their intention in the moment. We know that only in recent decades have historians incorporated feminist perspectives to reveal the narrowness of conventional historical narratives (e.g., Schlissel, Ruiz, & Monk, 1988). Overland Trail historians have used nineteenth-century first-person narratives recorded in diaries, journals, and daybooks to supplement their understanding of women's contributions to Western frontier settlements. Earlier, historians of the U.S. Old West relied on the Turner thesis and paid little attention to women until female historians of the West like Julie Roy Jeffrey, Sandra Myres, and Glenda Riley questioned and challenged masculinist interpretations of the West's historical record. Adding feminist perspectives throughout the 1980s and 1990s offered evidence to male historians that women's diaries were worth studying (Burt, 1998; Malone, 1991; Pascoe, 1991).

The earliest framers of public relations history benchmark the founding date of the profession with the early twentieth century. This favors the beginnings of railroad companies' commercial activities after the waves of Overland Trail pioneer migrations had concluded their westward journeys. This telling of public relations history reminds us that press agentry tactics proved useful among railroad barons and others charged with promoting land settlement by Caucasians/Whites in the West. The role of public relations in these dynamics is widely accepted (e.g., Broom & Sha, 2013), yet Kruckeberg and Starck (1988) opined that "[P]ublic relations historians do not adequately view the underlying reasons why public relations developed" (p. 8). These senior scholars also noted that "systematic efforts to attract or divert public attention are as old as efforts to persuade and propagandize" (Kruckeberg & Starck, 1988, p. 4). Rather than focus on the earliest roots of the public relations profession as defined in terms of propaganda and promotion techniques, the study reported in this book considers the potential social change as public relations. Considering nineteenth-century Oregon Trail women as social change agents in performing a community-building role in Oregon's Willamette Valley and beyond fills a significant gap in the history chapter of U.S. public relations and offers the female-dominated field of practitioners and students the opportunity to discover ways women played important roles in a key moment of U.S. history. As noted by Kruckeberg and Starck (1988), public relations historians have missed opportunities to offer underlying reasons for why the field evolved, expanded, and emerged as an essential component of society. The study reported in this book responds to this rhetorical urging to raise critical questions and to ponder whether the "history of public relations as it is commonly presented adequately or even accurately describe[s] why public relations exists today?" (Kruckeberg & Starck, 1988, p. 82).

Assuming a care perspective when examining the early community-building activities of the nineteenth century on the Western frontier – particularly the roles that women played – adds depth and nuance to understanding the roots of public relations embedded in U.S. social forces through new sets of stories and lived experiences. The *care perspective* reveals the potential for social change in undergirding the power of community-building skills to advance community welfare. The care perspective values attentiveness, responsibility, competence, responsiveness, respect for people and their situations, relationship building, and emotional connections (Burnier, 2003). Using a feminist theory lens and a new social history sensibility (Morrissey, 1992) to examine women's everyday experiences as *Community Builders of Meeting Houses and Schools* through caretaking promotes reflection on the ethics and degrees of gender equality across public and private spheres – all of which has implications for the practice of public relations today.

Explored in the next chapter are the outcomes of pioneer women's *Civilizing Function* in building new homesteading communities after arriving in Oregon's Willamette Valley and beyond – with grave implications for indigenous peoples.

References

Baines, C., Evans, P., & Neysmith, S. (1998). Women's caring: Work expanding, state contracting. In C. Baines, P. Evans, & S. Neysmith (eds), *Women's caring: Feminist perspectives on social welfare* (pp. 3–22). New York: Oxford University Press.

Blunt, A. (1994). *Travel, gender and imperialism: Mary Kingsley and West Africa.* New York: Guilford Press.

Boyer, K. (1998). Place and the politics of virtue: Clerical work, corporate anxiety, and changing meanings of public womanhood in early twentieth-century Montreal. *Gender, Place and Culture*, 5, 261–276.

Broom, G. M., & Sha, B-L. (2013). *Cutlip & Center's effective public relations* (11th edn). Upper Saddle River, NJ: Prentice-Hall.

Burnier, D. (2003). Other voices/other rooms: Towards a care-centered public administration. *Administrative Theory & Praxis*, 25(4), 529–544.

Burt, E. (1998). Challenges in doing women's history. *Clio: Newsletter of the History Division of the Association for Education in Journalism and Mass Communication*, Fall, 31(1), 17–19.

Butruille, S. G. (1993). *Women's voices from the Oregon Trail: The times that tried women's souls and a guide to women's history along the Oregon Trail.* Boise, ID: Tamarack Books, Inc.

Carter, K. (1999). An economy of words: Emma Chadwick Stretch's account book diary, 1859–1860. *Acadiensis*, 29(1), 43–56.

Collection of Oregon Pioneer Letters. The Margaret Bannard Letters, 1903. Accessed December 28, 2019 from https://bit.ly/37eHHhF.

Collection of Arvazna A. Cooper Papers, 1845–1900. Mrs F. W. Bayley, Letter. Eugene, OR: University of Oregon Libraries, Special Collections and University Archives.

Cope, M. (1998). She hath done what she could: Community, citizenship, and place among women in late nineteenth-century Colorado. *Historical Geography*, 26, 45–64.

Dewey, J. (1916/2018). *Democracy and education: An introduction to the philosophy of education*. Gorham, ME: Myers Education Press.

Dewey, J. (1927). *The public and its problems*. New York: Holt.

Exley, J. E. P. (1985). *Texas tears and Texas sunshine: Voices of frontier women*. College Station, TX: Texas A&M University Press.

Gilligan, C. (1982). *In a different voice*. Cambridge, MA: Harvard University Press.

Gower, K. K. (2007). Introduction. In D. M. Straughan (ed.), *Women's use of public relations or Progressive-era reform: Rousing the conscience of a nation* (pp. 1–8). Lewiston, NY: Edwin Mellen Press.

Grunig, J. E., & Hunt, T. (1984) *Managing public relations*. New York: Holt, Rinehart and Winston.

Grunig, J. E., & White, J. (1992) The effect of worldviews on public relations theory and practice. In J. E. Grunig (ed.), *Excellence in public relations and communication management* (pp. 31–64). Hillsdale, NJ: Lawrence Erlbaum Associates.

Hallahan, K. (2013a). Communication management. In R. L. Heath (ed.), *Encyclopedia of public relations* (2nd edn) (pp. 153–158). Thousand Oaks, CA: Sage.

Hallahan, K. (2013b). Community and community building. In R. L. Heath (ed.), *Encyclopedia of public relations* (2nd edn) (pp. 166–169). Thousand Oaks, CA: Sage.

Harris, K. (1987). Homesteading in northeastern Colorado, 1873–1920: Sex roles and women's experience. In S. Armitage & E. Jameson (eds), *Writing the range: Race, class, and culture in the women's west* (pp. 165–178). Norman, OK: University of Oklahoma Press.

Heath, R. L., & McKinney, D. B. (2013). Managing the corporate public relations department. In R. L. Heath (ed.), *Encyclopedia of public relations* (2nd edn) (pp. 530–534). Thousand Oaks, CA: Sage.

Heidegger, M. (1927). *Being and time*. New York: Harper & Rowe Publishers.

Held, V. (n.d.). The ethics of care. In D. Copp (ed.), *Oxford handbook of ethical theory* (pp. 1–44). New York: Oxford University Press.

Holmes, K. L. (1996). *Covered wagon women: Diaries and letters from the Western trails, 1851*. Lincoln, NE: University of Nebraska Press.

Hummel, R., & Stivers, C. (1998). Government isn't us: The possibility of democratic knowledge in representative government. In C. King & C. Stivers (eds), *Government is us: Public administration in an anti-government era* (pp. 28–48). Newbury Park, CA: Sage.

International Public Relations Association (2019). The International Public Relations Association wraps its values around a new definition of public relations, October 10. Accessed September 26, 2019 from https://bit.ly/2MvsTDb.

Jameson, E. (1987). Women as workers, women as civilizers: True womanhood in the American West. In S. Armitage, & E. Jameson (eds), *Writing the range: Race, class, and culture in the women's west* (pp. 145–164). Norman, OK: University of Oklahoma Press.

Jeffrey, J. R. (1998). *Frontier women: Civilizing the west? 1840–1880*. New York: Hill & Wang.

Johnson, N. C. (1995). Cast in stone: Monuments, geography and nationalism. *Environment and Planning: Society and Space*, 13, 51–65.

Kant, I. (1997). *Critique of practical reason*. Translated by Mary Gregor. Cambridge: Cambridge University Press.

Kruckeberg, D., & Starck, K. (1988). *Public relations and community: A reconstructed theory*. New York: Praeger.

L'Etang, J. (2014). Writing PR history: Issues, methods and politics. In B. St. John III, M. O. Lamme, & J. L'Etang (eds), *Pathways to public relations: Histories of practice and Profession* (pp. xix–xxxviii). Abingdon: Routledge.

Mackay, F. (2001). *Love and politics: Women politicians and the ethics of care*. New York: Continuum.

Malone, M. P. (1991). The new Western history: An assessment. In P. N. Limerick, C. A. Milner, & C. E. Rankin (eds), *Trails: Toward a new Western history* (pp. 97–102). Lawrence, KS: University Press of Kansas.

Martinelli, D. K. (2014). The intersection of public relations and activism: A multinational look at suffrage movements. In B. St. John III, M. O. Lamme, & J. L'Etang (eds), *Pathways to public relations: Histories of practice and profession* (pp. 206–223). New York: Routledge.

McGurty, E. M. (1998). Trashy women: Gender and the politics of garbage in Chicago, 1890–1917. *Historical Geography*, 26, 27–43.

Morrissey, K. G. (1992). Engendering the West. In W. Cronon, G. Miles, & J. Gitlin (eds), *Under an open sky: Rethinking America's Western past* (pp. 132–144). New York: W. W. Norton & Company.

Norwood, V. (1988). Women's place: Continuity and change in response to Western landscapes. In L. Schlissel, V. L. Ruiz, & J. J. Monk (eds), *Western women: Their land, their lives* (pp. 155–181). Albuquerque, NM: University of New Mexico Press.

Oregon State Parks (2010). Stories in stone: Cemeteries of the Willamette Valley. *Cultural Heritage Courier*, 8, Fall. Accessed December 30, 2019 from www.oregon.gov/oprd/HCD/docs/revised_courier_no3_2010_final.pdf.

Pascoe, P. (1991). Western women at the cultural crossroads. In P. N. Limerick, C. A. Milner, & C. E. Rankin (eds), *Trails: Toward a new Western history* (pp. 40–58). Lawrence, KS: University Press of Kansas.

Peak, W. J. (1983). "Community relations." In P. Lesly (ed.), *Lesly's public relations handbook* (3rd edn). Englewood Cliffs, NJ: Prentice-Hall, Inc.

Pearson, R. (1992). Perspectives in public relations history. In E. Toth & R. Heath (eds), *Rhetorical and critical approaches to public relations*. Hillsdale, NJ: Lawrence Erlbaum Associates.

Petersen, B. K., & Martin, H. J. (1996). CEO perceptions of investor relations as a public relations function: An exploratory study. *Journal of Public Relations Research*, 8 (3), 173–209.

Pickles, K. (1998). Forgotten colonizers: The imperial order daughters of the empire (IODE) and the Canadian North. *Canadian Geographer*, 42, 193–204.

Riley, G. (1984). *Women and Indians on the frontier, 1825–1915*. Albuquerque, NM: University of New Mexico Press.

Riley, G. (1988). *The female frontier: A comparative view of women on the prairie and the plains*. Lawrence, KS: University Press of Kansas.

Riley, G. (2003). *Taking land, breaking land: Women colonizing the American West and Kenya, 1840–1940*. Albuquerque, NM: University of New Mexico Press.

Robertson, J. R. (1905). Origin of Pacific University. *Oregon Historical Quarterly*, 6, 109–146.

Schlissel, L. (2004). *Women's diaries of the westward journey*. New York: Schocken Books.

Schlissel, L., Ruiz, V. L., & Monk, J. (eds) (1988). *Western women: Their land, their lives.* Albuquerque, NM: University of New Mexico Press.

Sklar, K. K. (1973). *Catharine Beecher: A study in American domesticity.* New York: W. W. Norton & Company.

Starck, K., & Kruckeberg, D. (2001). Public relations and community: A reconstructed theory revised. In R. L. Heath (ed.), *Handbook of public relations* (pp. 51–59). Thousand Oaks, CA: Sage.

Stivers, C. (2000). *Bureau men/settlement women: Constructing public administration in the Progressive Era.* Lawrence, KS: University of Kansas Press.

St. JohnIII, B., Lamme, M. O., & L'Etang, J. (2014). Realizing new pathways to public relations history. In B. St. John III, M. O. Lamme, & J. L'Etang (eds), *Pathways to public relations: Histories of practice and profession* (pp. 1–8). New York: Routledge.

Tronto, J. (1993). *Moral boundaries: A political argument for an ethic of care.* New York: Routledge.

Webber, B. (1990). Introduction and contemporary comments. *The Oregon Trail diary of twin sisters Cecilia Adams and Parthenia Blank in 1852* (pp. 82–83). Medford, OR: Webb Research Group.

5 *Civilizing Function*
Pioneer Women and Religion

In conjunction with a *Caregiver/Advocate* role and a *Community Builder of Meeting Houses and Schools* role, nineteenth-century homesteading women in Oregon worked as *Civilizer* in their new communities; as conduits for religious/faith practice. Oregon Trail westering experiences presented women with opportunities to expand upon the cult of the womanhood domestic framework in order to also serve as "molders of civilization" (Jeffrey, 1998, p. 130) through church and related benevolent social activities. These may also be interpreted as community-building activities and precursors to the present-day public relations profession. This chapter addresses the implications of women's *Civilizing Function* role, as it supported overall community-building efforts. Many historians of the U.S. West concur that once Overland Trail pioneers arrived at their final destination and began organizing their homesteads, it was the women who followed through with work related to transferring culture, organizing community, and civilizing the new accommodations (e.g., Norwood, 1988). Women tasked themselves with mending families broken by the migration, including loss by disease and death, illnesses, and travel accidents, by organizing churches (Schlissel, 2004). Feminist historians since the 1980s have written extensively about nineteenth-century pioneer women who organized prayer services on the Overland Trails and homesteader women who built churches in their new settlements (e.g., Riley, 1988). Church/faith activities provided an anchor for homesteading women's longing for a stable and familiar home like they had experienced back East. They served as a foundation for social reform in the wake of men's excessive drinking and gambling, as well as for converting Native Americans in conjunction with some pioneers' evangelical fervor.

Thinking of the nineteenth-century U.S. West in terms of *civilizing* is problematic, though. It presumes that the lands were unpeopled before pioneers from the Midwest and East journeyed there using Overland Trails. What had been less emphasized until recent decades is the fact that those trails were created and used by indigenous peoples whom many Caucasians/Whites eventually murdered, both accidentally and strategically, or violently relocated to reservations. The Homestead Act of 1862 itself was an invitation to displace indigenous people by characterizing the lands as available *public domain*. In the process of re-establishing rhythms of homelife for children that homesteading women hoped would replicate their own upbringing, making Caucasian/ White "settlements out of wilderness" (Schlissel, 2004, p. 149), they effectively displaced indigenous people and their communities.

Considering public relations practice in terms of normativity, social standards or the right thing to do can be complex in any time period setting. But normativity is especially troubling when considering the *Civilizing Function* of eighteenth-century pioneer women homesteading in Oregon and the ways this is relevant to community building that may be likened to early public relations history work. Today, the tasks public relations professionals perform as a management function, as advocates, and as relationship builders challenge each practitioner to perform due diligence so that they may be true to their own conscience and the field's ethical standards. Public relations theory building has been somewhat silent on the concept of *normativity* outside of contexts involving organizations – until recently. For example, there had been some attention to *normativity* when considering *diffused* publics that impact organizations temporarily (e.g., activism), as well as *normative* publics (similar goals, problems, values) (Bowen & Rawlins, 2013). Normativity had also been considered in the context of resource dependency theory wherein organizations liaise with other organizations with whom they share some common interest or problem (Sommerfeldt, 2013), and when organizations contrast collaboration over contestation as part of behavior guidelines in response to activist groups (Ciszek & Logan, 2018).

Consideration of *normativity* at the individual social identity level was incorporated into the public relations body of knowledge with the introduction of postmodern values. Holtzhausen and Voto (2002) pointed out that public relations practitioners tend to base their ethical decision-making on either "particularism" – the set of circumstances at hand which rely on strength of personal relationships to maintain commitments (Adler, 1997, p. 61), or on normative social standards of right and wrong. Postmodern values in public relations theory building illustrate that normative standards often are "unjust and only privilege those already in power" (Holtzhausen & Voto, 2002, p. 64). For example, when corporations defend the legitimacy of decisions that prove to be inconsistent with public relations practitioners' postmodern values and desires – or when corporations' decisions are later discovered to be harmful and/or unethical – a conundrum exists for practitioners torn between their own standards and what employers demand of them. Advocating for an unpopular position known to promote some greater good emphasizes the "emancipatory possibilities" of public relations (Holtzhausen & Voto, 2002, p. 77). Critical feminist (e.g., Aldoory, 2006; Vardeman-Winter, 2014), critical race (e.g., Logan, 2016; Pompper, 2005, 2014), and queer (e.g., Ciszek, 2016) theorists have encouraged public relations practitioners and researchers to rethink normativity that might privilege male, Caucasian/White, and cis social identities. In modern public relations practice, professionals can turn to codes of ethics to benchmark what constitutes accepted standards of right and wrong as promoted by trade organizations such as the Public Relations Society of

America (PRSA) and the International Public Relations Association (IPRA). For example, PRSA provides a statement of professional values with behavior guidelines based on principles of advocacy, honesty, expertise, independence, loyalty, and fairness (PRSA, n.d.). PRSA also offers a Provisions of Conduct that defines and provides examples of free flow of information, competition, disclosure of information, safeguarding confidences, conflicts of interest, and ways to enhance the profession (PRSA, n.d.).

This chapter examines eighteenth-century Oregon women's *Civilizing Function* role in: 1) Taming the Wilderness, 2) Religion and Spiritual Life, 3) Missionary Work and Moral Guidance, 4) Religion for Recovery and Relationship Building, and 5) Religion and the Paradox of Oregon's History with Race, and 6) Summary.

Taming the Wilderness

Homesteaders' views of their new home were gendered. Nineteenth-century women and men thought differently about their new situation and the ways to move forward in settling the land as part of their commitment under the Homestead Act of 1862. Lewis and Clark's Corps of Discovery expedition route in 1804 was north of the Oregon Trail across the northern part of the Rocky Mountains and through present-day Wyoming, Montana, and Idaho to present-day Oregon's Columbia River (including the Willamette River tributary) to the Pacific Ocean. However, the explorers' journey laid the groundwork for Caucasian/White people's migration westward. Pioneers' motives ranged, as discussed in Chapter 2. This chapter offers a deeper perspective on the gendered qualities of westward emigration with regard to personal faith systems. Jeffrey (1979) quipped that women tended to look at the wilderness and build churches, while men looked at the wilderness and build saloons. It is clear from diaries and journals of the nineteenth-century women of the Oregon Trail with their frequently spiritually inspired entries about keeping the sabbath and observing the landscape's flora, fauna, geographical formations, and serving as informal ambassadors to Native American communities – that these women were thinking about more than just farming.

Making time for prayer and reflection on the Oregon Trail and providing space for worship among homesteader settlements was considered a "female preserve" (Faragher & Stansell, 1975, pp. 158–159). The diaries, journals, and reminiscences examined for the current research project detailed Sunday entries about the sabbath, including notes about informal worship and prayer. Women's faith service organizing work was an extension of their *Caregiving/Advocacy* role on the Oregon Trail. Over the plains and mountains, 26-year-old Amelia A. Hammond Hadley regularly noted "sabbath" in her 1851 diary's Sunday entries, many of which noted the difficulties of the trip and explained how the journey's work continued even though Sunday was considered a day of rest, in order to affect wagon repair and meal preparation. Her Oregon Trail diary, which she titled "Journal of Travails," offered great detail about the challenges in finding fuel for campfires, food, water, and passing graves. On Sunday, April 27, 1851, Amelia A. Hammond Hadley compared what she encountered on her travels to what she considered normalcy:

> To day is the sabbath and finds us on a vast sea of prarie far away from dwellings or timber ... passed 14 teams for Oregon travelled along an Indian trail to day or in other words an Indian trail was followed by a road, which had been made to follow the trail. The inhabitants are very thin and perhaps in from 30 to 40 miles no meeting nor schools, nor many to have them what few there are have lived in ignorance so long they care for nothing except some sport of some kind, or Sunday amusement, something to pass away time.

In their Sunday, June 13, 1852 diary entry, twins Cecilia E. Adams and Parthenia Blank wrote that they, too, were disconcerted about faith services while on the Oregon Trail:

> W wind very hard. This is a lovely morning but has the appearance of rain which made us very anxious to ford the river so we started on. Found it rather dangerous crossing on account of quicksand. Mr. Miller's wagon came very near going down. P [sister Parthenia] and self waded through, took father for our pilot. We had a grand time as we had to follow down the river half-a-mile so that we traveled nearly a mile in the water. We feel all the better for our ducking. It took us nearly all day, but got across safe at last. Seems but little like the Sabbath. Find a few strange flowers. Made 6½; miles. Think of anne [their 14 year old sister who was still at home in Illinois with their mother, as it was her birthday].

By the time twins Cecilia E. Adams and Parthenia Blank wrote an August 29, 1852 diary entry, however, their party had enjoyed "a sermon from Captain Hyland who is a Methodist preacher," adding concern about finding sustenance for livestock: "Feed is not very good, but fear we shall have worse before we have better. Had a good sing today."

Amelia A. Hammond Hadley's Sunday diary entries served as spaces for recording laments about the trek and some homesickness. On Sunday, May 18, 1851, Amelia A. Hammond Hadley wrote:

> Started very early ... To day is the sabbath but does not seem much like it, has to travel to where we could get timber ... a good deal of thunder and lighting. The wind is cold have not had but one or two days that might be called warm.

Hadley and her family settled in Portland, Oregon, in 1851, their home became a meeting place for Methodist activities.

Chronicling Amelia A. Hammond Hadley's death after spending the rest of her life in Oregon, the Roseburg *Plaindealer* newspaper obituary noted Amelia A. Hammond Hadley's faith-based organizing activities in Oregon (Holmes, 1996):

> For many years her life has been that of an earnest and consistant (sic) Christian and she died in full fellowship with the M. E. Church South. Her hands were ready to every good work and the hearty sympathy and help of the community during her last painful sickness and the large number of friends who followed her to her last resting place fully attest the high esteem in which she was held by the entire community.

Religion and Spiritual Life

Carving out a new life meant women on the Oregon Trail often experienced cognitive dissonance throughout the journey; balancing a need to reach their destination with a need to stay connected to their spiritual life. On the Oregon Trail, many women bemoaned how they missed observing the sabbath (Jeffrey, 1998) because they found church activities and membership fulfilled their spiritual needs. So, ordering new settlements in the West to mirror their life in the East was a priority among homestead women. One element of such ordering was establishing Christian fellowship which communicated moral standards and clarified Christian values (Jeffrey, 1998). Establishing Sunday schools and religious meetings when no preacher was presiding was often the work of women (Harris, 1987). Construction of a formal worship building often lagged behind the building of a school unless a settlement's first community building served multiple duties, with timing depending on the number of families on hand and settlement finances.

Homestead women's *Civilizing Function* role also meant that their spirituality extended to organizing for social reform, especially ridding communities of men's excessive drinking and gambling (Jeffrey, 1998). Homestead women combined domestic activities like making everyday clothes with church gatherings and organized working bees for wool-picking or sewing while they also discussed social reform issues. Butruille (1993) explained that this form of organizing was strategic since women's time was limited, so they linked social activities with work. An adjunct to family care with spiritual dimensions for pioneer and frontierswomen outside of formal church walls was preserving and recording important benchmarks for posterity inside the private sphere – in the family Bible (e.g., births, deaths, weddings) (Riley, 1988) and sewing quilts with fabric from family members' clothing. In the early years of new settlements, women could see the part they had played in nurturing and supporting community growth through spiritual life and were satisfied with their contributions (Jeffrey, 1998). However, institutions like churches had fragile existences as populations shifted and consequently some churches disappeared. Women began benchmarking progress by comparing present to the past on the frontier, rather than comparing their new life in the West with their old life in the East.

Missionary Work and Moral Guidance

Nineteenth-century women's socialization to a female gender role and their perception of Native American cultures and value systems complicated relationship-building dynamics between the groups from the time Caucasian/White people first came to the North American continent. These dynamics continued to play out as pioneer women missionaries traveled westward on the Overland Trails and then settled in their frontier homes. It is obvious from reading women's diary and journal accounts that many homesteaders joined the Oregon Trail with preconceived notions about indigenous peoples – perhaps inspired by media accounts, adapted from other pioneers' views as they traveled westward and stopped at forts also serving as military installations (e.g. Fort Laramie, Fort Boise), and shaped by their own perceptions through brief encounters with other emigrants over the course of the Oregon Trail. Socialized to a female gender role that positioned them as the *weaker sex*, women viewed Native Americans predictably as they carried those ideas with them on the Overland Trails (Riley, 1984, 2004) and it set up a paradox. First, some married and single missionary women were inspired to join an Overland Trail wagon team in order to spread their religion/faith on the frontier and among Native Americans. Many of these women missionaries held "deep-seated and fairly inflexible perceptions of American Indians" that reflected "colonialist precepts, including a belief in white superiority" (Riley, 2004, p. 3). Fowler (1880) opined that women were best positioned to work together as "the great educator of the frontier," working with Native Americans to soften the "fierce temper of the pagan tribes" (p. 505). Second, frontier women expressed varying degrees of advocacy, or "sympathies for Indians on many different issues and in a wide variety of situations," including the view that Caucasians/Whites' seizure of Native Americans' lands was unjust (Riley, 1984, p. 206). A depth analysis of the U.S. "pro-Indian reform movement" which emerged after the Civil War (Riley, 2004, p. 9) is beyond the scope of the study reported in this book, but it is an important point to consider as this chapter explores pioneer women's community building with Native American peoples. There was a disconnect between the ambassador theme that emerged among their first-person accounts from the Oregon Trail before they had reached their destination and their Civilizing Function among indigenous peoples.

Feminist historians of Overland Trail journeys have found much evidence to support reading women's diary and journal texts as gendered (e.g., Riley, 2004), with Caucasian/White pioneer women paradoxically viewing Native American communities both as needing *civilization* and as deserving of protection. Many women on the frontier saw themselves as representing the world of civilization so then assumed a role of providing moral direction for Native Americans they met. Riley (1984) qualified this trend as women serving as "special liberators … missionaries" who were destined to eradicate Native Americans' "supposedly savage nature" (p. 16). Among Caucasian/White audiences, pioneer women's success in changing negative attitudes toward

Native Americans was mixed. Riley (2003) explained that women's speeches and writings attacked U.S. governmental policies and urged for new means of providing Native Americans with dignity and self-rule. Yet, their perceived *Civilizing Function* of amplifying the deeply held conviction that "white beliefs were superior" ended up hindering authentic relationships with Native Americans and causing confusion. Undoubtedly, some Caucasian/White women sought to develop positive relationships with Native Americans through bartering and trading food and apparel, sharing childcare tips, and hiring Native Americans for domestic help, but collegial relationships also had a damaging side-effect. Caucasian/White women's colonialist outlook undergirded urging Native American children to dress in Caucasian/White-style clothing, speak only English, and attend boarding schools. This ended up fostering distrust and fear among some indigenous peoples (Riley, 2003).

Pioneer women on a mission to spread the gospel ultimately found the goals they had set for themselves – "to create a West populated by industrious, faithful people living moral, pious, and temperate lives" (Jeffrey, 1998, p. 126) – to be grossly unrealistic, so that they frequently felt like failures. While there were single women motivated to travel westward by a promise of wedding bells (e.g., Bauman, 1986), some also responded to a formal faith structure that encouraged proselytizing. Unmarried female missionaries saw themselves as "part of a national effort to save the West for Protestantism and civilization" (Jeffrey, 1998, p. 46). Married women missionaries have been called "a decidedly eager group of pioneers" (Jeffrey, 1998, p. 44). Such women were anxious to take the gospel to the "heathen Indians" (Butruille, 1993, p. 17). Through this lens, pioneer women considered themselves as "guardians of morality, the protectors of ethics and civilization" (Riley, 1984, p. 250). Ultimately, women in the missionary life probably failed to see the contradiction in their attitudes toward Native Americans. As they advanced westward and met Native Americans for themselves, Caucasian/White women realized that what they had been told or learned was not necessarily reality (Riley, 1984). Moreover, many women missionaries discovered in their own lifetime that negotiating public and private sphere responsibilities could be highly challenging (Jeffrey, 1998) and that their own supposed moral superiority "could not be exercised with any regularity" on the frontier given the heavy work required (Riley, 1984, p. 250).

By the end of the nineteenth century, charitable work outside the home had become part of "women's province," a space where women could pursue a passion for helping others – and the emerging mass media often promoted the role of women as moral guardians (Riley, 1984, p. 9). The U.S. medical profession at that time refused to admit women, so perhaps pursuit of charitable works offered one of the only socially acceptable routes to pursue a passion to help others. By mid-century, a women's magazine *Godey's Lady's Book* in 1860 promoted charitable service for women to help the "poor and ignorant" (p. 556) as missionaries carrying Christianity's message throughout the world. U.S. scholars of women's experiences in the West have posited that it was women who defined high community standards and gave believers the courage to struggle on after at least five or six months walking the prairie and climbing mountains (Jeffrey, 1998). This had been the objective of the strategy leaders back East who used the media in the mid-1800s to spread their messages – like the *Wisconsin Herald*, the *New York Tribune*, and the *Iowa News*– to attract women to settle in the West (Riley, 1984).

Perhaps the most notorious of the stories about Caucasian/White women missionaries' interactions with Native Americans in Oregon Country/Territory is the story of Narcissa Prentiss Whitman and the Cayuse people. She is considered to be one of the first Caucasian/White women documented as crossing the Rocky Mountains (Jeffrey, 1991). In 1836, Whitman and her husband, Marcus, emigrated from Prattsburgh, New York, with another married missionary couple to an area in Oregon Country/Territory that would eventually become part of present-day Walla Walla in the state of Washington to found the Protestant Whitman Mission at Waiilatpu along the Walla Walla River. Before she married, Whitman taught physics classes and worked as an elementary school teacher at Franklin Academy, a co-ed school her father had helped to start. Whitman trained as a missionary before she got married and emigrated to the West, where she taught the Cayuse people Bible classes and domestic chores, often reporting in letters home that she found it a lonely and depressing life filled with "organiz[ing] each day so they could get by" (Gwartney, 2019, p. 16). Cultural differences and a measles outbreak contributed to hostilities that resulted in the Native Americans killing both Whitmans and several other Caucasian/Whites at the Mission in 1847, with the incident recorded in history as a "massacre" (Holmes, 2008). The Cayuse people proved reluctant to change their traditional ways, none converted to Christianity, men considered farming to be women's work (Jeffrey, 1998), and higher mortality rates among Cayuse children due to the measles outbreak were attributed to Marcus Whitman's favoring of Caucasian/White children at the mission who may have had limited immunity (Allen, 1959). The Cayuse people were concerned about the arrival of the pioneers and when they failed to convince the Whitmans and other missionaries to leave, they turned to violence (Jeffrey, 1998).

Religion for Relationship Building against a Backdrop of Limited Career Options

Desiring to both re-create a culture that they enjoyed back East and to embark on something new in the West, some women used religion as a backdrop for applying community-building skills to develop work outside their private sphere. As such, frontier women engaged in a number of public affairs initiatives in the form of organizing both economic and benevolent activities such as establishing mission stations, nursing the sick, and running women's clubs (Riley, 2003). Using the front parlor in their frontier home for community faith services, prayer meetings, ritual ceremonies, and revival meetings enabled women to develop relationship-building opportunities as they created communities through religious practice and waited for church buildings to be constructed. Accustomed to using her house as a Methodist worship meeting spot, Keturah Belknap set out for Oregon/Country territory in 1848 with her children, husband from Van Buren County, Iowa, and took charge of hosting camp sabbath services while on the Oregon Trail. When her family set up a homestead near Monroe, Oregon, they built a log schoolhouse that doubled up as a church (Holmes, 1983). Belknap died in 1913 aged 93, among the "earliest pioneers of the Oregon country" according to the Portland *Oregonian* newspaper (Holmes, 1983, p. 191). Other women like those in Sublimity, Oregon Country/Territory, "took advantage of the opportunity to act freely" and became key figures in providing religious services for their communities (Jeffrey, 1998, p. 120).

Many other homesteader women who did not work as missionaries nevertheless performed fundraising functions and served as Sunday school teachers in support of increasing the faith-based enterprise in Oregon. Frontier women organized prayer meetings and other church groups, created a Christian society in the West, and served as fundraisers for the church, which also helped to supplement their family income while the men did the preaching, visiting, and traveling (Jeffrey, 1998). Fundraising for church expenses also provided women with some degree of power, as Jeffrey (1998) found among records of the

Figure 5.1 Keturah Belknap and Husband
Source: Public Domain.

Ladies Guild of St. Paul's Episcopal Church in Oregon City, Oregon, wherein the rector requested help with building a rectory porch and "begs the women $450 to meet year-end expenses" (p. 121).

The techniques that frontier women used as part of their religion-inspired *Civilizing Function* may be compared to the community-building and advocacy techniques used by today's public relations practitioners. For example, missionary Mary Richardson Walker engaged in relationship building with members of the Spokane Native American community near present-day Walla Walla, becoming acquainted with the Chief and his wife by frying fritters together, building and teaching in a school for Spokane children, and learning the Spokane language – in order to acculturate the Spokane people to the "ways of the dominant, white culture" (Horner, 1982, p. 22). Walker had journeyed for five months from Maine to Oregon Country/Territory in 1838 with her new husband and another missionary couple, giving birth to her first child on the Oregon Trail. Considered "intelligent, articulate, and pious," Walker had worked earlier as a Maine schoolteacher (Horner, 1982, p. 22). After discovering limited career opportunities there, Walker applied to the Oregon Mission of the American Board of Commissioners for Foreign Missions for a missionary post (Horner, 1982, pp. 23–24), writing:

> I … have succeeded in combining the intellectual and domestic in a great degree than I ever knew any one else to attempt. Ever inured to household labor and care it is to me rather pleasant than irksome. I feel myself perfectly at home in the schoolroom, nursery, kitchen, or washroom or employed with the needle. I am wont the hardest duties on myself to lay, the public good not private interest to consult. I am aware that I possess an aspiring mind. But I have endeavoured [sic] and I hope with some success to cultivate a spirit of humility; to be willing to do something and be nothing if duty required.

Accepted for the position, Walker became the third Caucasian/White woman to travel West to Oregon Country/Territory as a missionary, a decision she had made before marriage and setting out on the Oregon Trail. Horner (1982) analyzed Walker's diary which spanned 46 years (1833–1879), learning that Walker had prioritized her morality guardian role over her wife and mother roles. Walker had worked with Narcissa Prentiss Whitman in 1838 before Whitman and her husband where killed by the Cayuse in present-day Washington. Ultimately, Walker realized that her romanticized ideas about proselytizing the Spokane failed to live up to her expectations, as she wrote in her diary: "They are very anxious … to devise some way to get to heaven without repenting and renouncing their sins … noisy and mischievious [sic]… I am sorry to find them so ill disposed." Horner (1982) concluded that Walker experienced "guilt, confusion and frustration" (p. 27) in her limited dealings with the Spokane people. The Walkers left the formal missionary life in 1848 and settled in present-day Forest Grove, Oregon, where they became farmers while their children attended school and Walker "took on the role of a mother and pioneer preacher's wife" (Horner, 1982, p. 29) and died in 1878 aged 86.

Religion and Oregon's Challenging Encounter with Race

Among the pioneer women's diaries, journals, and reminiscences examined for this book, the entries related to "Indians" offered many conflicting accounts of Oregon Trail journey encounters with Native Americans that may shed light on their faith system. Women who actively worked to build relationships with Native Americans, as well as those who preferred to remain detached observers, offered many entries in diaries and reminiscences expressing curiosities and fears about Native American encounters on the Oregon Trail. For example, twin diarists Cecilia E. Adams and Parthenia Blank noted toward the end of their journey on September 15, 1852 from the Boise River Valley, a tributary of the Snake River, in present-day Idaho, that bartering exchanges were good:

> This is a fine, clear stream, and there are plenty of Indians scattered along the banks. They bring us a great many salmon trout ... These Indians have a great many fine ponies, and most of them have guns and ammunition, and many of them have almost a complete suit of clothes, which they have got of the emigrants. They will trade a very good pony for a good rifle or a coat. Our company traded 2 guns for 2 ponies.

Interestingly, Cecilia E. Adams and Parthenia Blank recorded a few days later, on October 8, 1852 that their party traveled the Umatilla River in Oregon Country/Territory and came upon a Native American community that had been associated with the Whitman mission at Waiilatpu, where missionaries were killed five years earlier in 1847. The sisters wrote:

> ... the headquarters of the Cayuse Indians. They are more civilized than any we have seen before. Bought a few potatoes of them. They are killing some very fat cattle and sell the beef at 15 to 20 cents per pound.

Pioneer women's faith systems and the ways they perceived racial difference between themselves and people of color revealed several disconnects. Regarding African Americans, a rarely told story is one of thousands of African Americans freed from slavery after the Civil War's end in 1865 who joined the trek westward on the Oregon Trail to claim land of their own (Freedman, 1983). For some freed slaves, journeying to the West was more attractive than moving to the North or remaining in the South. Porterfield (2004) noted the first African-American homesteader in Nebraska settled in 1870, another in Oklahoma in 1889, and another in Kansas in 1877 creating a new town named Nicodemus that attracted 20,000 African Americans and earned them the nickname "exodusters" (Porterfield, 2004, p. 31). In Oregon, policymakers simultaneously prohibited slavery, and also legislated limitations on the freedoms of African Americans. Many emigrants who settled in Oregon's Willamette Valley were former Southerners with pro-slavery attitudes (Riley, 2003) and perhaps policymakers hoped to avoid issues connected with slavery by prohibiting the continuation of immigration of African Americans to the area (Tyler, 2016). An antislavery attitude had been institutionalized by local government in 1844, but five years later a territorial legislature adopted a measure excluding African Americans from Oregon Country/Territory and a constitutional convention reaffirmed the measure in 1857. Oregon became a U.S. state in 1859 and during the Civil War some Oregonian men supported slavery and fought Union troops. Mathes (1990) explained that during the Civil War, some sought to move African-American Oregonians to a state all of their own. So, Oregon's earliest policies on racial issues are troubling, indeed.

Summary

Oregon Trail pioneer women's community-building work via a *Civilizing Function* may be considered an outgrowth of the cult of womanhood domesticity to which they had been socialized. Moreover, religious life gave women purpose beyond their immediate family circle. Riley (1994) dispelled a widely held myth that nineteenth-century single women actually were dependent, weak, and traveled West only to find a husband among a "surplus of male settlers," making them a wife, or an "appendage" of a man (p. 5). Oregon Trail pioneer women who became Western frontier settlers were indoctrinated in religious teachings and these, intermingled with nineteenth-century traditional female gender roles, culminated in a support system. Voices of pioneer women as recorded in their diaries, journals, and reminiscences suggest that the Oregon Trail journey experience had well prepared women to transition from a stable immobile lifestyle back East – to settling in a new frontier in the Oregon Willamette Valley and beyond, equipped with confidence to both lead and support the literal building of a new community.

While the tone of pioneer women's first-person narratives is often optimistic, training a feminist theory lens on their lived experiences suggests that even women who considered themselves to be missionaries in the service of their deity did not always find the work fulfilling. Some pioneer women questioned the outcomes and ultimate goals of the approximately 2,000-mile journey. No doubt, Caucasian/White women's attitudes toward Native Americans were shaped by years of popular discourse negatively framing indigenous people with prejudicial images, so that serving as "special liberators of American Indians" (Riley, 1984, p. 16) may have felt logical when considering the import of religious teachings. Shifts in tone across women's diaries may suggest that personal experiences on the Oregon Trail and observations and encounters with Native Americans showed a willingness to form their own opinion or to alter a prejudiced one of believing that Native Americans possessed a "savage nature" (Horner, 1982, p. 22). Possessing an open mind and displaying preparedness to learn – despite socialization or dogmatic training – are traits of an ethical public relations practitioner today.

Impacts of ideologies on nineteenth-century dictates about what was considered proper women's work is explored next in Chapter 6 as a foundation for discovering pioneer and homesteading women's agency and leadership.

References

Adler, N. J. (1997). *International dimensions of organizational behavior.* Cincinnati, OH: SouthWestern College Press.

Aldoory, L. (2006). A (re)conceived feminist paradigm for public relations: A case for substantial improvement. *Journal of Communication,* 55(4), 668–684.

Allen, O. S. (1959). *Narcissa Whitman: An historical biography.* Hillsboro, OR: Binfords & Mort.

Bauman, P. M. (1986). Single women homesteaders in Wyoming, 1880–1930. *Annals of Wyoming,* 58, 39–49.

Bowen, S., & Rawlins, B. L. (2013). Publics. In R. L. Heath (ed.), *Encyclopedia of public relations* (2nd edn) (pp. 706–762). Thousand Oaks, CA: Sage.

Butruille, S. G. (1993). *Women's voices from the Oregon Trail: The times that tried women's souls and a guide to women's history along the Oregon Trail.* Boise, ID: Tamarack Books, Inc.

Ciszek, E. L. (2016). Digital activism: How social media and dissensus inform theory and practice. *Public Relations Review,* 42(2), 314–321.

Ciszek, E. L., & Logan, N. (2018). Challenging the dialogic promise: How Ben & Jerry's support for Black Lives Matter fosters dissensus on social media. *Journal of Public Relations Research,* 30(3), 115–127.

Faragher, J., & Stansell, C. (1975). Women and their families on the Overland Trail to California and Oregon, 1842–1867. *Feminist Studies,* 2(2/3), 150–166.

Fowler, W. W. (1880). *Women on the American frontier.* Hartford, CT: S. S. Scranton & Co.

Freedman, R. (1983). *Children of the wild west.* New York: Clarion Books.

Gwartney, D. A. (2019). *I am a stranger here myself.* Albuquerque, NM: University of New Mexico Press.

Harris, K. (1987). Homesteading in northeastern Colorado, 1873–1920: Sex roles and women's experience. In S. Armitage & E. Jameson (eds), *Writing the range: Race, class, and culture in the women's west* (pp. 165–178). Norman, OK: University of Oklahoma Press.

Holmes, K. L. (1983). *Covered wagon women: Diaries and letters from the Western trails, 1840–1849.* Lincoln, NE: University of Nebraska Press.

Holmes, K. L. (1996). *Covered wagon women: Diaries and letters from the Western trails, 1851.* Lincoln, NE: University of Nebraska Press.

Holmes, K. L. (2008). *Best of covered wagon women.* Norman, OK: University of Oklahoma Press.

Holtzhausen, D., & Voto, R. (2002). Resistance from the margins: The postmodern public relations practitioner as organizational activist. *Journal of Public Relations Research,* 14, 57–84.

Horner, P. V. (1982). Mary Richardson Walker: The shattered dreams of a missionary woman. *Montana, The Magazine of Western History,* 32(3), 20–31.

Jeffrey, J. R. (1979). *Frontier women: The trans-Mississippi West, 1840–1880*. New York: Hill & Wang.
Jeffrey, J. R. (1991). *Converting the West: A biography of Narcissa Whitman*. Norman, OK: University of Oklahoma Press.
Jeffrey, J. R. (1998). *Frontier women: Civilizing the West? 1840–1880*. New York: Hill & Wang.
Logan, N. (2016). The Starbucks race together initiative: Analyzing a public relations campaign with critical race theory. *Public Relations Inquiry*, 5(1), 93–113.
Mathes, S. (1990). *Helen Hunt Jackson and her Indian reform legacy*. Austin, TX: University of Texas Press.
Norwood, V. (1988). Women's place: Continuity and change in response to Western landscapes. In L. Schlissel, V. L. Ruiz, & J. J. Monk (eds), *Western women: Their land, their lives* (pp. 155–181). Albuquerque, NM: University of New Mexico Press.
Pompper, D. (2005). "Difference" in public relations research: A case for introducing Critical Race Theory. *Journal of Public Relations Research*, 17(2), 139–169.
Pompper, D. (2014). Interrogating inequalities perpetuated in a feminized field: Using critical Race Theory and the intersectionality lens to render visible that which should not be disaggregated. In C. Daymon & K. Demetrious (eds), *Gender and public relations: Critical perspectives on voice, image and identity* (pp. 67–86). Abingdon: Routledge.
Porterfield, J. (2004). *The Homestead Act of 1862: A primary source history of the settlement of the American heartland in the late nineteenth century*. New York: Rosen Publishing Group.
Public Relations Society of America (PRSA) (n.d.). PRSA code of ethics. Accessed January 1, 2020 from www.prsa.org/ethics/code-of-ethics.
Riley, G. (1984). *Women and Indians on the frontier, 1825–1915*. Albuquerque, NM: University of New Mexico Press.
Riley, G. (1988). *The female frontier: A comparative view of women on the prairie and the plains*. Lawrence, KS: University Press of Kansas.
Riley, G. (1994). *Frontierswomen: The Iowa experience*. Ames, IA: Iowa State University Press.
Riley, G. (2003). *Taking land, breaking land: Women colonizing the American West and Kenya, 1840–1940*. Albuquerque, NM: University of New Mexico Press.
Riley, G. (2004). *Confronting race: Women and Indians on the frontier, 1825–1915*. Albuquerque, NM: University of New Mexico Press.
Schlissel, L. (2004). *Women's diaries of the westward journey*. New York: Schocken Books.
Sommerfeldt, E. J. (2013). Resource dependency theory. In R. L. Heath (ed.), *Encyclopedia of public relations* (2nd edn) (pp. 795–796). Thousand Oaks, CA: Sage.
Tyler, J. H. (2016). The unwanted sailor: Exclusions of Black sailors in the Pacific Northwest and the Atlantic Southeast. *Oregon Historical Quarterly*, 117(4), 506–535.
Vardeman-Winter, J. (2014). Issues of representation, reflexivity, and research-participant relationships: Doing feminist cultural studies to improve health campaigns. *Public Relations Inquiry*, 3(1), 91–111.

Part III
Ideologies, Women's Work, and the Female Frontier

6 Understanding Pioneer Women's *Agency and Leadership*

Prior to feminist Old West ground-breaking late-twenty-first-century research, U.S. history predominantly relegated women to the female roles of *daughter* as part of a father's family and *wife* as part of a husband's. For many years the earlier Turner thesis framing suggested that Oregon Trail women lacked agency and acted as submissive wagon train inhabitants reliant on men. Moreover, U.S. history narratives have devoted substantial attention to unmarried women driven to emigrate West *to find a husband* since *marriage* was the socially accepted role for nineteenth-century women and there was a shortage of women in settlements in the West. For most middle-class Caucasian/White women, marriage and mothering was the most appropriate role for a young woman and she would be relegated to the private sphere for domestic work for the rest of her life without being fully engaged in making family decisions about economic matters (Riley, 1994b). But close reading of pioneer women's diaries, journals, letters, and reminiscences reveal how the Oregon Trail transformative experience prompted an expansion of the eighteenth-century female gender role for community-building work. As specifically noted in Chapter 5, propagation of faith enabled emigrant women to perform a *Civilizing Function* in their new communities as they took the lead in missionary work and the organizing of revival meetings, prayer meetings, and sites for congregational worship. Exploring the community-building experiences of women throughout a continent-crossing-journey-through-settlement time frame promotes more than simply adding women to the Western drama or reducing women to *just* wife and mother. Necessity required that they develop their own style of *Agency and Leadership* within a female gender role social status.

In public relations research and practice, the concepts of *Agency and Leadership* are intrinsically linked for community building. Community building is enhanced by public relations leadership (Starck & Kruckeberg, 2001). Stogdill (1950) operationalized *leadership* as "the process of influencing the activities of an organized group in its efforts toward goal setting and goal achievement" (p. 5). People find their work most meaningful when they have a sense of *agency*, or have the ability to make choices over the way their work is performed. People tend to experience higher degrees of satisfaction and sense of self when they feel directly connected to work tasks at hand – or agency in their work (Mumby & Kuhn, 2019). Degrees of strategic thinking, decision-making, and managing became embedded in pioneers' daily routines over the five-to-six-month journey to Oregon Country/Territory and these processes are central to public relations practice and theory building today. For women on the Oregon Trail, the open air had replaced the formal kitchen and bedroom walls back home that had segregated women to the private sphere and excluded them from public sphere action. Perhaps for the first time, democratic leadership processes became visible to women, so they could observe decision-making and organization among the men who predominantly made Oregon Trail travel decisions. Moreover, pioneer women were able to develop their own style of *Agency and Leadership* in completely new settings as survival and settlement in a new land required.

Considering the new challenges offered by urbanization and industrialization in the Progressive-era 1890s–1920s U.S., historians promoted the "status for women" theme to more fully and broadly "embrac[e] the American experience" (Waller, 1978, p. 206). They advocated for incorporating voices of women even though U.S. history and "understanding of the American character" generally was framed in a male context (Waller, 1978, p. 206). In recent decades, women's lived experiences have become legitimate subjects for study, including those of the Oregon Trail. In the spirit of liberal reform, historians sought to revise the old ways of history telling and increasingly began thinking that women had gained an "enhanced role" (Waller, 1978, p. 206). The launch of a formal feminist movement has been dated at the time of the Seneca Falls Convention in 1848 and this key event coincided with the greatest waves of westward migration on the Oregon Trail. Women didn't gain the right to vote until 1920 with the 19th Amendment to the U.S. Constitution; a key event associated with opening the floodgates for married Caucasian/White women to also join the paid workforce in substantial numbers.

Oregon Trail historians have written about ways that emigrants organized themselves once the wagons pulled out of Missouri – Westport, Independence, St. Joseph. Across the approximately 2,000-mile journey lay dangers associated with the terrain, sorrow about leaving loved ones and familiar community behind, uncertainty about resource supplies for survival, and risk-filled encounters with indigenous communities. Also, most emigrants lacked formal training and experience in organizing, persuasion, oratory, and management; skills that became necessary both on the Oregon Trail and when creating new settlements in the Willamette Valley and other areas across Oregon. The first few weeks of the westward journey were what Feltskog (1969) characterized as "town meetings on wheels" (p. 13) as the emigrants began developing "frontier democracy" (p. 13) which was put to the test as the wagon trains turned slightly northwestward along the Oregon Trail around Lawrence, in modern-day Kansas, and the emigrants realized the impact of fatigue on people's morale and trust, as well as the bodies of livestock.

On the Oregon Trail, emigrants selected leaders via a simple process of candidates (men) setting out in the morning and other wagons lining up behind the leader of their choice so that the man at the front of the longest line won the leadership position (Butruille, 1993). This type of citizen activity (L'Etang, 2014) has escaped the scrutiny of U.S. public relations history researchers who traditionally have favored organizational (especially corporate) developments on a progressive march toward present-day professional public relations practice. Indeed, a small dedicated group of public relations researchers have advocated for deeper examination of gendered aspects of leadership. The study reported in this book builds upon their encouragement in an attempt to expand U.S. public relations history's benchmarking of public relations as a "twentieth century phenomenon" (Wilcox, Ault, & Agee, 1986, p. 32) with an embedded framework for narratives shaped by predominantly Caucasian/White men. While the original source documents examined for the study reported in this book do not offer experiences of women leading wagon trains, they do offer narratives of other important leadership and agentic work emigrant women performed that we may consider to be the early beginnings of community building in public relations. Adding marginalized voices to the formative years of public relations provides new avenues for reconceiving public relations' trajectories and histories (Watson, 2014). Interrogating contested constructions of history telling and history making also contributes to public relations theory building (Fitch & L'Etang, 2017).

Deeply embedded gender role stereotypes can contribute to an incomplete view of leadership and agency in the public relations history story as communicated in our body of scholarship and textbooks. L'Etang (2014) reminded us of Lippman's (1922) conclusion that stereotyping fuels public opinion as we make sense of what we observe by splicing together new information to the old we have stored in our memory. Popular culture artifacts have amplified stereotypical images of U.S. Western pioneer women as having high morals and being dutiful to husbands and fathers and, therefore, being subservient and lacking in their own agency. Evidence of this limited scope may be found in George Caleb Bingham's early-1850s painting of Daniel Boone escorting settlers, which prominently featured an archetypical Madonna-like female figure on a white horse, and Ella Farman's 1860 poem published in the *New York Evening Post*, "Idyl of a Western Wife," which promoted the rustic "housewife merry" fondly speaking of her home, husband, and the countryside. However, lumping together all women as "lesser (although admittedly necessary) appendages to the male undertaking of going West" contributed to long-accepted stereotypes (Riley, 1994b, p. 5) of women as secondary background characters which downplayed and contributed to overgeneralizations about women's roles. Meanwhile, Native Americans displaced by the U.S. emigrants have been portrayed historically as "enemies, as bloodthirsty evildoers, people whose traditions, whose families, whose losses were given no room in our textbooks" (Gwartney, 2019, p. 37).

This chapter offers replacements for negative female gender role stereotypes with a revised view of agentic women possessing leadership skills which were forged by Oregon Trail and Oregon settlement experiences: 1) Leadership on the Plains through Suffrage, 2) Decision-Making for Network Building, 3) Strategic Planning for Endurance, 4) Managing to Stay Alive and Thrive, and 5) Summary.

Leadership on the Plains through Suffrage

The gendered qualities of leadership have fascinated researchers across several academic disciplines in recent decades. A primary inspiration for gendered leadership scholarship in public relations was an attempt to understand why there has not been gender parity at the top-most managerial levels in an otherwise feminized field (e.g., Grunig, Toth, & Hon, 2001). We know that *relational leaders* are people who have an open mind, care about the other people they work with, and are willing to advocate for others. For such leaders, *care* means readiness to collaborate and to respect multiple perspectives while "remaining in caring relationships over time" (Regan & Brooks, 1995, p. 27). In public relations research, Aldoory and Toth (2002) found that women's socialized traits – empathy and collaboration – translate to a *transformational* leadership style which is marked by qualities like charisma, or "the power to captivate and energize a following" (McWhinney, 1997, p. 188). Interplay between leadership and gender is impacted by variables such as constraint of job description, job roles, position in the hierarchy, and status (Aldoory & Toth, 2002). Women are expected to be more communal and nurturing in their leadership style (Eagly & Karau, 2002), so the argument that feminine traits in conjunction with a transformational style may make women more accepted as leaders (e.g., Maher, 1997) offers a useful framework for examining the lived experiences of nineteenth-century women traveling the western plains and building new communities in Oregon as part of settlement. Reading pioneer women's original first-person texts through this lens provides the opportunity to consider community building as important work before professional public relations emerged as an occupational field that relied upon formal organizational contexts and the proliferation of mass media.

More broadly, feminist geographers struggled to bring greater attention to the equitable treatment of gender when writing history. As discussed in Chapter 2, feminine images in conjunction with the masculinized West clearly illustrate the limited ways women have been represented as almost exclusively existing as subservient to men, as paragons of virtue, or being totally invisible. The framing of women relative to men offers one explanation for public relations history's general failure to consider the acts, achievements, and contributions of women prior to the twentieth century. Study findings reported in this book offer a nuanced reading of Oregon Trail pioneer women's diaries, journals, and reminiscence documents which provide hints of transformational leadership which may be considered a precursor to formal public relations practice and represent an opportunity to add women's stories to public relations' community-building history.

In the historical accounts of many (if not most) professional fields, women's voices have not figured prominently as administrative leaders navigating social power dynamics. For example, public administration research (like public relations study) has been relatively quiet about gendered power dynamics or women's contributions in history (Butruille, 1993). One variable may be a dearth of surviving written records. Even for the study reported in this book, nineteenth-century pioneer women's diaries, journals, and reminiscences offer only so much detail about leadership and power forces at work in their own family or among the families compiling wagon trains. Nineteenth-century pioneer women were processing adjuncts to their female gender role shaped by the cult of true womanhood ideas about women's "piety, purity, submissiveness, and domesticity" (Welter, 1966, p. 59), while they also were learning how to write about themselves as new members of the public sphere. Jeffrey (1998) noted that the "primacy of family life, symbolized by the notion of home as retreat, worked against recording situations that might reveal power dynamics" (p. 81). For example, Elizabeth Ward reminisced about her Oregon pioneer life and reticence in writing about personal issues:

> [O]f many things connected with family I do not care to speak in these pages, such as my marriage, the loss of my first child, or the birth of my second, which meant much to all of us and was a great event in our lives, and is something that especially belongs to ourselves.
> (Jeffrey, 1998, p. 81)

Thus, assessments about power dynamics within emigrant Overland Trail families may be "strong hints" rather than "direct evidence" (Jeffrey, 1998, p. 81).

Perhaps one of the most celebrated (albeit, ill-fated) women leaders among the Oregon Trail pioneers was Narcissa Prentiss Whitman, who was greatly admired across the heartland less for her church affiliation and mission in Oregon Country/Territory than for her achievement – as a woman – in crossing the Rocky Mountains and being the first Caucasian/White woman to give birth in the West. Her feat and that of the other missionary woman in her company, Eliza Spalding, communicated to those back East that women could make the cross-continent journey as well as men had – while pregnant for half the trip. Whitman's leadership was testament that the Oregon Trail "was suddenly a real thing, an actual passage for people who had before considered it folly or simply too dangerous for women and children" (Gwartney, 2019, p. 86). Whitman and Spalding had so inspired other women in 1836 that they, too, began packing trunks and equipping wagons. For many pioneer women, we must consider *subtle* evidence of transformational leadership qualities in the pages of their daybooks, journals, and diaries. To support scrutiny of diaries and other narratives, the critical communication perspective of leadership is most useful (Mumby & Kuhn, 2019, p. 304):

> ... a coordinated social process through which people communicatively construct and experiment with new possibilities for thought and action. Such possibilities are recognized by the group or organization as moving beyond self-interest and meeting a collective, higher good. Within this communication process, individuals may be constructed as leaders who help guide and facilitate decision-making and action.

As noted in previous chapters, pioneer women successfully served as boundary spanners as they networked within and across wagon train groups and as ambassadors with indigenous communities where they visited homes and engaged in bartering activities. Central to these activities is good communication skills which contribute to transformational/charismatic leadership (Den Hartog et al., 1999).

The Oregon Trail pioneer woman possessing the most celebrated communication skills and transformational leadership style as "one of the most important women in the history of Oregon" (Shirley, 1998, p. 39) was Abigail Scott Duniway, also known as the mother of woman suffrage in the Pacific Northwest (Graber, 1978). Traveling with her family on the Oregon Trail at the age of 17, her lifelong work as a women's rights advocate and newspaper editor and writer was instrumental in gaining voting rights for women as she was a "vigorous" campaigner (Lake, 1994, p. 393), orator, and journalist. Duniway helped to found a State Equal Suffrage Association and "her philosophy was a collage of progressive social and political ideas" (Abigail, 1995, p. 1). Duniway is one of only six women inscribed in the legislative chambers of the Oregon State Capitol in Salem out of the 158 citizens considered "prominent in Oregon's early development" (Holmes, 1983, p. 47).

Born on an Illinois frontier farm, Duniway emigrated to Oregon's Willamette Valley with her family, setting out on April 2, 1852. On the six-month, 2,400-mile trip, Duniway maintained a travel diary, a job assigned to her by her father. Like many other Oregon Trail women who kept diaries, Duniway noted at day's end details about forts, rivers, cattle, grass conditions, and picturesque scenery. She also recorded her mother's death from cholera on the Oregon Trail:

> How mysterious are the works of an all-wise and overruling Providence! We little thought when last Sabbath's pleasant sun shed upon us his congenial rays that when the next should come it would find us mourning over the sickness and death of our beloved Mother!

Her mother's death and Oregon Trail memories of women's constant pregnancy and difficult sibling births impressed Duniway to one day advocate for women's rights. The Scott family arrived in the Willamette Valley on September 28, 1852 to stay with maternal relatives, as Duniway noted in her diary's last entry: "We found them all in good health and well satisfied… They were of course glad to see us."

Influenced by her frontier experiences, Duniway became engaged in suffrage leadership as an adult. In her autobiography, she wrote of the monotony associated with traditional female gender roles soon after she settled and married, performing domestic tasks and working as a school teacher. Duniway (1914) posited that frontier life actually encouraged women to challenge their socially designated *place*: "To bear two children in two and a half years from my marriage day ... a general pioneer drudge, with never a penny of my own." Duniway rejected many conventional ideas about women's traditional role limitations – and at age 25, published the first commercially printed book in Oregon, *Captain Gray's Company, or Crossing the Plains and Living in Oregon* (Duniway, 1859) about her westward travel experiences. She eventually built and sold a school, worked as an artist and businesswoman opening a millinery shop in Albany, and later moved to Portland to establish a weekly newspaper in 1871, *The New Northwest*, as "a forum for her feminist views" (Shirley, 1998, p. 48). By this time, Duniway was supporting her invalid farmer husband and six children. Duniway may have had only one year of formal schooling but was well-informed and passionate about public issues, trends, and social reform, including women's issues, abolitionism, temperance, and immigration. She devoted four decades to community service in Oregon, Washington, and Idaho, and delivered at least 1,750 public speeches throughout her activist career, 1871–1884 (Lake, 1994). When Oregon became the ninth state to recognize women's right to vote, the governor invited Duniway, aged 78 and "architect of woman's suffrage in Oregon" (Shirley, 1998, p. 53), to sign the official Oregon women's suffrage proclamation on November 30, 1912. She died on October 11, 1915, just five years before ratification of the 19th Amendment to the U.S. Constitution giving women the vote.

Rights for women in the West advanced more rapidly than those for women in the East, and Western colleges and universities were coeducational. Women gained suffrage in Wyoming and Utah soon after the Civil War ended and 10 of the 11 Western states gave women the vote by 1914 – while only 1 eastern state enfranchised women. Duniway (1914) had spent four decades fighting for the cause of women's rights (Lake, 1994), writing: "Nowhere else, upon this planet, are the inalienable rights of women as much appreciated as on the newly settled borders of these United States" (p. 403). However, Jeffrey (1998) was reluctant to suggest that political enfranchisement led to full equality for Western women or a dramatic change in their gender roles. Moreover, it is noteworthy that Caucasian/White women's suffrage efforts in the West did not include advocating for women of color (Jeffrey, 1998).

Decision-Making for Network Building

Oregon Trail pioneer women's *Agency and Leadership* role in community building emerges from pioneer women's diaries, journals, and reminiscences via stories associated with making decisions and building networks. In the

Figure 6.1 Abigail Scott Duniway
Source: Public Domain.

nineteenth century, few people tended to live in isolation for long, but rather were part of groups of family, neighbors, and friends who depended upon one another. According to the first-person texts of Oregon Trail pioneer women, their openness and willingness to build networks among families and individuals offers testament to their forming of micronetworks that collectively supported the macronetwork of the entire pioneer community on the journey and through early settlement. As network theory suggests, opening communication lines to integrate multiple perspectives promotes interaction between individuals and groups at input, processing, and output levels (Littlejohn, 2002; Stohl, 1995).

At the family level, historians offer mixed assessments of decision-making along gender lines when the chance to migrate West presented itself. Nineteenth-century law gave the husband the right to decide where the family lived (Butruille, 1993), but stereotyping all westward-bound women as weak and dependent has obscured more nuanced understandings of the Oregon Trail community-building experience. Even though men typically made decisions about economic matters (Jameson, 1987), women were not inactive onlookers. Women had a significant share of responsibility in the care and survival of family members, which involved making routine and long-term decisions (Harris, 1987) among both immediate family and strangers. Yet, women were careful to maintain the appearance of male superiority. Working "behind men's backs" and avoiding direct confrontation (Jeffrey, 1998, p. 82) enabled pioneer women to develop a work style based on influencing, negotiating, and working for their goals indirectly, but sometimes arguing (Jeffrey, 1998) as they also made many decisions on their own. Butruille (1993) reported that some women's diaries included accounts of talking back to husbands and throwing things at them, hollering at trail bosses, making demands at gunpoint, and refusing to cook and clean – and some "decided what the hell and wore pants … got uppity" (p. 117). Nineteenth-century pioneer women's work as negotiators and conflict negotiators in conjunction with community building offers an example of Vasquez's (1996) issue development approach to public relations as part of boundary spanning. On the Oregon Trail and once settled in the Oregon's Willamette Valley, it was women who moved across both private and public spheres, across natural habitats, and among Native Americans building communities. Possibly even less is known about the decision-making activities of unmarried women who migrated to Oregon Country/Territory. Riley (1994b) found that even though marriage was considered the ultimate destination for young women, many single women traveled on their own to the Iowa frontier as laborers, missionaries, and teachers. For women emigrating to Oregon Country/Territory, being a wife and/or mother required adapting those roles and building their decision-making skills to accommodate the contexts of wagon train life on the Oregon Trail and of new settlement spaces once they reached Oregon.

Some diaries also include notes that could be interpreted as a critique of decisions made by others that affected not only women's comfort, but their *Caretaker/Advocate* role tasks. Even though letters written home to family and friends amplified enthusiasm in anticipation of favorable farming conditions at the journey's end (Riley, 2006), pioneer wagon trains often experienced frustration and fear given that they had little guidance in finding their way and routinely pursued impassable canyons and wasted valuable time before winter set in which depleted provision stores (Schlissel, 2004). For example, en route to Oregon Country/Territory, 17-year-old Jane (Jennie) Paul Eakin Hanna made two notes in her diary about her family wagon train taking "the wrong road." On July 16, 1866 she wrote: "We are on the right road again." Just a few weeks shy of arrival in Oregon's Willamette Valley, Hanna noted on August 10, 1866 along the south side of the Columbia River: "We got on the Umatilla road by mistake and wandered over the prairie but found the right road at last." The first pages of the twins Cecilia E. Adams/Parthenia Blank diary of 1852 are missing to history, so it begins with a May 19 entry explaining that her party "were on the road to St. Joseph instead of the Mormon trace [trail]."

Lydia Allen Rudd began the Oregon Trail journey in mourning after recently losing a baby daughter, so adjusting to life on the Oregon Trail also meant searching for an outlet to express her emotions as she contemplated how to move on. She concluded her diary with a poem, "To Friend Margaret," which includes the verse:

> That curly hair and forehead high
> Which God to her had given
> We never will see them more
> Until we meet her in heaven

For Lydia Allen Rudd, travel with her husband Harry from the Missouri River to Oregon Country/Territory in May–October 1852 required her to act as household head given that Harry Rudd was ill throughout much of the overland journey. According to the Homestead Act, married women could not apply for land unless they were considered head of the household. There was a small minority of women who independently registered as homesteaders and farmed without male assistance (Schlissel, 2004), forging ahead to carve their own definition of opportunity on a homestead in Oregon Country/Territory. Applicants had to be 21 years old and citizens or immigrants who had filed for citizenship. With a sick husband, Lydia Allen Rudd's concern about proving head of household status in her final October 27, 1852 diary entry underscored her low spirits: "I expect that we shall not make a claim after all our trouble in getting here on purpose for one I shall have to be poor and dependent on a man my life time." Yet, after arriving in Salem, Oregon, Rudd sought to secure land in her own name under provisions of the Donation Land Act which allowed a settler to claim another 320 acres for his wife (Schlissel, 2004).

Unlike most of the other women whose diaries and reminiscences offered first-person accounts of Oregon Trail travel starting points at or near Missouri, a widow named S. D. Evans began her journey to Roseburg, Oregon, from Washoe, Nevada, in 1861 two years after her husband was killed in California. S. D. Evans' reminiscences' narrative details several accounts of decision making as she made the journey "with nothing" but her two children and two hired men who drove the ox team. She wrote extensively about Native American encounters, mostly violent, but some involving barter exchanges. She sought escort from a military officer at Fort Crook in present-day California for protection from any Native American violence, but was turned down.

> He didn't think it necessary to send an escort with us for a few days so we had to go alone. The military didn't want to be bothered looking after people passing through the country and it was tedious work escorting travelers with ox teams as they could make only about twenty miles a day. The truth of the matter was, they did not want to be bothered with anything.

S. D. Evans later agreed to let a man named "Whiskers" travel with her family as a guide and protection against any Native American attacks.

> One day as we were eating dinner a man rode up, leading a mule with a pack. We asked him to have dinner and he joined us. He was the roughest looking man I ever saw; long tousled hair that hadn't been cut or combed

for months and long stringy whiskers that would have made a good Santa Claus of him if he could have ever been cleaned up ... He saw from the questions we asked that we were uneasy about Indians and said if we would haul his pack he would stay with us to Yreka. We were glad for his company and agreed.

Information exchange and keeping up with issues and current events was important to the westward emigrants, as open space, rugged terrain, raging rivers, and dust kept them separate even though the wagon trains moved en masse, sometimes filling the horizon for as many miles as the eye could see – 10 to 20 miles per day. Maintaining connections was especially important for women. Through diary writing and journaling, women "emphasize the ties they feel with another, whether that other is a dead relative, a cherished friend, a place yearned for, or an aspect of themselves remembered but seemingly lost" (Huff, 1989, p. 10). Emigrating women could also write letters home since couriers from settlements rode up to wagon trains with the latest newspapers and camp reports – while rumors passed from wagon to wagon (Feltskog, 1969). Women's time spent with others on the Oregon Trail included information exchanges about childcare, apothecary, and food preparation. Female companionship on the wagon train was central to these tasks for Oregon-bound women and they made diary entries about visiting and meeting others as they expanded their network. When 17-year-old Jane (Jennie) Paul Eakin Hanna set out with her family in 1866 for Oregon's Willamette Valley from Bloom, Illinois (now Chicago Heights) she had no idea how important her developing network building skills would become. Throughout her diary, she noted writing letters to loved ones back home which she posted at military and trading outposts. Many of the emigrant women were conflicted, writing about anticipating a bright future, while simultaneously looking backward with hearts broken because they were missing home and family left behind. Jane (Jennie) Paul Eakin Hanna recorded several new encounters with other pioneer women: "four young ladies visited our camp this evening," "about twenty Oregon wagons camped with us tonight. Two women visited our camp," "Camped on the Big Sandy and wrote letters," "Arrived at the Swift River about noon and got the last wagon over about dark. We women all came over in one wagon," "Rested in camp. Wrote letters," "Crossed the Willamette River on a ferry boat. We are at the end of our long journey at last where Uncle Andrew and Aunt Maria and Uncle Robert Pattison and Aunt Isabel live. Took tea with Aunt Isabel tonight."

At a time before the proliferation of mass media, emigrant women relied on a much broader network than just those traveling in their own wagon train and others intercepted on the journey. Traveling from Burlington, Iowa, Harriet A. Loughary and her family relied on letters from home as part of their social network for news about the Civil War. Early in the family's westward journey, Harriet A. Loughary wrote in her journal on April 22, 1864 that her husband set out from the wagon train to retrieve mail from Council Bluffs, Iowa, and included commentary about draft dodgers:

… Returns in the evening with letters from home and news from the seat of war, which was a great treat to us. Large numbers of emigrant wagons are centering here … The whole country is dotted with tents and covered wagons as to resemble an army in quarters … mostly families on the way to Oregon and California. A great many Copperheads from Missouri hiding away from duty rendered their state by the Conscription Act.

Later, on August 2, Harriet A. Loughary and her wagon train happened upon news traveling in the opposite direction – a circus caravan headed eastward from Oregon to Idaho. Harriet A. Loughary wrote in her journal: "Still going down the Payette river Met to day a circus from Oregon going to the mining towns." One historian noted that the Dan Rice Circus was actually the first to use "The Greatest Show on Earth" slogan and also the first to follow the Oregon Trail to the Boise Valley (McGill, 2010, p. 132). Twenty-three-year-old twin sisters Cecilia E. Adams and Parthenia Blank also networked with friends and extended family from home, relying on letters from Missouri in 1852. On Monday, June 21, the sisters wrote: "Today 5 men direct from Oregon on their way east visited and waited. They gave us the privilege of writing home." On Friday, July 9, they wrote: "West wind today. Started on very pleasant roads, very sandy. Passed by the fort. Left four letters at the Post Office. Saw some Indians. Found some wild currants – two kinds black and yellow ones." Missionary Narcissa Prentiss Whitman took a portable writing desk on the Oregon Trail for letter writing that she hoped would fortify networks with colleagues and loved ones back home. Gwartney (2019) wrote that Whitman's desk was put in a trunk and tossed over a cliff by a hired man weary of carting her personal belongings. In addition to being useful in maintaining networks, the act of writing letters provided pioneer women with consolation in the form of reminding them of home.

Once they arrived at their West coast destination, women homesteaders adapted to their new home and lifestyle in Oregon by extending their social networks and also expanding what they had considered to be their traditional female gender role. In a study of northeastern Colorado homesteaders, Harris (1987) found that resource allocation decisions were shared within a marriage, with women having significant power to direct expenditures associated with developing the homestead. Indeed, frontier life afforded women greater opportunity to form relationships with others than if they had stayed at home in the Midwest or the East (Lindgren, 1991). When families settled in Oregon and began tending their homestead, pioneer women dealt with a very different set of circumstances than they had been accustomed to when making decisions in the private sphere back East. Women who were paid for work such as selling eggs or cheese, or outsourcing their domestic labor could improve their networking and relationship-building skills while they made some money. Paid occupations on the frontier put women in contact with others and some husbands even defined relationships with wives as *partnerships* (Lindgren, 1991).

Public relations researchers have found that network theory helps to explain and predict people's need and desire for information, given that more information translates to better relationships and more ethical decision making (Heath, 2013). Looking back over time, historical accounts have much to offer our understanding of the way network theory also occurred outside the boundaries of formal organizations. Indeed, the community-building work performed by pioneer women on the Oregon Trail and as part of Oregon settlement also offers important application points, expanding network theory's utility to historical events as well as contemporary ones.

Strategic Planning for Endurance

Perhaps the most challenging terrain of the Oregon Trail for the emigrants was navigating the desert and mountains of Oregon Trail/Territory throughout the final month of the westward journey when supplies had dwindled. Pioneer women's diaries detail the strategic planning that went into their scavenging for fire fuel and food, watering and feeding livestock, navigating steep mountains, working to nurse sick family members, keeping an eye on children to keep them from harm, and forging the Columbia River loading, unloading, and drying wagon contents. More broadly, brainstorming wagon train operations regarding which ferries to trust while bartering with frontier people and Native Americans was a daily routine. Pioneers who arrived later in the season, in September or October, encountered rain, snow, and mud in Oregon. Butruille (1993) noted that women arrived having survived disease, starvation, and the elements: "By the time she reaches her destination, she hardly recognizes herself... not the same woman who left her home 2,000 miles away" (p. 91).

The tone of Abigail Scott Duniway's 1852 diary grew dark as she wrote about crossing Oregon's Cascade mountain range, being penniless, hunting for lost cattle, dealing with broken wagons, and walking in worn-out shoes. By 1863 Duniway had settled in Oregon, was married with several children, working as a novelist and schoolteacher and her husband had co-signed for a friend's business loan. The deal went sour and the Duniways had to sell the family farm and move to the small town of Lafayette, Oregon. After they settled in, husband Ben Duniway was injured in a wagon accident and never fully recovered. Abigail Scott Duniway made the strategic decision, as the family breadwinner, to enlarge her school and create a dormitory for female boarders in the loft of their family home for additional income.

In "Reminiscences of Plains Crossing, 1852," Julia Thomas wrote in 1907 about enduring the death of her child, her husband's mountain fever and abandonment by two hired hands (George and Horatio Cook) on the Oregon Trail in present-day Idaho:

> Sept. 5 babie died. Sept. 12 we crossed the Snake River from that time on the journey was more like a troublesome dream or perhaps nightmare. My husband's health began to fail. The hands got impatient and got them ponies and left us going on ahead.

She also reflected on the strategic planning to successfully transport her family to Oregon's Willamette Valley on the other side of the Cascade Mountains after crossing the Columbia River near The Dalles:

> The children were getting to complain and I almost gave up and said to myself must I hear my children ask for something to eat and not get it. That is almost to much but what am I spared for when so many are called away. Just then some men that had come out to meet the emigrants and get worn out cattle for but little hitched on to our waggons and hauled us to waters pretty soon Mr. Gould came up with the oxen and the 2 cows. One of the cows plunged in the spring and we lost her and from there to the dalles we came and sold one yoke of oxen for 20 dollars and got my husband to the Cascades in a waggon base towed …

Before arriving in Oregon, Amelia Stewart Knight of Monroe County, Iowa, confided to her diary a hard lesson learned about keeping strategic thinking skills sharp. On Monday, August 8, 1853, she wrote about accidentally leaving a child behind when the wagon train set out for the day, assuming the child was with a family member in another wagon:

> We have to make a drive of 22 miles, without water today. Have our cans filled to drink. Here we left unknowingly our Lucy behind, not a soul had missed her until we had gone some miles when we stopped a while to rest the cattle; just then another train drove up behind us with Lucy … It was a lesson to all of us.

When Keturah Belknap, with her husband and baby, emigrated via the Oregon Trail in 1848 from Iowa to settle in Oregon, she filled a diary with strategic planning details that consumed her days, from saving money to buy land, buying only certain groceries like coffee and sugar, to making clothes for her family with wool from their sheep. She wrote:

> We will put the old ground into wheat this fall and break some more land for corn. Will have twenty acres of wheat in and now its spring of 1840. The work of this year will be about the same. I have been spinning flax all my spare time thru the winter, made a piece of linen to sell, got me a new calico dress for Sunday and a pair of fine shoes and made me one home-made dress for everyday.

Twin sisters Cecilia E. Adams and Parthenia Blank, at age 23, noted a strategic decision on the part of their wagon party on Wednesday, August 18, when it was decided that their family would wait for new wagon trains to catch up with theirs to make a larger group when entering an indigenous peoples community:

> As we are just on the borders of the Digger Indians' territory, both companies thought best to increase our strength by combining our forces.

We now have 14 wagons in our company … We are now in the valley of the Snake River.

This Native American community may have been Shoshone people in present-day Idaho and the term "digger" is considered a derogatory term used to describe the practice of digging for edible roots (Shoshone Indians, n.d.)

Managing to Stay Alive and Thrive

This study's investigation of community building as enveloped within Oregon Trail women's diaries, journals, and reminiscences has shed new light on the one-dimensional stereotypes of the *Prairie Madonna, drudge*, and subservient *little woman* stereotypes for women. Rather, these thousands of women were strong and managed to stay alive and thrive while also taking care of others. The *Prairie Madonna* was primarily "an interior creature" committed to chores about the house and family, according to Jordan (1992), yet she could also handle a gun or help with the stock when the cows broke down a fence or a husband was away when Native Americans attacked. Another negative stereotype is the *drudge* who was nearly worked to death overcome with physical and mental exhaustion, and was haggard and thin. Such popular culture representations characterized women as barely dealing with life on the frontier and having mental states edging toward insanity (Riley, 1988). Dick (1937) characterized plains women as "leathery, stooped, and lifeless figures" (p. 144) determined to either return home or persevere until their bodies gave out. Authors of captivity narratives also capitalized on the weak-and-unfortunate-woman-destroyed-by-the-frontier theme. The findings of the current study reported in this book found no evidence of Oregon Trail pioneer women seeing themselves as either *Prairie Madonnas, drudges*, or *victims*.

On the contrary, Oregon Trail women's first-person narratives offered realistic accounts of their lived experiences, but were also seasoned with optimism for westward emigration and a new life in Oregon. On Sunday, July 6, 1851, journeying from Illinois to Umpqua Valley, Oregon, 26-year-old Amelia A. Hammond Hadley made careful notes in her diary after passing Fort Laramie in present-day Wyoming about gathering food that reminded her of home, which she distinguished by calling it "the states." Her last diary entry on Saturday, August 23, 1851 was about re-adjusting to home life indoors as she wrote about a reception hosted at the Foster farm, a first stop in Oregon where emigrants could buy vegetables and other supplies. Amelia A. Hammond Hadley titled her diary ironically "Journal to Oregon of Travails." Historians have suggested that she probably meant "travels" rather than "travails" given that her spelling throughout the diary is inconsistent. However, Holmes (2008) was unable to avoid calling this title a "Freudian slip" since much of Amelia A. Hammond Hadley's lived experiences as documented in her diary were about the journey's challenges (p. 117).

Back in the nineteenth century, Oregon Trail women proved their powers of endurance and ability to stay alive and thrive. Even though they sometimes wrote in their diary about feeling low, most managed to conclude entries on an optimistic note, which is the mark of someone seasoned to dealing with challenging situations and moving forward. Today, public relations trade journals and websites regularly list the personal characteristics or qualities needed to be a "successful PR professional" – including flexibility, meticulous learning, collecting information, seeing the bigger picture, building relationships, strong writing, honesty, attention to detail, and developing a thick skin (e.g., Chari, 2017). It may be argued that the personal qualities of Oregon Trail women can be viewed as a basis for the successful practice of professional public relations. Homesteaders who arrived in the Willamette Valley after the mid-1850s often considered doing a bit of backtracking by moving to the east of the Cascade mountain range since the best land in the Willamette Valley had already been taken. By 1861, a few ranchers occupied the Powder River area and another area known today as La Grande (del Mar, 2005).

While many of the diaries investigated for the current study are the voices of young women in their late teens or early 20s, the writing of Mary Colby is that of a 44-year-old woman who made the Oregon Trail journey a little later in life in 1850, from St. Joseph, Missouri. She wrote letters to close relatives once she, her husband, and two children finally settled in Lebanon, Oregon, about a change of heart. While she said she did not like Oregon when they took their claim, she explained that she had warmed to her new accommodations: "the longer I live here the better I like it … cannot say that I wish to go back to the States to live at present if ever."

Nineteenth-century female gender roles dictated that women manage family housekeeping and childrearing – while men cultivated fields, constructed buildings, and shopped for supplies. Frontierswomen built upon this foundation to expand their roles into conservators of family, religious, and racio-ethnic traditions, recording family history, as well as creating sewing and quilting groups with other women that eventually developed into organizing for social reform efforts (Riley, 1988). In new settlements, women also managed and oversaw children as the family's valuable labor force, teaching children tasks like food processing, candlemaking, spinning, weaving, and soap making (Riley, 1994b). These informal organizing events in the private sphere may be considered a precursor to strategic management activities so common today among public relations practitioners (Piasecki, 2000).

Summary

Examining women's narratives documenting their Oregon Trail travels and settlement in the Willamette Valley and beyond against what we know about the Western frontier from popular culture and some history books reveals plenty of disconnects. Ideology-fueled stereotypes have limited and erroneously shaped our understanding of women and the Old West. Reading nineteenth-century pioneer women's lived experiences promotes new ways of looking at people long considered to be submissive and compliant secondary characters. On the contrary, these pioneer women who settled in Oregon performed exceptionally important community-building *Leadership/Agency* roles and, in the process, expanded upon the traditional cult of true womanhood female gender roles. Oregon Trail women were agentic leaders – perhaps not always in the ways we think of this function today as leading employees and organizations – but they took the initiative and survived exceptionally challenging circumstances to keep communication lines open by networking with others, including indigenous communities. Rather than holding the Oregon Trail pioneer women to some idealized *Prairie Madonna* standard – or minimizing their identities to *drudge* or *subservient little woman* appendage to a man – pioneer women's voices ring out from their diaries, journals, and reminiscences to consider their decision making acts, as well as their strategic planning, and ways they managed to not only stay alive but to thrive and develop Oregon communities. Shirley (1998) referred to pioneer women as "more than petticoats."

Findings such as these supplement the gaps left by nineteenth-century newspapers' inattention (Lindgren, 1991) to homesteading women's *Agency and Leadership*. From the transformational direction of Abigail Scott Duniway who built a school and devoted four decades of her life to human rights issues in the Pacific Northwest so as to meet "a collective, higher good" (Mumby & Kuhn, 2019, p. 304), to Lydia Allen Rudd and S. D. Evans who abruptly became homesteading household heads when their husbands died, to Jane (Jennie) Paul Eakin Hanna, Harriet A. Loughary, and twin sisters Cecilia E. Adams and Parthenia Blank who networked among wagon train bands traveling in both directions so they could post and receive letters with extended family back home and develop a social network for Civil War news, such women were pioneers in more than some romantic sense. They supplemented the traditional gender role they had been socialized into with an *Agency and Leadership* role for the benefit of emerging shared Oregon communities. Indeed, the Oregon Trail daughter was more than part of her father's family and the *wife* was more than her husband's spouse – something feminist geographers have argued for decades as part of an explicitly feminist approach to the subfield of Western U.S. history.

The study findings reported in this book offer new ways of considering nineteenth-century pioneer women's community-building work as a recent addition to the history chapter of public relations and a precursor to the development of formal professional public relations practice. To marginalize the voices and experiences of women while amplifying those of a privileged set of Caucasian/White early-twentieth-century men propagates a limited and inaccurate understanding of the past. The investigation of Oregon Trail pioneer women's important roles as revealed throughout this book provides a re-imagining and, hopefully, inspires other researchers to expand public relations history in the U.S. and elsewhere. These new findings may also encourage authors of public relations textbooks to consider expanding the time frame for the founding of public relations beyond the twentieth century since this would promote inclusion of more women's voices to overcome what has become a male-centric telling of public relations history.

In Chapter 7 the importance of women's emotional connections in contributing to social cohesion is explored – as this fostered a paradox in pioneer women's role as frontierswomen in Oregon's Willamette Valley and beyond.

References

Abigail Scott Duniway led the fight for Oregon women. (1995). *Eugene Weekly*, February 23, 1(9), 10.

Aldoory, L., & Toth, E. L. (2002). Gender discrepancies in a gendered profession: A developing theory for public relations. *Journal of Public Relations Research*, 14(2), 103–126.

Butruille, S. G. (1993). *Women's voices from the Oregon Trail: The times that tried women's souls and a guide to women's history along the Oregon Trail*. Boise, ID: Tamarack Books, Inc.

Chari, V. (2017). The 10 characteristics of a successful PR professional. Accessed February 1, 2010 from https://bit.ly/2ufjXfg.

del Mar, D. P. (2005). Early contact. The Oregon History Project. Accessed February 17, 2020 from https://bit.ly/32drNTz.

Den Hartog, D. N., House, R. J., Hanges, P. J., Ruiz-Quintanilla, S. A., Dorfman, P. W., et al. (1999). Culture specific and cross-culturally generalizable implicit leadership theories: Are attributes of charismatic/transformational leadership universally endorsed? *The Leadership Quarterly*, 10(2), 219–256.

Dick, E. (1937). *The sod house frontier, 1854–1890*. New York: Appleton-Century.

Duniway, A. S. (1859). *Captain Gray's company, or crossing the plains and living in Oregon*. Portland, OR: S. J. McCormick.

Duniway, A. S. (1914). *Path-breaking: An autobiographical history of the equal suffrage movement in Pacific Coast states*. Portland, OR: James, Kerns & Abbott.

Eagly, A. H., & Karau, S. J. (2002). Role congruity theory of prejudice toward female leaders. *Psychological Review*, 109, 573–598.

Feltskog, E. N. (ed.) (1969). *The Oregon Trail*. Madison, WI: University of Wisconsin Press.

Fitch, K., & L'Etang, J. (2017). Other voices? The state of public relations history and historiography: Questions, challenges and limitations of "national" histories and historiographies. *Public Relations Inquiry*, 6(1) 115–136.

Graber, K. (ed.) (1978). *Sister of the Sioux: The memoires of Elaine Goodale Eastman*. Lincoln, NE: University of Nebraska Press.

Grunig, L., Toth, E. L., & Hon, L. C. (2001). *Women in public relations: How gender influences practice*. New York: The Guilford Press.

Gwartney, D. A. (2019). *I am a stranger here myself*. Albuquerque, NM: University of New Mexico Press.

Harris, K. (1987). Homesteading in northeastern Colorado, 1873–1920: Sex roles and women's experience. In S. Armitage & E. Jameson (eds), *Writing the range: Race, class, and culture in the women's west* (pp. 165–178). Norman, OK: University of Oklahoma Press.

Heath, R. L. (2013). Network theory. In R. L. Heath (ed.), *Encyclopedia of public relations* (2nd edn) (pp. 603–605). Thousand Oaks, CA: Sage.

Holmes, K. L. (1983). *Covered wagon women: Diaries and letters from the Western trails, 1840–1849*. Lincoln, NE: University of Nebraska Press.

Jameson, E. (1987). Women as workers, women as civilizers: True womanhood in the American West. In S. Armitage & E. Jameson (eds), *Writing the range: Race, class, and culture in the women's west* (pp. 145–164). Norman, OK: University of Oklahoma Press.

Holmes, K. L. (2008). *Best of covered wagon women.* Norman, OK: University of Oklahoma Press.

Huff, C. (1989). That profoundly female, and feminist genre: The diary as feminist practice. *Women's Studies Quarterly*, 17(3/4), 6–14.

Jeffrey, J. R. (1998). *Frontier women: Civilizing the west? 1840–1880.* New York: Hill & Wang.

Jordan, T. (1992). *Cowgirls: Women of the American West.* Lincoln, NE: University of Nebraska Press.

Lake, R. A. (1994). Abigail Scott Dunway. In K. K. Campbell (ed.), *Women public speakers in the United States, 1800–1925: A bio-critical sourcebook* (pp. 393–408). Westport, CT: Greenwood Press.

L'Etang, J. (2014). Writing PR history: Issues, methods and politics. In B. St. John III, M. O. Lamme, & J. L'Etang (eds), *Pathways to public relations: Histories of practice and Profession* (pp. xix–xxxviii). Abingdon: Routledge.

Lindgren, H. E. (1991). *Land in her own name.* Norman, OK: University of Oklahoma Press.

Lippman, W. (1922). *Public opinion.* New York: The Macmillan Company.

Littlejohn, S. W. (2002). Theories of human communication (7th edn). Belmont, CA: Wadsworth/Thomson Learning.

Maher, K. J. (1997). Gender-related stereotypes of transformational and transactional leadership. *Sex Roles*, 37, 209–225.

McGill, J. (2010). Did Harriet Loughary see the elephant? *Overland Journal*, Fall, 28(3), 129–132.

McWhinney, W. (1997). *Paths of change: Strategic choices for organizations and society.* Thousand Oaks, CA: Sage.

Mumby, D. K., & Kuhn, T. R. (2019). *Organizational communication: A critical introduction* (2nd edn). Thousand Oaks, CA: Sage.

Piasecki, A. (2000). Blowing the railroad trumpet: Public relations on the American frontier. *Public Relations Review*, 26(1), 53–65.

Regan, H., & Brooks, G. (1995). *Out of women's experience: Creating relational leadership.* Thousand Oaks, CA: Corwin Press.

Riley, G. (1988). *The female frontier: A comparative view of women on the prairie and the plains.* Lawrence, KS: University Press of Kansas.

Riley, G. (1994). *Frontierswomen: The Iowa experience.* Ames, IA: Iowa State University Press.

Riley, G. (2006). Sesquicentennial reflections: A comparative view of Mormon and gentile women on the westward trail. In D. L. May & R. L. Neilson (eds), *The Mormon History Association's Tanner Lectures: The first twenty years* (pp. 153–171). Urbana, IL: University of Illinois Press.

Schlissel, L. (2004). *Women's diaries of the westward journey.* New York: Schocken Books.

Shirley, G. C. (1998). *More than petticoats: Remarkable Oregon women.* Helena, MT: Falcon Publishing, Inc.

Shoshone Indians (n.d.). Accessed August 15, 2019 from http://mojavedesert.net/shoshoni-indians.

Starck, K., & Kruckeberg, D. (2001). Public relations and community: A reconstructed theory revised. In R. L. Heath (ed.), *Handbook of public relations* (pp. 51–59). Thousand Oaks, CA: Sage.

Stogdill, R. M. (1950). Leadership, membership and organization. *Psychological Bulletin*, 47, 1–14.

Stohl, C. (1995). *Organizational communication: Connectedness in action*. Thousand Oaks, CA: Sage.

Vasquez, G. M. (1996). Public relations as negotiation: An issue development perspective. *Journal of Public Relations Research*, 8, 57–77.

Waller, R. A. (1978). A thematic approach to teaching United States history. *The History Teacher*, 28(2), 201–210.

Watson, T. (2014). Introduction. In T. Watson (ed.), *Asian perspectives on the development of public relations: Other voices* (pp. 1–3). Basingstoke: Palgrave Macmillan.

Welter, B. (1966). The cult of true womanhood, 1820–1860. *American Quarterly*, 18, 152.

Wilcox, D. L., Ault, P., & Agee, W. K. (1986). *Public relations: Strategies and tactics*. New York: HarperCollins.

7 Expanding Women's Role
Emotional Connection for Social Cohesion

Another important theme that emerged from eighteenth-century pioneer women's first-person narratives was *Emotional Connection for Social Cohesion*. Acts of making emotional connections supported Caucasian/White women's community-building efforts and broadly benefitted wagon train members and Oregon's Williamette Valley communities. However, the theme sharply contrasts with a broader view of the negative impact of emigrants as they traveled across the plains and homesteaded in the Pacific Northwest displacing indigenous peoples and altering the landscape in their path. While a feminist and humanist communitarian reading of the ways eighteenth-century pioneer women built upon the cult of true womanhood tradition through *Emotional Connection for Social Cohesion* suggests degrees of liberation when entering the public sphere, this theme simultaneously underscores pioneer women's complicity in colonization. The disconnect creates space to consider the importance of contemporary public relations practitioners' ethical responsibility to society and all stakeholders.

The *Emotional Connection for Social Cohesion* theme exposes tensions between pioneer women's emergence from the private sphere into the public sphere – and the effects of colonization. It would be disingenuous to ignore genocide, warfare, disease, removal and relocation, and other destruction to ways of life among indigenous communities (Thornton, 1987) as a result of nineteenth-century U.S. frontier policy and the land clearing and settlement of homesteaders. To celebrate Oregon Trail pioneer women and their lived experiences as community builders without recognizing these negative impacts could constitute an egregious error and further disrespect the pain inflicted on indigenous communities. While exploring the full range of the effects of Caucasian/White emigrants effects on and their relationships with Native Americans in Oregon's early statehood years is beyond the scope of the current study reported in this book, this chapter will not shrink from pointing out the harsh impacts as part of the contextual backdrop.

The humanist, communitarian concept was introduced to the public relations literature when Kruckeberg and Starck (1988) posited that community building, as facilitated via communication, provides a solid foundation for public relations theory building and professional practice. A theoretical perspective rooted in the Chicago School of Social Thought, humanist communitarianism views community as a requirement for a healthy social structure (e.g., Dewey, 1927). Today, we recognize that ethical public relations practitioners use communication tools to shape public opinion without causing harm and that communication and community are inter-related and cannot be disaggregated (Kruckeberg & Starck, 1988). The humanist, communitarianism concept offers much utility for examining and interpreting public relations before large organizations and widespread mass media developed, including the addition of women's contributions to early public relations history. This chapter adds an *Emotional Connection for Social Cohesion* theme to the roles performed by Oregon Trail pioneer women: *Caretaker/Advocate, Community Builder of Meeting Houses and Schools, Civilizing Function*, and *Agency and Leadership*. The *Emotional Connection for Social Cohesion* theme is consistent with a humanist, communitarian approach to fostering a living environment and "sense of community" (Vujnovic & Kruckeberg, 2013, p. 163) that benefits all and assures "survival and prosperity" (Kruckeberg & Starck, 1988, p. 25).

The chapter examines these important components of a paradox when interrogating women's expanded role on the Oregon Trail journey through to settlement: 1) *Emotional Connection and Social Cohesion* Theme, 2) Female Frontier and Recording the Landscape, 3) Apprehension Toward Native American People and Communities, 4) The Violent Side of Oregon's Homesteading History, 5) Stereotyping, and Captivity Narratives, and 6) Summary.

Emotional Connection for Social Cohesion Theme

An *Emotional Connection for Social Cohesion* theme emerged from the analysis of pioneer women's first-person texts, as it captured their feelings toward husbands, family members, other pioneers, some Native American communities, and the landscape itself as a deeper context for women's community-building work. Through emotional bonds, pioneer women embraced familiarity with reduced degrees of strangeness in order to address conflict. The *Emotional Connection for Social Cohesion* theme is consistent with network theory's trust concept given that emotional bonds among group members characterized by friendship and closeness contribute to the building of networks (Van den Bossche, Gijselaers, Segers, & Kirschner, 2006). The emotional connections nurtured and developed over the course of the five-six-month westward trek and as emigrants settled in Oregon's Willamette Valley and beyond promoted increased familiarity, trust, and ultimately social cohesion. Once settled in Oregon, women's emotional connections ripened into social organizing work which gave them responsibility and purpose outside the domestic sphere.

One means of dealing with homesickness and uncertainty or discomfort with emigration was for women on the Oregon Trail to seek comfort together in building on a female subculture. As part of their traditional domestic sphere duties, pioneer women bonded together, pooling enterprising talents, and resisting forces that threatened individual and community survival. Amidst the stresses and tensions associated with the approximately 2,000-mile journey to Oregon, female émigrés found themselves in a new and changing geographic territory while they performed familiar domestic sphere chores. One strategy for further developing the female subculture was for women to schedule laundry duties together across the wagon train camp in order to share water hauling and fire-building chores. Women prepared meals together, pooled wild game killed by the men, and shared food provision supplies to vary meals. Women's first-person texts detailed numerous instances of forming sewing groups on "lay-by" days, or days off from travel, when wagons were being repaired, livestock needed a rest, or the weather was too bad to travel. A January 14, 1901 reminiscences report by J. A. Newell recounted how old clothes "went into 'piece quilts' the prevailing fancy work. Though many did beautiful embroidery and wore it." When Keturah Belknap and her family set out for Oregon/Country territory from Iowa on October 27, 1848, the two-horse wagon featured a double-thick muslin and linen cover that she sewed together "real good and strong and I have to spin the thread and sew all these long seams with my fingers." Pioneer women embraced their work, celebrated their own skills, bonded with other women, and shaped a female collective identity to accommodate the demands of the journey. Women performed much more work than they were accustomed to doing back home and lacked the necessary information, as individuals, to do the work required of them alone. Women pieced together the few fragments of female subculture left to them out in the wilderness and built a community through emotional connections.

An *Emotional Connection for Social Cohesion* theme characterized the ways women acted independently of men of the patriarchal world for "a sense of self-worth" for "socially essential work" (Faragher & Stansell, 1975, p. 161). Pioneer women supported others in the face of danger as people engaged in conflict and pulled further apart while crossing the plains and mountains, forging deep and rapid rivers, dealing with animals, battling the weather, and bartering with or fighting Native American people. Strengthening interconnectivity (Stoker & Stoker, 2012) to get a free flow of information enabled women to navigate their destiny in ways that served the public interest, community, and society in a similar way to Heath's (2000) explanation of links between public relations and trust and Bivins' (1993) conflation of individual and societal interests in the service of morality: "The point becomes not *whose* interest is being served, but rather that *all* interests have an opportunity to be served" (p. 121).

An *Emotional Connection for Social Cohesion* theme, as it relates to the Oregon Trail lived experience, also lends a historical component to what we already understand about female management styles. Among public relations research, Aldoory (1998) found that women public relations practitioners' communication styles and rhetorical strategies focused on relationship building, cooperation, and consideration. In a nineteenth-century community-building context, women's Oregon Trail diaries, journals, and reminiscences texts suggest pioneer women used the language of friendship and partnership to strategize for social cohesion through intimacy and bonds – techniques associated with a transformational-style approach (Pincus & DeBonis, 1994) which is consistent with female socialization (Bass, 1990). A transformational style means working collectively to address a higher order purpose (Rosener, 1994), especially during trying times. Catharine Beecher, a mid-nineteenth-century philosopher and public school advocate opined that female friendships provide comfort during periods of "mental stress" (Sklar, 1973, p. 43). So, an *Emotional Connection for Social Cohesion* theme characterizes pioneer women's transformational style of deep friendships with other women as part of their own female subculture – which further promoted community building.

Meeting new friends and maintaining close personal friendships while journeying westward on the Oregon Trail may have been easy in comparison to the arrival and settlement work in Oregon. The covered wagons moved slowly and many women actually walked alongside and visited other women in wagons covering an expanse of four or five miles to get out of each other's dust as they moved en masse toward Oregon and California. Women turned out to be each other's best companions as women "found security and well-being through their relationships with other women," seeing their duties as different from and perhaps "superior to man's" (Jeffrey, 1998, p. 19). Women on the Oregon Trail wore long skirts as was traditional nineteenth-century fashion, but also used them as a modesty screen when they created space for one another to take care of bodily functions as they stood back to back with their skirts fanned out (Butruille, 1993). This ritual, performed quickly, proved especially useful as diarrhea, a common ailment on the Oregon Trail journey, did not discriminate along gender lines. In the evening, women's food preparation and camping responsibilities included working together to scavenge for campfire burning materials, collect water, and gather berries, roots, herbs, and other edibles. Most wagon trains hosted regular "lay-by" days, so that cattle could rest and repairs could be made. This gave women time to commune while birthing, tending the sick, and burying the dead. Giving birth and looking after other women constituted a ritual that depended on female support on the Oregon Trail and frontier, comparable to nurse midwifery activities in communities from which women had emigrated (Riley, 2006). Jeffrey (1998) noted that "to be alone at such a moment was a dreadful fate" (p. 87), with such women otherwise experiencing an "intense sense of isolation" (Harris, 1987, p. 174).

Another way to look at the *Emotional Connection for Social Cohesion* theme is to consider one Oregon Trail pioneer woman's expression of how she worked at hiding her emotions. Arvazna A. Spillman-Cooper wrote in a reminiscences document, "Our Journey Across the Plains from Missouri to Oregon," of her 1863 journey that she tried not to show emotion to avoid causing her family concern: "I kept it all to myself, and shed a few tears when others were asleep, and kept up appearances so well, that no one suspected that I was not reasonably happy." The worst way for woman to travel on the Overland Trails was in the company of only men. This was the lonely experience of S. D. Evans, a widow who began her journey to Roseburg, Oregon, from Washoe, Nevada, in 1861 two years after her husband was killed in California. With her two small children and two hired men who drove the ox team, Evans made it to Oregon – as she wrote a reminiscences narrative some years later: "We had a farm in Oregon in Douglas Co. near Roseburg, and in August, 1861 we concluded to go there."

In Oregon's early frontier years, Caucasian/White women were keen to reestablish deep emotional relationships with other women in an attempt to replicate their lifestyle prior to emigration (Harris, 1987). Jeffrey (1998) found from examining Oregon's 1850 census records that in the most rural areas the ratio was 37 men to every 100 women. Kinship ties among emigrants who settled in Oregon were particularly strong, with at least 40% of households reporting family relationships with one or more other Oregon households as "marriage bound families together and family, relatives, and old friends emigrated to swell the circle of love" (Jeffrey, 1998, p. 95). While only one of the original documents examined for the current study was written by a single (widowed) woman, homesteaders in North Dakota who were single women forged cooperative relationships with friends and neighbors as they managed their homestead (Lindgren, 1996). Some historians have found evidence of single women homesteaders in today's Wyoming and Colorado who "sought economic freedom through land ownership … who sought to earn a living by means other than those of schoolteacher, maid, or factory worker" (Patterson-Black & Patterson-Black, 1978). As women settled in Oregon, deep trusting friendships with other women formed a solid foundation for expanding women's role in the public sphere through women-directed church groups, reform associations, philanthropic activities, and communal child-rearing. Frontier women formed networks to discuss social issues in their developing new communities, as well as fashion. The confidences and gossip women shared helped to lighten the load of domestic tasks with a forum for expressing anxieties, exchanging information, and negotiating male-dominated society (Jeffrey, 1998).

Oregon Trail pioneer women's *Emotional Connection for Social Cohesion* theme also characterized the relationships between wives and husbands as partnerships. Once arrived and building homesteads in Oregon, women got busy working side by side with husbands clearing the land and building homesteads. Wives drew closer to husbands for companionship given that often there were great geographic distances between homesteads where other women lived. The findings of earlier studies of Overland Trail experiences suggested that the journey actually "eased the distance between wives and husbands as they moved westward" (Butruille, 1993, p. 133). Working out of doors drew couples together as emigrant women expanded their domestic work to also include tending the livestock and keeping an eye out for grass to feed the cattle. Engaging in more visibly open public sphere duties that were thought to be male-dominated arenas enabled women to work more closely with husbands and fathers. Their first winter in Oregon, married couples either stayed with family who had emigrated earlier, or worked together hastily building crude cabins, shacks, sheds, and lean-tos (Butruille, 1993).

Female Frontier and Recording the Landscape

The *Emotional Connection for Social Cohesion* theme that emerged from Oregon Trail women's first-person texts also characterized women's communing with nature, even though they had very little free time to themselves. Oregon Trail pioneer women occupied nearly every waking moment with childcare and domestic tasks, yet some found moments to write in their diary or journal about entertaining activities that broke the tensions of five-six-months of slow travel across the continent in the spring rain and under the hot summer sun. Leisure-time activities among people "enhance their sense of community," according to the humanist, communitarian concept used by today's public relations practitioners tasked with community building (Kruckeberg & Starck, 2004, p. 141). Interestingly, several pioneer women reported the pleasure they took in music, dancing, and drawing flora and fauna discovered across the natural landscape while walking amidst nature. These forms of enjoyment offered a much-needed respite from the pressures on the Oregon Trail as pioneer women simply picked wild flowers, went swimming, or learned new skills like horseback riding (Butruille, 1993).

Recording the landscape became part of women's lived experience on the Oregon Trail. Pioneer women's emotional connection with the landscape is particularly easy to see in the case of twins who shared a diary. Joseph McMillen, asked his twin daughters Cecelia Emily McMillen Adams and Parthenia McMillen Blank, to keep a journal on the Oregon Trail; a task the two married young women took seriously and seemed to enjoy. Their lively and descriptive writing included poems and apparently Mrs. Cecilia Emily McMillen Adams was "a born musician and artist" (Holmes, 2008, p. 150). Such was the opinion of her husband, Dr. William Adams, who wrote to a friend on June 1, 1905 about his 23-year-old wife as she traveled the Oregon Trail three years into her marriage, along with other family members. The McMillen twin sisters also enjoyed one another's company, taking pleasure in combining domestic duties with walking trips of discovery. On June 3, 1852, Adams penciled a poem: "Home what so sweet! So beautiful on Earth! Oh! So rare As kindred love and family repose!" On June 10, 1852 the sisters wrote about the landscape as they walked along the Platte River scoping out a location to wash clothing, describing a "very rapid stream filled with sand bars" and "a few wild roses and yellow daisies." They noted passing two grave sites: "On the headboard was written with a pencil 'Mary Morris aged 19 and M. C. Morris aged 9 yrs.' We saw good clothing scatter around which caused us to think they had died with some contagious disease." The following days on June 11 and 12, 1852, the sisters wrote of joy in having time "to get to write or read" as well as to see the sites as "P and self walked on several miles. We came to an old deserted Indian village." Later that month on June 26, 1852, the sisters detailed new flora, prairie dogs, and natural wonders:

> Find prickly pears in great abundance. The flowers of one kind resemble the double yellow hollyhocks and the other kind resemble the pink china aster. The pink ones are very beautiful. Passed through another dog town today. They resemble the fox squarrel in shape and color. It is almost impossible to kill one of them. They are so very shy. Passed some deep ravines. Passed 9 graves. Very sandy roads. Find some beautiful looking springs but dare not use the water. Keep near the Platte. Good grass, no wood. Made 18 miles.

By late July the McMillen party had reached Independence Rock in present-day Wyoming, and the twins recorded in their diary:

> Very warm ... Keep on the Sweetwater River. Find gooseberries. They are very sour indeed ... Parthenia and I climbed a very steep rock some 400 to 500 feet high and got very tired indeed. Found a great many names. Today we can see the snow-capped mountains for the first time. Roads in some places very bad. Keep the Sweetwater River. Very poor grass. Made 17 miles.

In early August, the McMillen's wagon train encountered Chimney Rock in present-day Nebraska and on August 3, 1952, the McMillens' diary recorded:

> To day we come to the river opposite Chimney Rock which has been visible most of the way for the last 35 miles ... It consists of a large square column of clay and sand mixed together with a base of conical form apparently composed of sand, round base cone, and appears as if the column had been set up and the sand heaped around it to sustain it.

Later, on August 14, 1852, once in Oregon, one of the McMillen sisters poetically described the land: "The grasshoppers are so thick that they look like snow in the air coming very fast."

On the journey from Illinois to Umpqua Valley, Oregon, 26-year-old Amelia A. Hammond Hadley made careful notes in her diary and found a creative outlet in detailing views, landscapes, and observations about other emigrants who had passed before her – as a way of keeping up her morale or of sharing it with others. Early in her journey on Monday, April 28, 1851, Amelia A. Hammond Hadley optimistically noted the larger emigrant groups who had passed that way before:

> ... the amount of emigration you will see at almost every little stream a place where some one has camped, a great number of trees and stumps

Figure 7.1 Chimney Rock
Source: Deposit Photos.

marked, a great many names of persons, for Oregon & California. It is realy amusing to read them, now and then coming across persons you know. We help to mark also some of them. Find everything pleasant, ourselves well and hearty. Timber principaly oak and elm.

Amelia A. Hammond Hadley continued detailing the landscape on May 24, 1851:

Prickely pears grow spontaneous and 3 kinds of cactus, they look beautiful. The Platte is a delightful stream all though back from the stream on each [bank?] in most places they are huge sand bluffs which look like snow drifts being so white and not an atom of vegetation on them but on the banks of the river plenty of grass and some little skirts of timber.

She also cataloged flora on July 6, 1851: "There are any quantity of wild currents of which are yellow, red, & black. The red ones are like our currents in the states, are quite a luxury, could gather a bushel in a short time." Amelia A. Hammond Hadley was the same honeymooning bride who had noted the virtues of buffalo chips as campfire fuel and beautifully described the scenery her wagon train encountered, including her own sketches in the back of her diary, much like a naturalist might. Some girls and women supplemented regular notes about weather and terrain with doodles. Faragher and Stansell (1975) qualified such activities as a "psychological lifeline to their abandoned homes and communities" (p. 158). On Sunday June 1, 1851, Amelia A. Hammond Hadley noted the changing landscape:

> This road lends over the bluff called Cobble Hills, and one would certainly think from their rude construction they were rightly named, after leaving these and traveling some miles farther we discover some hills, or bluffs, Called Ancient Bluffs ruins which are decidedly grand and beautiful for such as love such a scenery. It looks like ruins of old castles and buildings of all sises and descriptions one in particular runs up some 100 ft and almost square, and the top of it covered with grass, the ruins being principaly rock, makes it look more strange, here is part of a company who are in search of their cattle which have taken a stampede animals are wild an easy frightened up the Platte, but to return these hills are the most delightful of any thing I have seen visitors have to be very careful on account of the many rattlesnakes lurking among the clefts of the rocks.

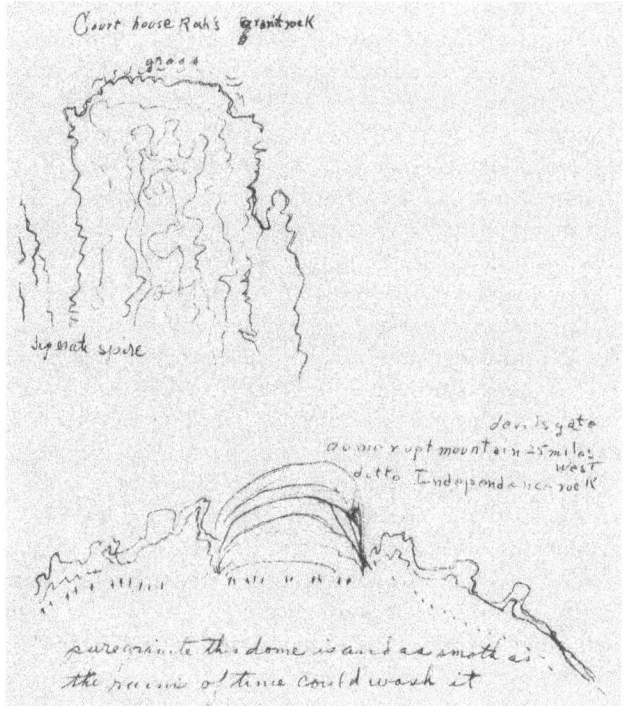

Figure 7.2 Amelia A. Hammond Hadley's Journal
Source: A43, Special Collections and University Archive, University of Oregon Libraries, Eugene, Oregon.

Apprehension toward Native American People and Communities

While some Oregon Trail pioneer women worked at being *Ambassador/Liaison* among indigenous peoples and their communities, as addressed in Chapter 3, others were apprehensive about Native Americans and hit the Oregon Trail with cautious or negative mindsets. The 350,000 homesteading emigrants who journeyed 2,000+ miles westward to Oregon or California generally followed natural landscape river routes that had been used for many years by indigenous peoples and Caucasian/White trappers. Even today, the major highway systems of Interstate 80 and Interstate 84 follow these early travel corridors and it is common to see parts of it marked by triangular brown and white "Oregon Trail National Historic Trail" signs featuring a covered wagon graphic posted across Oregon and Idaho. Sometimes indigenous peoples aided emigrants with stuck wagons, helped to round up escaped cattle, and rescued those at risk of drowning.

The hero narrative of homesteading settlers is an exceptionally powerful trope that endures, even though facts about Oregon's history and its indigenous peoples tell a different story. Even while events unfolded, several Oregon Trail women wrote about the negative impact of wagon trains on the land and waterways as they traveled toward Oregon – for example carcasses and raw sewage created by wagon trains over time, and discarded broken wagons, clothing, and household items such as stoves abandoned to lighten loads. Arvazna A. Spillman-Cooper reflected in a 1902 reminiscences document on how her extended family's journey to Oregon in 1863 included many encounters with oxen, horses, and livestock that had died along the trail due to lack of food, water, exhaustion, and poisoning from drinking alkali water: "We saw many dead animals all along through the worst section, while we did not lose one." Julia Thomas wrote in 1907 in her "Reminiscences of Plains Crossing, 1852," about the challenges associated with finding enough grassland to feed cattle, due in part to the natural landscape, but also because so many wagon trains had passed through before and livestock had already devoured dwindling supplies: "This was the fourth of July but from this time on I can give no dates although I kept a diary but the teams were failing and grass scarce." Harriet A. Loughary shared a similar observation in her 1864 diary entry: "As a result of the alkali, found one of our buck oxen dead from drinking too much of this water." Seldom did the pioneers actually bury livestock that died. Elizabeth Julia Ellison Goltra maintained a journal in 1853 while journeying from Missouri and explained: "One of our oxen laid down and died, saw a great many dead cattle along the road today." Moreover, burying dead people also proved challenging on the Oregon Trail. The widow, S. D. Evans wrote in her reminiscences document in 1861:

> At one of our camps we kept smelling something every time the wind would blow from a certain direction. The next morning one of the men

went out looking around and found a dead man in a ditch with some grass and sticks over him.

Some Oregon Trail pioneer women – like Jane (Jennie) Paul Eakin Hanna, Amelia A. Hammond Hadley, and Arvazna A. Spillman-Cooper – wrote of extending a hand of friendship and maintaining an attitude of respectful curiosity about the indigenous people they met along the Oregon Trail. However, others recorded the high degrees of distrust, fear, and trepidation about encountering "Indians." The early missionaries, in particular, believed Western lands were theirs for the taking. For example, in 1837 Narcissa Whitman believed that attempts to convert the Cayuse and to farm the land was done "in the name of Progress and Providence," justifying "colonial indifference" about entire Native American cultures (Gwartney, 2019, pp. 12, 15). Several of the first-person original source documents examined for this study highlight the ways that Oregon's indigenous peoples resisted Caucasian/White settlement and the changes the emigrants affected. At least one diary examined for this research project, that of S. D. Evans who traveled west in 1865, was full of bias against indigenous people because she believed that her husband had been murdered by them in California. This inspired S. D. Evans' 500-mile westward trek from Idaho to Oregon, as she recalled in her reminiscences document: "a wild uninhabited country, where thieving, murderous Indians skulked ready to murder any unprotected party that should fall in with." S. D. Evans told a story about encountering a male "Indian" who begged for food for himself and his "sick squaw" and in exchange for "a shirt one of the men had to spare," he offered trail information. S. D. Evans wrote that this same man later attacked her party: "We knew him by the shirt he had on that had a big patch we remembered." S. D. Evans also wrote about a violent encounter with "Indians" throwing rocks down on her party: "Fortunately, none of the rocks struck us, for the Indians were so high on the hill they couldn't time them very well and they all went behind us." As Oregon Trail emigrant numbers swelled throughout the 1850s, relationships between the two cultures generally worsened. Unruh (1979) estimated that the most violent conflicts unfolded west of the Rocky Mountains, where the most dangerous conditions of the overland journey lay. Around 360 U.S. emigrants were killed by Native Americans between 1840 and 1860, while Caucasian/Whites killed around 425 Native Americans during the same period (Unruh, 1979).

Several women's diaries and other writings offered conflicting accounts of interactions with and observation of Native Americans, with several references to Indians' begging and stealing. Historians' accounts dispute popular film representations of murderous attacks on pioneer wagon trains by Native Americans. Rather, Unruh (1979) noted that mutual aid shaped the relationships more often than violent hostility or "murderous attack" (p. 180), but that thievery was quite common. While the McMillan twin sisters wrote of barter exchanges for much-needed food and footwear, some Oregon Trail women's diaries, journals, and reminiscences noted Native Americans stealing, perhaps considered noteworthy given their religious training about the sinfulness of stealing. Amelia A. Hammond Hadley wrote in her diary several sightings of "Indians," mostly as a curiosity, as on May 11, 1851:

> Camped on the Loup Fork on account of crossing very rainy and cloudy, and considerable cold, find plenty of grass, and little timber have had no trouble with the Indians as yet, they are afraid to tackle us an ox train back of us they attacked and took 2 oxen and 2 sacks of meal. Have seen some antelope and plenty of wolves.

Elizabeth Julia Ellison Goltra wrote in her diary on May 5, 1863 while traveling from Missouri, offered a contrasting account of, "Met some Indians on the road. Gave them some bread and meat," and then by August, "We are among the most hostile tribe of Indians on the route, many emigrants have been killed here." Amelia A. Hammond Hadley lamented on July 9, 1851 about lack of federal government support to ensure emigrant safety:

> The Indians are every day commiting some depredation or other, they steal and rob from every train and those dirty french put them up to it. I think if congress knew how bad they were they would protect the emigration as I have said it is cruel, for them to hold out inducements for people to settle Oregon and leave them unprotected and to fight theyr way as best they can …

Indeed, the emigrants stopped at military fortifications like Fort Laramie in present-day Wyoming for shelter and protection but did not always find it. Nor did they find much government-sponsored defense once settled in Oregon where "protection from Native tribes and delineated ownership of land" with punishment for those who crossed boundaries often was nonexistent (Gwartney, 2019).

Even the McMillen twins, whose diary was usually filled with the joys of discovery mixed with longing for home, included fear-filled entries about the perceived risks associated with travel across Native American communities. On June 7, 1852, they wrote:

> To day we saw four Indian's graves. They were quite open … They were buried on the surface of the earth and mounds erected over them and an opening had been made in the side probably by the emigrants. As we were looking at them we saw four Indians comeing towards us on horseback which caused us to be leaveing they had been stealing sheep from the Emigrants.

Then on July 22, 1852, the McMillen twins wrote: "The Indians are gathered around us to day they look very savage but we are well prepared for them we go in large companies …"

A distinct pattern emerged among pioneer women's emotions about Native Americans which shifted throughout the course of the five-to-six-month journey. Many pioneer women started by being curious at the outset of the journey, fear by midpoint, but concluded with gratitude for Native Americans' willingness to barter, sell provisions, and offer assistance with hazardous river crossings. Oregon Trail diaries are especially useful because often they reveal changes in women's perceptions about Native Americans as they moved westward. The tone of some women's diary and journal writings about Native Americans seemed to alter once they had reached Fort Laramie in present-day Wyoming. While some women considered their relationships with Native Americans to be "collegial," men played an "adversarial" role (Riley, 2004b, p. 173) and perhaps women were swayed by a husband's or father's attitude as the trip lumbered on.

In the years after early emigrants' settlement, some women blamed Caucasian/White men for frontier conflict and became generous benefactors supporting indigenous communities (Riley, 1984). Reminiscing in 1907, Julia Thomas wrote of an ever-present fear and concern about "Indians" in 1859 when she and her husband and four small children set out for the plains with two wagons, a yoke of oxen, and four cows: "[W]e were often told that hostiles were just ahead of us," but she wrote nothing further about experiencing any conflict or violence. Once settled in Oregon, J. A. Newell wrote a reminiscences letter in 1903 about only positive reactions to community building in Oregon among Native Americans: "There was in those days little of any danger from Indians in the Willamette and Columbia valleys (except from over friendliness). They were almost the only resource for hired labor working well 'til by some unknown motive to quit." On the Oregon Trail and in emerging new settlements, Caucasian/White women's female gender roles adapted in ways that moderated their beliefs about race and social class and supported community-building outreach through bartering, exchange of home remedies and recipes, and actual hiring of Native American women and men as domestic help.

The Violent Side of Oregon's Homesteading History

It has been argued that U.S. westward migration facilitated the growth of public relations as a profession during the 1870s and 1880s in conjunction with industrial growth and railroads' need to encourage waves of emigrants to migrate to the Midwest and beyond. Railroad companies were "selling America" via publicity in the form of persuasive romantic imagery to transform the Western wilderness into settlements (Piasecki, 2000, p. 59), effectively displacing indigenous communities in the process. While these image-laden messages served railroad operators and politicians (Emmons, 1971), emigrants became crucial actors "within the utopian discourse relating to the settlement and the civilizing of the western frontier" (Piasecki, 2000, p. 59). The less-told story is the violent side of Oregon's homesteading history and indigenous people's suffering as a result of the "near genocide by colonists ... near destruction of our peoples and their cultural life ways" (Lewis, 2014, p. 414).

In the twenty-first century, we have an even clearer understanding of the complexities associated with Westward migration and homestead settlement. Historians like Jeffrey (1998) cautioned against rejecting or demonizing Caucasian/White pioneer women, given their "admirable spirit and energy" in the face of adversity, resolving: "That they were unable to see beyond the boundaries of their culture should remind us of the difficulty of that task – in the past and in our own day" (p. 9). Examining at least some of the effects Oregon Trail emigrants had in disrupting the ecological balance and indigenous peoples' cultures offers an important dimension for this book's exploration of early public relations in the form of community building. Nevertheless, what cannot be overlooked is that while Caucasian/White women's community-building work in successfully fostering positive relationships between emigrants and some Native American communities reveals women's stories in ways that contribute to the history chapter on early U.S. public relations, we must temper this discovery with problematizing the consequences of women's contributions to the impact on Oregon's original inhabitants. When writing about the history of public relations and its precursors, we must understand that selective recall, emphasizing some facts at the expense of others (Dennis, 2014), is disingenuous. Many feminist historians have grappled with contextualizing women's lived experiences in the context of the times in which the women lived. However, Gwartney's (2019) writings about 1837 missionary Narcissa Prentiss Whitman, who expressed depression and disenchantment associated with proselytizing and acting on her right to alter the lives and lands of the Cayuse people, concluded that she wouldn't forgive Narcissa Prentiss Whitman "for building a good part of her cage" (p. 12).

Emigration fever took hold by the 1840s when the U.S. jointly claimed Oregon Country/Territory with Great Britain –the greater the number of U.S. citizens occupying the land, the stronger the case for acquiring more Pacific Northwest land on the continent (Butruille, 1993). There was little, if any, concern about displacing indigenous communities. This is with hindsight in 2020 and unfortunately, the perspectives of many Native American peoples largely are unknown. Pre-1970s, it was rare for historians to include the perspectives of indigenous peoples when writing Oregon history because tribal oral histories were considered unreliable (Lewis, 2014). Deep reading of first-person accounts of Caucasian/White women in the form of diaries, journals, and reminiscences also has its limitations, but these are the only available record of their lives and their interpretation of the Oregon Trail and settlement saga (Jeffrey, 1998).

Plains traffic on the Overland Trail roughly doubled between 1820 and 1840 (Jeffrey, 1998), and en route to Oregon, the effects of the emigrants were felt. Caucasian/White pioneers encountered many communities of indigenous peoples along the early miles of the Oregon Trail, including the Fox, Sauk, Shawnee, and Potawatomi of the lower Missouri Valley. Further on, they encountered the Cheyenne, Pawnee, Shoshone, Nez Perce, Cayuse, Northern Paiute, and many more. During the heavy migration years, convoys of wagon trains that were miles wide negatively impacted the natural landscape along crucial waterways and overcrowding in well-traveled areas polluted shallow drinking holes and springs with human and livestock waste (Butruille, 1993). Waterways used by indigenous communities for millennia became breeding grounds for infectious diseases including typhoid, tuberculosis, malaria, dysentery, pneumonia, measles, smallpox, yellow fever, and cholera. Beginning with Lewis and Clark's Corps of Discovery expedition, "isolated attempts" were made by U.S. government officials to vaccinate Native Americans (Thornton, 1987, p. 100).

Starting in the fifteenth century, European invasions contributed to the annihilation of 95% of the population of the American continents, or roughly 20 million people, within a few generations (Diamond, Harrison, & Lambert, 2005). Specifically, there were nearly 10 million indigenous peoples living in the area now known as the U.S. before European settlers started arriving and present-day Oregon ranks fifteenth with about 4.1 million Native Americans living in the state in 2019 (Native American population, n.d.). The U.S. Census Bureau reports that Native Americans comprise nearly 6.79 million, or 2.09% of the U.S. population (Native American population, n.d.). Nineteenth-century Overland Trail migrations contributed to the extermination of indigenous communities – whether directly when pioneers used Indians for target practice or killed them in the name of self-defense, or indirectly through the spread of disease to which indigenous communities had no immunity. Moreover, centuries of "persecution and discrimination" led to Native Americans losing their land and resources as they were forced onto reservations lacking in natural resources (Native American population, n.d.). Additionally, Caucasian/White Overland Trail emigrants killed wild animals such as bison (buffalo) for food, tools, clothing, and bedding; a species crucial to the Native American way of life (Butruille, 1993), while some emigrants shot them merely for sport (Jernigan, 2018).

When missionary emigrants arrived in Oregon early in the nineteenth century, proselytizing efforts such as those of Presbyterians at the Whitman Mission at Waiilatpu had limited success, as did missionaries elsewhere in Oregon when indigenous communities refused to accept an influx of Caucasian/Whites on their lands. On November 30, 1847, failed pleas to convince Narcissa Whitman, her husband Marcus, and several others to leave after 11 years erupted into violence as Cayuse people experienced a deadly measles epidemic and eventually resisted outside pressures to change their traditions and way of life. A band of Cayuse killed the missionary couple and 14 others, believing that Marcus Whitman had deliberately poisoned their community in order to grab land for the increasing numbers of Caucasian/White emigrants (Lavender, 1963). This course of events inspired the Cayuse War, driving out the Presbyterians but stiffening the resolve of Catholic priests determined to convert the Cayuse without violence (del Mar, 2005). The Cayuse War ended with the arrival of regular U.S. Army troops and five Cayuse men surrendering to government officials who hosted a trial, convicted and hanged the men in Oregon City, and buried them in an unmarked grave on June 3, 1850 (Proclamation from Governor George Abernethey, n.d.). Several military-supported wars with Native Americas resulted in massive destruction to indigenous communities throughout the nineteenth century. Said a Sioux named Black Elk: "Wherever we went the soldiers came to kill us, and it was all our own country" (Thornton, 1987, p. 91).

On the whole, the Caucasian/White emigrants "gave little more than a passing thought to the peoples they were displacing" (Jeffrey, 1998, p. 67) as missionaries continued travel to Oregon throughout the rest of the 1830s (Feltskog, 1969). Missionaries tasked themselves with assimilating indigenous peoples whom they considered "uncivilized (savage, not Christian, and not fully human)" (Lewis, 2014, p. 422). Such a philosophy steeped in Caucasian/White superiority "created upset, and even chaos, among Indians" (Riley, 2003, p. 201). Consequently, the effects of their reform efforts were mixed. Riley (2003) explained that nineteenth- and twentieth-century Caucasian/White women – through their writings and public speeches – had some success in changing people's minds about Native Americans as they pleaded for enabling indigenous peoples to live in dignity and with more self-rule.

In Oregon, Caucasian/White people have bequeathed indigenous communities a legacy of literal and figurative death. Native Americans experienced epidemic illnesses, land reductions, and forced marches onto reservations – as well as degradation of tribal cultures, legally through policy and court decrees, and in scholarship that failed to consult them and adequately represent their lived experiences in historical writing. Caucasian/White homesteaders ended up taking over the best lands – either for farming or to pan for gold alongside rivers – and then organizing to "completely eliminate tribes from the land" (Lewis, 2014, p. 420). Homesteading farmers drained, burned, and plowed fertile land to accommodate wheat, cattle, sheep, and potatoes. Encouraging Native American children to assimilate by discarding their traditional fashion, speaking only English, and attending boarding schools was overwhelmingly futile. Assimilation was actually written into treaties with Native American communities (Lewis, 2014, p. 423). The Willamette Valley – considered to be the end of the Oregon Trail – was home to the Kalapuyan people. Anthropologists estimate that at its peak, the Kalapuyan community population reached 13,500 people (Robbins, 2002a). After 1841, U.S. emigration became more intensive and the Kalapuyan people "simply became unable to feed their population" (Thornton, 1987, p. 125). By 1844, only a few hundred indigenous people were left in the Willamette Valley (Ratcliff, 1973). By 1854, Kalapuyan people were forced to give their Willamette River Valley lands to the U.S. government. Thornton (1987) opined that "genocide of American Indians was probably most blatant" (p. 107) in southern Oregon Territory and northern California mid-nineteenth century in conjunction with gold discovery in 1849 and the subsequent invasion by miners and settlers.

Many emigrants who headed for Oregon's Willamette Valley encountered violent encounters with Native American peoples. For example, what has come to be known as the "Snake River Massacre" took place in 1854 when the Shoshone killed 19 emigrants in the Snake River country as part of the "Ward Massacre," and in 1860 again killed 28 as part of the "Utter-Van Odum Massacre" (Allen, 2005). The events were recorded in the *Oregon Argus* on November 24, 1860 according to the experiences of Joseph Myers, one of the survivors. As colonizers, Caucasian/White settlers had begun relocating indigenous communities to established reservations in the seventeenth and eighteenth centuries and operations exploded in "massive proportions" in the nineteenth century (Thornton, 1987, p. 113). Throughout the 1850s, Oregon Country/Territory's indigenous communities were relocated to the Siletz and Grand Ronde reservations, lands deemed far enough away from the Willamette Valley and too close to the Pacific Ocean to be of significant agricultural potential. Robbins (2002b) explained that the two reservations were established by presidential executive order, which was all that was required to open lands to settlement, and were not subject to treaty stipulations. These actions and others in conjunction with U.S. President Andrew Jackson's Indian Removal Act further marginalized Native American communities and severely limited their access to traditional hunting grounds and immediately began negatively impacting their way of life. Oregon's own "Trail of Tears" involved Native Americans walking 33 days in winter through towns inhabited by new emigrants as Caucasian/Whites hatefully attacked them (Lewis, 2014). They experienced suffering in the reservations in the form of starvation and disease as the U.S. Indian Bureau failed to provide adequate food and shelter. Mortality rates that were higher than birth rates became the pattern through the early twentieth century (Robbins, 2002b). Meanwhile, U.S. policies opened millions of acres of land to private, non-Native American ownership and provided space for Oregon Trail homesteaders to settle. In the 1860s, some Native Americans worked as migrant agricultural workers in the Willamette Valley and as domestic help to homesteaders. The U.S. Congress's Doolittle Committee concluded in 1867 that emigration "is filling every valley and gorge of the mountains with the most energetic and fearless men in the world" (Thornton, 1987, p. 133), such that lawlessness inspired homesteaders to disregard Indian reservation boundaries and engage in conflicts that left "the Indian … overwhelmed if not destroyed" (Prucha, 1975, p. 103).

Indeed, Oregon Trail homesteaders who emigrated West changed Oregon forever. From 1800–1900, 350,000 American Indians were decimated (Thornton, 1987). Native Americans' villages and camas fields were turned into pastures and native grasses to oats and wheat. Emigrants broke down stream banks, enabled livestock to pollute the streams, destroyed native grasses, and burned and cleared fields, destroying woods and filling the air with smoke. In September 1874 the editor of the Jacksonville, Oregon, *Democratic Times* newspaper lamented: "It seems as though no year shall pass but what the woods are set afire and the country deluged with smoke" (Atwood & Gray, 2003). In addition to farming, emergent logging and mining enterprises altered the landscape. Place names were changed, too. For example, *Di'tani* became *Table Rock* and *Me-tus* became *Humbug Mountain* as Caucasian/White, emigrants also gave new names to waterways such as *Wagner Creek* and *Hunter Creek* (Atwood & Gray, 2003).

Even historians documenting the tragedies experience difficulty in writing about them. Dennis (2014) explained:

> We are attuned to this as historians, and yet, the implications of such developments are often overwhelming. Death on a large scale is particularly potent, unsettling, and socially dangerous. Historically, it can be so threatening that we sometimes act to control or neutralize its effects, deny or obscure the death itself, or put it to work politically.
>
> (p. 282)

Stereotyping and Captivity Narratives

Emigrant women's challenges inspired mass media producers of books, magazines, and newspapers back East to cash in on tales of "the weak and unfortunate woman who was destroyed by the frontier" (Riley, 1988, p. 8). These stories included tales of Caucasian/White women being abducted and/or sexually abused by Native Americans. While many historians (e.g., Pearce, 1947) and anthropologists (e.g., Strong, 2012) take such captivity narratives with a pinch of salt, they do offer insights into how colonizers constructed *the other*. For 300 years, captivity narratives became a long-established genre as Caucasian/White women sold their stories about being held captive by Native Americans (Riley, 2004). Intersectionally, gender combined with ethnicity/race in ways that the mass media exploited to produce some generally titillating stories (Riley, 1988). These captivity narratives forged negative stereotypes of indigenous communities, increasingly deviating from factual accounts (Pearce, 1947). As Caucasian/White women, they were privileged colonizers and captivity narratives appealed to a wide market and sold well (Riley, 1984). By 1892, Emeline Fuller's tale of torture which she claimed to have witnessed en route to Oregon, became a best seller (Riley, 1988, p. 9). In sum, by the end of the nineteenth century captivity narratives fueled anti-Native American sentiments and contributed to the negative stereotypes of indigenous people west of the Mississippi River. Framing Native Americans as brutal and uncivilized rationalized U.S. policies and actions that led to genocide and theft of indigenous lands. On the other hand, some nineteenth-century captives' stories were about the ways in which indigenous peoples' cultures were not inferior as popularly supposed, as some had unhappy homecomings back among Caucasians/Whites (Van Der Beets, 1972) and underscored the reality that "the frontier was not empty of culture or people" (Jeffrey, 1998, p. 29). Persistent stereotypes of Native Americans as "defilers of White virgins" (Merskin, 2014, p. 187) were popular in captivity narratives of the past, yet it has been argued that racist representations persist in product and brand names, sports team mascots, and geographic landmarks (Coombes, 1998).

Summary

This chapter examined the *Emotional Connection and Social Cohesion* theme as it characterized pioneer women's relationships with husbands, other family members, wagon train members, as well as some Native American communities. Pioneer women's first-person narratives add a new dimension to community building in the history chapter of early U.S. public relations. Juxtaposing the positivity of women's *Emotional Connection for Social Cohesion* theme in community building against the reality of being complicit in an Oregon homesteading enterprise that violently impacted so many Native Americans offers an opportunity to think more critically about ways the public relations profession continues to grapple with ethical decision making. Emigrants' encounters with the indigenous communities of the prairies beyond Independence, Missouri, through the Pacific Northwest were inevitable, greatly transforming Native American communities. Overland Trails from the Platte River to the Sweetwater River had been "an Indian Road" for centuries when fur trade mogul John Jacob Astor and subsequent parties started using it in the early 1800s (Feltskog, 1969, p. 18). This backdrop must be factored into the positive findings that nineteenth-century pioneer women experienced a shift from operating only in the domestic private sphere to lived experiences in the public sphere.

Among the six elements that Kruckeberg and Starck (1988) identified as essential to the *community* concept, as they reflected on the Chicago School of Social Thought's usage of the term, is the principle that "an individual ordinarily belongs primarily to one community" (p. 56). In the context of women's role on Oregon Trail overland journey and subsequent homesteading experience in Oregon, this study's findings suggest that women underwent a transformation that required reassessing their traditional domestic duties and expanding their awareness of public sphere events so that they could play a more active community-building role through a deeper partnership and friendship with their own family and others. By recording the landscape, Oregon Trail women engaged with nature for survival, for posterity's sake, and as part of their own awakening to possibility of becoming more of a part of the overland enterprise and its social activities. In the process of recording observations and thoughts in their diaries, journals, and reminiscences, Oregon Trail women revealed their perceptions of Native American communities and provided evidence of the ways their attitudes toward indigenous peoples shifted over the course of the Westward trek as they met them in person.

Because public relations today requires practitioners to be ethical in all things, regarding the impact of their work in all contexts (Fawkes, 2012), it is impossible not to consider the complicity of Oregon Trail women in negatively impacting on Native Americans' way of life across the plains and in

Oregon – and the paradox this presents. Their role as colonizers must be ever present as a critique of community building integral to the violent side of homesteading history in Oregon. Of course, these events and dimensions of the Oregon Trail phenomenon as explored in this book took place prior to the establishment of formal public relations practice. However, the work women performed *was* community-building work and contributes a new dimension to the history chapter of public relations in the U.S. So, Fawkes' (2012) global ethical perspective offers a useful lens through which to examine this episode of U.S. history as Oregon Trail emigrants left the U.S. behind en route to the Willamette Valley and other parts of Oregon occupied by indigenous peoples. Today, public relations practitioners are encouraged to erase boundaries separating the inner and outer, public and private ethics by interrogating their own ethical identities. On the one hand, contemporary practitioners are loyal to clients and employers who pay them, but they also are responsible to the widest possible social good and harmony. Fawkes' (2012) saint/sinner binary dualism encourages modern public relations to "develop and internalize stronger ethical arguments among practitioners" (p. 871). One way to affect ethical arguments is to consider the impact of community-building work.

Close reading of the diaries, journals, and reminiscences of women who ultimately settled in the Willamette Valley area revealed how the overland journey and settlement experience necessitated women's transformation within mainstream nineteenth-century ideas about the role of women – to become community builders in ways both subtle and direct. On the other hand, pioneer historian Jeffrey (1998) resolved that emigrating frontier women expected to "labor hard and long to achieve their goals" (pp. 95–96). Kruckeberg and Starck (2004) expanded their early research on the ways public relations and creating community interplay by underscoring the importance of becoming "conscious of common interests" (p. 141), which helps with networking and problem solving. As explored in this chapter, emigrating women tended livestock and became responsible for watching for grasslands, collecting grass and storing it in wagons in preparation for parts of the journey when the landscape turned barren. This work brought women into partnerships with the men driving the teams of oxen and put them in the service of the entire wagon train community since livestock were essential to the overland enterprise. Similarly, women's community-building work advanced the "welfare, social order, and progress goals" (Kruckeberg & Starck, 2004, p. 141) of the wagon train and Willamette Valley settlement enterprises.

The humanist, communitarianism concept introduced into the public relations literature at the end of the twentieth century pondered "Why cannot the public relations practitioner help foster personal friendships?" as one of eight ways contemporary public relations practitioners can heighten a sense of community among publics and in organizations (Kruckeberg & Starck, 1988, p. 67).

The final chapter offers concluding thoughts and direction for discovering more women's voices for the history of public relations.

References

Aldoory, L. (1998). The language of leadership for female public relations practitioners. *Journal of Public Relations Research*, 10(2), 73–101.

Allen, C. (2005). *Snake River massacre account by one of the survivors*. The Oregon History Project. Accessed February 17, 2020 from https://bit.ly/2STbQ0d.

Atwood, K., & Gray, D. J. (2003). *Claiming the land*. The Oregon History Project. Accessed February 17, 2020 from https://bit.ly/2HuSsBp.

Bass, B. M. (1990), From transactional to transformational leadership: Learning to share the vision. *Organizational Dynamics*, 18, 19–31.

Bivins, T. H. (1993). Public relations, professionalism, and the public interest. *Journal of Business Ethics*, 12, 117–126.

Butruille, S. G. (1993). *Women's voices from the Oregon Trail: The times that tried women's souls and a guide to women's history along the Oregon Trail*. Boise, ID: Tamarack Books, Inc.

Coombes, R. J. (1998). *The cultural life of intellectual properties: Authorship, appropriation, and the law*. Durham, NC: Duke University Press.

del Mar, D. P. (2005). *Early contact*. The Oregon History Project. Accessed February 17, 2020 from https://bit.ly/32drNTz.

Dennis, M. (2014). Natives and pioneers: Death and the settling and unsettling of Oregon. *Oregon Historical Quarterly*, 115(3), 282–297.

Dewey, J. (1927). *The public and its problems*. New York: Holt.

Diamond, J. (Writer), Harrison, C. (Director), & Lambert, T. (Director) (2005). *Guns, Germs and Steel*. Washington, DC: Public Broadcasting Service.

Emmons, D. M. (1971). *Garden in the grasslands: Boomer literature of the Central Great Plains*. Lincoln, NE: University of Nebraska Press.

Faragher, J., & Stansell, C. (1975). Women and their families on the Overland Trail to California and Oregon, 1842–1867. *Feminist Studies*, 2(2/3), 150–166.

Fawkes, J. (2012). Saints and sinners: Competing identities in public relations ethics. *Public Relations Review*, 38, 865–872.

Feltskog, E. N. (ed.) (1969). *The Oregon Trail*. Madison, WI: University of Wisconsin Press.

Gwartney, D. A. (2019). *I am a stranger here myself*. Albuquerque, NM: University of New Mexico Press.

Harris, K. (1987). Homesteading in northeastern Colorado, 1873–1920: Sex roles and women's experience. In S. Armitage & E. Jameson (eds), *Writing the range: Race, class, and culture in the women's west* (pp. 165–178). Norman, OK: University of Oklahoma Press.

Heath, R. L. (2000). A rhetorical perspective on the values of public relations: Crossroads and pathways toward concurrence. *Journal of Public Relations Research*, 12, 69–91.

Holmes, K. L. (2008). *Best of covered wagon women*. Norman, OK: University of Oklahoma Press.

Jeffrey, J. R. (1998). *Frontier women: Civilizing the west? 1840–1880*. New York: Hill & Wang.

Jernigan, M. (2018). What animals were found on the Oregon Trail? *USA Today*, May 31. Accessed February 15, 2020 from https://bit.ly/2SPRzbY.

Kruckeberg, D., & Starck, K. (1988). *Public relations and community: A reconstructed theory*. New York: Praeger.

Kruckeberg, D., & Starck, K. (2004). The role and ethics of community building for consumer products and services. In M-L. Galician (ed.), *Handbook of product placement in the mass media: New strategies in marketing theory, practice, trends, and ethics* (pp. 133–146). New York: Best Business Books.

Lavender, D. (1985). *Westward vision: The story of the Oregon Trail*. Lincoln, NE: University of Nebraska Press.

Lewis, D. G. (2014). Four deaths: The near destruction of Western Oregon tribes and native lifeways, removal to the reservation, and erasure from history. *Oregon Historical Quarterly*, 115(3), 414–437.

Lindgren, H. E. (1996). *Land in her own name*. Norman, OK: University of Oklahoma Press.

Merskin, D. (2014). How many more Indians? An argument for a representational ethics of Native Americans. *Journal of Communication Inquiry*, 38(3), 184–203.

Native American population 2020. (n.d.). Accessed August 15, 2019 from http://worldpopulationreview.com/states/native-american-population.

Patterson-Black, G., & Patterson-Black, S. (1978). *Western women in history and literature*. Crawford, NE: Cottonwood Press.

Pearce, R. H. (1947). The significances of the captivity narrative. *American Literature*, 19, 1–20.

Piasecki, A. (2000). Blowing the railroad trumpet: Public relations on the American frontier. *Public Relations Review*, 26(1), 53–65.

Pincus, J. D., & DeBonis, J. N. (1994). *Top dog*. New York: McGraw-Hill.

Proclamation from Governor George Abernethey (n.d.). The Oregon History Project. Accessed February 17, 2020 from https://bit.ly/2HyNQKM.

Prucha, F. P. (1975). *Documents of United States Indian policy*. Lincoln, NE: University of Nebraska Press.

Ratcliff, J. L. (1973). What happened to the Kalapuya? A study of the depletion of their economic base. *The Indian Historian*, 6, 27–33.

Riley, G. (1984). *Women and Indians on the frontier, 1825–1915*. Albuquerque, NM: University of New Mexico Press.

Riley, G. (1988). *The female frontier: A comparative view of women on the prairie and the plains*. Lawrence, KS: University Press of Kansas.

Riley, G. (2003). *Taking land, breaking land: Women colonizing the American West and Kenya, 1840–1940*. Albuquerque, NM: University of New Mexico Press.

Riley, G. (2004). *Confronting race: Women and Indians on the frontier, 1825–1915*. Albuquerque, NM: University of New Mexico Press.

Riley, G. (2006). Sesquicentennial reflections: A comparative view of Mormon and gentile women on the westward trail. In D. L. May & R. L. Neilson (eds), *The Mormon History Association's Tanner Lectures: The first twenty years* (pp. 153–171). Urbana, IL: University of Illinois Press.

Robbins, W. B. (2002a). Resettlement and the new economy. A changing landscape and the beginnings of White settlement. Accessed February 17, 2020 from https://bit.ly/2uKwvff.

Robbins, W. G. (2002b). *A new legal landscape*. The Oregon History Project. Accessed February 17, 2020 from https://bit.ly/38BXIzi.

Rosener, J. B. (1994). Ways women lead. In N. A. Nichols (ed.), *Reach for the top: Women and the changing facts of work life* (pp. 13–23). Boston, MA: Harvard Business Review.

Sklar, K. K. (1973). *Catharine Beecher: A study in American domesticity*. New York: W. W. Norton & Company.

Stoker, K., & Stoker, M. (2012). The paradox of public interest: How serving individual superior interests fulfil public relations' obligation to the public interest. *Journal of Mass Media Ethics*, 27(1), 31–45.

Strong, P. T. (2012). *American Indians and the American imaginary: Cultural representation across the centuries*. New York: Routledge.

Thornton, R. (1987). *American Indian holocaust and survival*. Norman, OK: University of Oklahoma Press.

Unruh, J. D. (1979). *The plains across: The overland emigrants and the trans-Mississippi west, 1840–1860*. Chicago, IL: University of Illinois Press.

Van den Bossche, P., Gijselaers, W., Segers, M., & Kirschner, P. A. (2006). Social and cognitive factors driving teamwork in collaborative learning environments. Team learning beliefs, & behaviours. *Small Group Research*, 37(5), 490–521.

Van Der Beets, R. (1972). The Indian captivity narrative as ritual. *American Literature*, 43, 548–562.

Vujnovic, M., & Kruckeberg, D. (2013). Communitarianism. In R. L. Heath, *Encyclopedia of public relations* (2nd edn) (pp. 161–164). Thousand Oaks, CA: Sage.

8 Concluding Thoughts and Direction for Discovering More Women's Voices for Public Relations History

Failure to include women's lived experiences as community builders among the pages of public relations history prior to the twentieth century has presented an exceptionally limited view; an effect of uneven power distribution among those who practiced public relations, as well as those who write about its history. Long overdue is a more nuanced history of the development of public relations before the twentieth century; one that focuses on contexts such as when women discovered ways to move beyond the cult of true womanhood with gender roles that relegated them to the domestic private sphere. While it is unlikely that most nineteenth-century Oregon Trail women strategically set out to completely dismantle domestic arrangements, they did ultimately discover the means to expand their role and set the tone for homesteading for years to come in ways that enabled women to get out of the kitchen occasionally. There was no real turning-back point for westward emigrants beyond Independence, Missouri, given that "they were stepping off into the unknown" (Burns & Burns, 1992). Broken wagons meant riding weary horses or walking for much of the 2,000+-mile trip in shoes barely up to the task through spring, summer, fall, and sometimes winter. Out of necessity, women acquired a variety of additional skills in trial-by-fire manner. Once in the Willamette Valley of Oregon, women had to continue improvising since their stoves had been abandoned to lighten the load en route. No doubt, they experienced moments of doubt. For Narcissa Prentiss Whitman, however, there was no evidence that the ill-fated missionary woman "begged to return to her little village in upstate New York" with all the comforts of home even when she lost her two-year-old daughter to drowning at the Mission and "became as impenetrable as stone" (Gwartney, 2019, pp. 87, 97). Spirits just as strong as Whitman's were evidenced among the narratives in the diaries, journals, and reminiscences of nineteenth-century pioneer women examined for the study detailed in this book.

Findings for the study were examined in the context of this research question – *What roles did women on the Oregon Trail play that may be considered early public relations community building?* – have illuminated new means for adding nineteenth-century pioneer women's lived experiences to the history chapter of public relations.

Using the nineteenth-century U.S. westward movement as a lens – one of the great migrations in history (Hurt, 2004) – the research findings reported here unfolded in three parts. The foundational part, "Overview," set the stage for a critique of the ways that establishing the "history of public relations as beginning in the twentieth century has de facto excluded women's voices. The voice concept means "the ability to speak and to have one's speech heard and be taken into account in social and political life" (Rakow & Wackwitz, 2004, p. 95). Chapters 1 and 2 offered a theoretical underpinning and historical context for the study of Oregon Trail pioneer women's community-building role by grounding the phenomenon in a critique of the ways the American West continues to capture popular attention as a masculinized space. These chapters also offered a re-assessment of Grunig and Hunt's (1984) four evolutionary models' progress orientation as confining early public relations history to the works of Caucasian/White men in the public sphere. Vasquez and Taylor (2001) offered a five-stage framework, which begins with an inclusive and flexible *foundational* stage, as an alternative. Part II, "Gendering and Expanding Roles as Early Public Relations Work," revealed key themes describing women's specific roles on the Oregon Trail as *Caretaker/Advocate* (food preparer, healer, childcare provider, livestock care provider, conflict negotiator, ambassador/liaison), as *Community Builder of Meeting Houses and Schools*, and as fulfilling a *Civilizing Function*. These important roles offer precursors to what we now consider to be qualities associated with professional public relations practice. Building upon these essential roles as the outcome of doing what was necessary to survive an incredibly dangerous Oregon Trail journey, pioneer women accepted their fate with aplomb and then actively worked to create homestead and settlement communities in Oregon. While frontier men worked the fields and sometimes left to work the mines, frontier women served as arbiters of morality and ethics whilst organizing charity work, building schools, establishing community networks through social and church gatherings, developing mutually beneficial relationships with Native Americans, and maintaining ties with family and friends back East. As emigrants, women actively expanded their traditional nineteenth-century domestic role, as explored in Part III, which thematically explored the interplay among *Ideologies, Women's Work, and the Female Frontier*. Two additional themes characterize pioneer women's community building on the Oregon Trail through settlement via their *Agency and Leadership* and *Emotional Connection for Social Cohesion*. Ultimately, what emerged among the findings was an inevitable paradox as Caucasian/White pioneer women's interactional qualities made them complicit as colonizers altering indigenous peoples' way of life forever. Moreover, commercial interests benefitted from the population influx west of the Mississippi with expanded markets and profits, organized faith institutions sought to save souls, and mass media capitalized on stories whether authentic, exaggerated, or false. Altogether sad, unfortunate, and shameful colonization outcomes underscore modern public relations practice's responsibility for ethical behavior and careful attention to the impact of public relations work on the whole community. Shining a contemporary light on historical events promotes understanding, responsibility, growth, and ultimately stronger relationships rooted in respect. The University of Oregon community learned this lesson the hard way when protestors took matters into their own hands in response to the Black Lives Matter social protest actions in June 2020 when they toppled and defaced the Pioneer Mother and Pioneer Father statues outside the university administrative offices to make a statement about symbols of racism and oppression.

The remainder of this chapter offers some concluding thoughts and ways of discovering more women's voices for public relations history: 1) Significance of Research Findings, 2) Moving Forward with the U.S. Public Relations History Expansion Enterprise, 3) Taking the Public Relations History Expansion Impulse Global, and 4) Final Thoughts.

Significance of Research Findings

The findings of this study highlight the early community building that took place when waves of would-be homesteaders accepted a challenge inspired by U.S. President Thomas Jefferson's 1803 Louisiana Purchase and Louis & Clark's Corps of Discovery, which was were charged to find a Northwest Passage the following year. Many of the early explorers journaled during the first decade of the nineteenth century and included details about two Native American women (Sacajawea and Watkuweis) whose expertise immensely benefitted the westward journey to the Pacific Ocean. Only a couple of decades later, U.S. pioneer women journaled about their own journey of discovery – both on the 2,000+-mile Oregon Trail journey and as settlers and homesteaders in Oregon's Willamette Valley and beyond.

The use of a humanist, communitarian perspective and a feminist communicology lens to examine pioneer women's community-building work has revealed a new dimension to U.S. public relations history prior to the "seedbed era" (Broom & Sha, 2013, p. 83), beyond Grunig and Hunt's (1984) progress models, and before progressivism amplified in Hiebert's (2017) Ivy Lee biography. Because nineteenth-century women's gender role placed them physically and figuratively outside the public sphere, their work and voices fell outside any formal framework of public relations history when the "seedbed era" of public relations was germinating between 1900 and 1916. Gender constitutes society and is used for power (Aldoory, 2006) so that critiquing the ways the history of early U.S. public relations was gender myopic now establishes a context for activism – by expanding the definition of public relations to emphasize community building and by expanding the timeframe to precursors well before the twentieth century in order to incorporate the voices of women and other social identity groups. The heretofore limited framework that has narrowly grounded the beginnings of the history of public relations in the work of two or three Caucasian/White men, coinciding with the emergence of the Progressive Era's large-scale industry and the growth of the mass media has, perhaps inadvertently, excluded the lived experiences of women. At the same time, the findings reported in this book refute Cutlip's (1994) claim that public relations history telling's dearth of women is "a fact of history, not a choice of mine" (p. xi). By adding stories about and perspectives of women across history's timeline, today's public relations students, who are predominantly women, have the opportunity to see figures like themselves rather than having to rely on the framing of early professional public relations as a masculine space shaped by male founding fathers. Furthermore, male public relations students who see women in the telling of public relations history open their worldview on the field as one that is diverse, equitable, and inclusive. The implications of a more critical view of public relations history should inspire female public relations practitioners to strive for and achieve their maximum potential in their chosen profession which is normatively flexible by definition, according to Public Relations Society of America, in the form of its commitment to diversity and inclusion (Public Relations Society of America, n.d.).

As it turns out, crafting ways of seeing that are blind to the experiences of women and people of color on the frontier has been rather typical, when it comes to examining nineteenth-century Western emigration in the U.S. Our Western past is a place "where women were notable by their absence or rarity," (Morrissey, 1992, p. 139). In particular, preoccupation with frontiers*men* and masculine images long negated the publication of Western women's diaries and letters, and the involvement of women in representing the American West as media correspondents, lecturers, authors of emigration experiences, or as subjects of essays, interviews, or sketches. According to Riley (1984), perhaps most nineteenth-century Americans and Europeans "could not surrender their prejudicial images of women and American Indians to pursue a more accurate portrayal of them as rational, capable beings" (p. 251). Even historians have dismissed pioneer women's struggles and successes as trivial (Vuolo, 1975). Because the West, as a "field of Americana," still holds public fascination (Malone, 1991, p. 100), the research findings reported in this book require turning one's gaze backward to the emigration/colonial experience in order to examine the roles of women on the Oregon Trail and homesteading settlement – and to own the implications of colonialism's effects on indigenous communities. Community building happened in the U.S. well before the nineteenth century, preceded organizational and mass media contexts, and women played equally important roles as men. Through their diaries and journals, pioneer women were among the first historians to record the Western experience; well positioned to discover how liberating the migration West could be in terms of expanding their participation in the community-building public sphere.

No doubt there will be some readers who are skeptical of an approach to public relations history that spotlights women at a time in the U.S. when women were relegated almost exclusively to the private domestic sphere while men navigated the public sphere. The public sphere is a realm of social life where public opinion can be formed (Hohendahl & Russian, 1964), state government serves as an executor of the political public sphere (Habermas, 1991), and consists of institutions such as the mass media. Private, domestic spheres with kitchens and bedrooms have been regarded as secondary spaces and the women tending them have historically been deemed subordinate (e.g., MacKinnon, 2006). Today, a public sphere landscape wherein world leaders' inaction in addressing social issues such as the causes of climate change underscores women's limited role in decision making while they, too, experience the impact of these issues and have much to say (Byerly, 2018). More central to public relations theory building and practice is how for too long such a mindset has rendered women's contributions to the development of professional public relations invisible or at the margins. Unfortunately, our important public relations textbooks' history chapters often begin by defaulting to the twentieth-century emergence of industries and mass media which were managed and run by men actively working in the public sphere. Ongoing failure to consider the community-building work of women as active agents has not served our field of practitioners or our students well. While this book responds to a call to "grow public relations history" (Lamme, L'Etang, & St. John III, 2009, p. 156), the degree to which public relations scholars, students, practitioners, and critics of the field are willing to seriously consider the addition of pre-twentieth-century women's community-building work interpreted as early public relations remains to be seen.

Expanding public relations history to include marginalized voices may be considered an activist turn. L'Etang (2016b) suggested that public relations as activism offers a means to "position PR more favorably within the moral universe" (p. 208). This impulse is present among scholars who use the critical paradigm to advance diversity studies in public relations in the U.S. and the U.K., in particular. These inquiries are mainly concerned with the underrepresentation of specific social identity populations and the power dynamics among those who may be overrepresented. Digging into history to investigate power discrepancies is a tenet of the social identity intersectionality approach of critical race theory (Crenshaw, 1991). Too little U.S. diversity research in public relations has reached back to examine the historical roots of the problem. However, beyond U.S. shores, researchers like Munshi (2005) have used postcolonial theory to examine the experiences of minority groups othered in discourse with less input than majority groups.

Oregon Trail women's adaptation to roles of *Caretaker/Advocate* (meal preparer, apothecary, childcare provider, livestock caretaker, undertaker, conflict negotiator, ambassador/liaison), as *Community Builder of Meeting Houses and Schools*, and their *Civilizing Function*, with the additional themes characterizing pioneer women's *Agency and Leadership* and their *Emotional Connection for Social Cohesion* – all constituted community building. This work enabled women to expand upon traditional domestic duties in the private sphere to make their mark outside the home. Women of the Oregon Trail set out on the westward journey as part of a family enterprise and soon modified their traditional female role within the nuclear family to include caretaking and advocating for others.

They continually cooked, cleaned, gave birth, attended to children, nursed and visited the sick and dying, and buried the dead. This work enabled women to share and learn from one another, as part of a care ethic that inspired women who may have started out as strangers from different backgrounds but transitioned them into community members who became socially and personally interdependent on one another. In her important work on the homesteading achievements of North Dakota's nineteenth-century women, Lindgren (1991) alliteratively characterized the outcomes of using a closed mindset to marginalize women's contributions in terms of a marriage, madness, and marginality syndrome: "Women are portrayed as depending on marriage for fulfillment, as unable to cope with severe adversity, and as marginal or secondary contributors to the important business of society" (p. 210). So, implying that homesteading women who traveled the Oregon Trail fulfilled subordinate roles by doing "only women's work" is an incomplete assessment of the depth and degree of the homesteading processes. I concur with Lindgren (1991) that pioneer women were "main characters" (p. 233) in the immigration and homesteading saga. These women planted the seeds for community building now considered integral to public relations, which has become a feminized field dominated by women at every hierarchical level except top-most management suites (e.g., Aldoory & Toth, 2002; Pompper & Jung, 2013).

Using a feminist theory approach to retrieve, analyze, and amplify stories of community-building women who may have been underappreciated during their lifetime and largely forgotten in death promotes engaging with these women's lived experiences afresh to revise the history of public relations. In the process, we may incorporate new ways to investigate the power of public relations today and to discover additional means to look at the present and future for making public relations even more diverse, inclusive, and ethical. Evidence unfolded in this book's research findings reveals that although Oregon Trail pioneer women's labor was unpaid and they were not affiliated with formal organizations, they nevertheless worked as community builders enabling the wagon trains and early settlement communities to connect with their past back East, make sense of a new present, and plan for the future. In a recent *Journal of Public Relations Education* report, DiStaso (2019) referred to history books as pinpointing the beginning of the history of public relations in the early twentieth century and Edward Bernays as writing the first public relations textbook and teaching the first class in 1923 (Broom & Sha, 2013). Even though educators who participated in the annual survey rated *PR history* knowledge/skills/abilities more highly than practitioners (DiStaso, 2019), I hope that public relations practitioners might also concur that limited perspectives on our history could short change students who are working to build confidence, strategic management and leadership skills, and the inclusive outlook required for ethical public relations practice. Public relations has been qualified as a "small and young academic domain" that benefits from being made even more legitimate by virtue of its "different stories about the history of a widely used communication practice" (Wehmeier, 2015, p. 106).

Projecting feminist sensibilities on the past and doing women's history is both rewarding and risky work. The field of Western women's history emerged during the 1970s among historians who identified women's perspectives as distinct from those of men while recognizing that Western history traditionally had been masculinized, narrow, and inadequate (e.g., Schlissel, Ruiz, & Monk, 1988). In other words, women's narratives were constricted as shaped by the "cult of domesticity" (Morrissey, 1992, p. 135). Historically significant women may not necessarily identify with women's issues or feminism (Golombisky & Holtzhausen, 2005) and what cannot be ignored are the pressures of the "pervasive *sentimental* domestic ideology of the day" (Kolodny, 1984, p. 166) (emphasis in original). What we know from the writings of mid-nineteenth-century feminists (e.g., Davis, 1853) is that middle-class Caucasian/White women at that time were concerned about the outsourcing of domestic tasks to paid servants and shifting primary energies from home to industrialization's factory work. Catharine Beecher (1865) recommended redefining domestic professionalism as "includ[ing] three departments – the training of the mind in childhood, the nursing of infants and of the sick, and all the handicrafts and management of the family state" (p. 710). All three of these tasks with associated skill sets played out on the Oregon Trail journey and as part of settlement work in Oregon's Willamette Valley and beyond. I'd like to think that many, if not most, of the Oregon Trail women who left behind diaries, journals, and reminiscences chronicling experiences that fueled this study would want to be associated with ideals of feminist historical geographers who make reference to the past with a primary concern for the present. Diaries are, after all, considered to be "that profoundly female, and feminist genre" (Huff, 1989, p. 6). I suspect that the struggle for women's suffrage was first successful in the West for a reason.

Moving Forward with the U.S. Public Relations History Expansion Enterprise

Offering findings based on the discovery of themes in Oregon Trail women's diaries, journals, and reminiscences – and interpreting everything in the context of early public relations community-building work – makes this book a valuable contribution to the public relations body of knowledge. In the words of Szyszka (1997), historical study is a theory building block and the keystone in our search for the identity of public relations. Moreover, I posit that this brand of public relations history research underscores Byerly's (2018) wider feminist communication theory approach to embracing structural aspects of problems in order to systematically analyze a phenomenon and reveal a path forward for social change. Unfortunately, the backlash to feminism and career threat from those who perceive critical approaches as an attack on men or the omission of specific social identity groups can be quite real. My approach is to supplement our understanding of early public relations history rather than attempt to tear down what we already know and esteem.

Hence, I hope this study inspires other public relations researchers to publish experiences and perspectives of multiple individuals and groups who have not been included in narratives about the early foundation years of public relations. Revisionist history writing means adding what should not have been excluded in the first place by questioning stereotypes and eradicating bias (McPherson, 2003). More specifically to public relations history writing, a "contested subject" (Vardeman, Kennedy, & Little, 2019, p. 97), critics have revealed multiple problems with traditional readings as the foundations for practice and theory building (e.g., L'Etang, 2014). In the spirit of feminist historical geographers' theory building, this book echoes pleas for an end to the "erasure of women effaced from geographies of the past" (Morin & Berg, 1999, p. 326) in public relations. Already, we know that women of color and women practicing the Mormon faith considered the West to be a refuge and chance to escape discrimination (e.g., Riley, 2006). No doubt their long-forgotten stories, from a social identity intersectionalities critical view, have also got much to teach us about community building. By extension, I include in this invitation a plea to consider BIPOC people's historical contributions to the development of public relations and its professionalism, supporting theory-building work that uses as its basis projects such as Hill's "Hidden Figures in Public Relations History" podcast (Finneman, 2016), Kern-Foxworth's critique of stereotypical representations of Aunt Jemima and Uncle Ben in corporate messaging (1994) and lack of ethnic inclusion in public relations textbooks (1990), and Vardeman and colleagues' (2019) analysis of social movements as each has played out on a global stage. Incorporating the experiences of men of color in the history of public relations is equally important. For example, the important contributions of Ofield Dukes, a prominent Washington D.C. organizer for Black Public Relations Society have yet to be fully explored in textbooks' telling of public relations history. In our zeal to understand public relations history, we must resist the urge to focus exclusively on the twentieth century. For example, crucial to Lewis and Clark's Corps of Discovery charge to find a Northwest Passage was the contribution of York, a Black man enslaved to William Clark, who was exceptionally helpful in negotiating with indigenous peoples as he also hunted, cared for the sick, and helped discover new plants and animals (Natanson, 2020). All of these tasks may also be considered community-building work. Tragically, Clark refused to grant York his freedom after the journey.

Advancing the public relations history expansion enterprise also benefits from considering the precursors and roots of public relations beyond the work of people who advocated for nonprofit organizations and for-profit corporations. The organizational standpoint naturally defaults to time periods consistent with progressivism and the Industrial Revolution, focusing on the ability of public relations to solve business problems for even greater profits or fundraising revenue. Adding money to the equation potentially downplays the fundamental relationship- and community-building normative ethics in public relations. So, the *partial organization* concept also has significant potential for public relations history research because it is broader and promotes consideration of "all the elements of organization that exist outside formal organizations" so that we may examine the complex interplay and relationships in social life (Ahrne & Brunsson, 2010, pp. 2–3). So, historical investigations of community and relationship building that existed as partial organization are just as relevant as contexts associated with modernity's formal networks and institutions, or full organizations. In other words, researchers need not be restricted by public relations history's traditional dependence upon brick-and-mortar organizational contexts.

Considering public relations history as something greater than what is written in textbooks is not a new or isolated exercise. As Kern-Foxworth (1990) and Duffy (2000) posited, public relations textbooks must continually evolve to persist as relevant pedagogical tools given their socializing role and power in shaping viewpoints about people and issues (Van Dijk, 1989). Well-established among public relations textbooks is a focus on corporate settings and the influences on professional public relations practice according to the great men approach. More specifically, public relations instructors critically consider the history chapters of public relations textbooks, supplementing lessons found there with their own materials. For example, in my classes, I add to public relations history lessons the community-building work of the Reverend Barbara Harris, a Philadelphia African-American practitioner-activist who began her career at the public relations firm of another African-American practitioner, Joseph Varney Baker, and became its president in 1958. She also became the first female bishop in the Episcopal Church, as well as a public relations executive at Sun Oil Company. Many other public relations instructors also liberally supplement the history chapters of popular introductory public relations textbooks to add or expand upon the inclusion of contributions made by people of color and women, to offer historical contexts other than those of industry, to add activism dimensions from public relations history, to include Museum of Public Relations resources, and to offer public relations history perspectives from nations beyond the U.S. (Ertem-Eray & Pompper, 2020). Of course, some instructors consider textbooks as merely a starting point for developing lectures and course materials for students. However, given that the PRSA lists textbooks as part of the public relations body of knowledge and that the PRSA endorses a responsibility to embrace diversity, it is logical to conclude that the history chapters of public relations textbooks should offer broader views on who is included as making history and who contributed to the development of this field of practice – without excluding pre-twentieth-century time frames.

Taking the Public Relations History Expansion Impulse Global

The historical development of the discipline must not depend exclusively on the history of public relations in the U.S. New pathways are needed. There is much to know about the history of public relations around the globe, but little of this is reflected in U.S. introductory textbooks on public relations (Ertem-Eray & Pompper, 2020). Public relations history, from a U.S. perspective, favors corporate contexts (L'Etang, 2014; Miller, 2000). Attributing the fostering of the origins and development of professional public relations to the U.S. may have inadvertently negated the inclusion of the practice's predecessors in other countries just because these were not actually called *public relations*.

Only in recent years have researchers emerged to stake claims that public relations precursors pre-date the twentieth century and that it is not necessarily a U.S. import. Bournemouth University's sponsored Public Relations History Conference has inspired this type of inquiry with foci on history and events, national histories, and historiography, and related topics (Watson, 2013). Moreover, recent publications of books on the history of public relations have transcended U.S.-centric contexts by examining the work of U.K.-based spiritual leaders (Spaulding & Dodd, 2014), social responsibility across ancient kingdoms (Tilson, 2014), church-state conflict in Ireland (Carty, 2014), international public relations and World War II (Kunczik, 2014), communication in Dark Ages Europe (Moore, 2014), reputation management in ancient Rome (Schnee, 2014), public relations and Thailand's transition to modernization (Tantivejakul, 2014), public relations in Nigeria (Ibraheem, Ogwezzy-Ndisika, & Akanni, 2014), Ubuntu and professionalism in Uganda (Natifu & Zikusooka, 2014), social transformation in Turkey (Bicakci & Hurmeric, 2014), agency and change in Australia (Crawford & Macnamara, 2014), and more.

The study of the nineteenth-century Oregon Trail westward migration is but one example of mass population shift and colonization, with extreme cultural and environmental effects. The topic of migration is relevant to the experience of many nations around the world today and historically, so that the research findings shared in this book may open up many fruitful avenues of interesting comparative community building around the world.

Final Thoughts

Inspired by an understanding that public relations is fundamentally a profession that serves the public interest and benefits society by facilitating dialogue (Kruckeberg & Starck, 1988) – and that the public interest impacts *all* social identity groups – this study was designed to offer a new outlook on the history chapter of public relations. First, the history of public relations has been dominated by portrayals of Caucasian/White men. Public relations is a gendered profession and discrepancies endure in the field even now that the profession's lower and middle ranks are dominated by women while men dominate top management positions (e.g., Aldoory & Toth, 2002; Pompper & Jung, 2013). Limited historical views on the development of professional public relations has perpetuated biased beginnings for our history that play out in establishing who belonged then and who belongs now. Second, by the end of the twentieth century, public relations researchers' definition of the field was also limited by considering the work primarily in terms of formal industry and organizations – defined as a process of working in the public interest to "develop mutual understanding between organizations and their publics" (Grunig & White, 1992, p. 53). By failing to consider *informal* means for facilitating relationship building among diverse people beyond organizational walls, certain voices and perspectives have been further silenced. We also must rethink the telling of our history to offer new avenues of discovery for inclusionary perspectives and greater diversity. No doubt there are many other phenomena to be investigated to offer greater awareness of women's community-building role across history.

More broadly, dominant ideologies stereotyping Caucasian/White women as weak but morally superior limited the telling of complex stories about women's lived experiences on the Oregon Trail and as homesteaders in Oregon and beyond. Jeffrey (1998) reminded us that "there was considerably more variety in the behavior of women than ideology would suggest" (p. 18). Eighteenth-century considerations of women as being regarded chiefly for domestic labor in the private sphere limited the aspirations of all women, even those considered "intellectual" and of the middle or upper classes (Riley, 1984, p. 3). Caucasian/White women who pioneered their way to Oregon's Willamette Valley and beyond experienced a transformation in roles. Within the constraints of what was considered acceptable for female behavior, they found their voice. Ordinary women participated in exceptional circumstances, enabling them to advocate on behalf of others and themselves. I wonder to what degree women were cognizant of how socialized they were to accepting what was expected of them, socially? Were they even able to fully articulate what they were feeling or the gravity of their circumstances? Caucasian/White pioneer women became trendsetters in their community-building work which now offers public relations history a story of women who networked and enhanced or developed skills for being assertive, agentic, caring, and creative leaders who paradoxically were incredibly supportive of others while simultaneously being complicit in the colonization of indigenous peoples' lands. Hence, we must also remember that dominant ideologies across at least two centuries also produced racist accounts of Native Americans – and these ultimately contributed to the annihilation of cultures.

In addition to limited storytelling, public relations theory-building enterprises have also limited the inclusion of women's voices in our history chapter. To reinvigorate our conceptual understanding of public relations theory building, Gower (2006) called for incorporating new theories from other disciplines, exploring new options, and questioning our knowledge base. In this spirit, research findings reported in this book suggest that Caucasian/White women were laying the foundation for community building while emigrating on the Oregon Trail and homesteading in Oregon. In 1984, the four evolutionary models' progress orientation for characterizing public relations history (Grunig & Hunt, 1984) made sense for justifying a twentieth-century present because it mirrored de rigueur practices and reflected the dominance of organizations and the mass media. As a consequence, informal aspects such as community building – where less powerful voices ring – probably received less attention because this work falls outside the four evolutionary models' progress orientation. Alternatively, the public relations five-stage development framework – foundations, expansion, institutionalization, maturation, and professionalization – offers space for describing public relations' development in terms of foundations (Vasquez & Taylor, 2001, p. 321) rather than framing it as anyone's idea of progress. The five-stage framework offers greater flexibility than the four evolutionary models given that the stages are not mutually exclusive, may be applied in any socio-political context, and sets the tone for defining public relations in the twenty-first century by avoiding ethnocentrism as an outcome of power dynamics.

While the act of formally grounding maturation of professional *public relations* in the twentieth century limited broader curiosity about its historical precursors, this benchmark *has* been useful in the U.S. for underscoring the importance of history as a component of the accredited public relations (APR) exam. A study guide PowerPoint presentation divides public relations history into seven eras, beginning with the "seedbed era" of 1900–1916 and ending with the "digital age and globalism" era of 1986 to present (PRSA, n.d.). Gower (2007) has pointed out that frameworks for examining public relations professionalization are limited by corporate boardroom and government service contexts. By definition, this narrows the conversation to men's work in the public sphere given that women in the nineteenth century were considered predominantly for their wife, mother, and housekeeping functions in the private sphere. So, to examine women's role in developing what might be considered that which eventually would evolve into professional public relations tactics, the study findings reported in this book posit that one must approach the task of telling public relations history with a fresh, un-blinkered perspective. Moving forward, PRSA is urged to consider revising its history timeline for greater equity, diversity, and inclusion.

Findings such as those presented in this book offer new contributions to the history chapter of U.S. public relations by chronicling nineteenth-century community building among westering emigrant women as a precursor to professional public relations practice. For too long, the rich history and function of public relations has been under-appreciated across the communication discipline. Defining public relations history by considering fundamental informal community building promotes embracing the lived experiences of women and other marginalized voices prior to the twentieth century. Doing so could strengthen our discipline and inspire other related fields to take notice of our tradition and potential for interdisciplinary collaboration for social change. However, we must avoid misappropriating voices (hooks, 2000) and carefully navigate the power dynamics between ourselves in positions of privilege and the people and phenomena we study (Pompper, 2010). Public relations scholars around the globe who undertake the challenge of incorporating women's experiences into the history chapter could benefit from a feminist communication theory commitment that the enterprise must be political, polyvocal, and transformative (Rakow & Wackwitz, 2004). It is important to name the phenomenon being investigated, to methodologically explain how data are collected and gathered, and to undergird the project with theory to help explain the foundation of the inquiry, any assumptions, and the hypotheses or research questions. As a critical theory, feminist communication theory promotes discerning and revealing mechanisms of communication which give shape to power relations along gender lines.

To aid in the next steps of expanding the history of public relations, including theory testing, the explanatory propositions which have contributed to the problem of the shortage of women in the history of public relations are offered: 1) Given that *public relations* defies universal or global definition, the greatest latitude must be accorded to investigations of its precursors across time periods and contexts, 2) Deeper investigations are required to overcome the strong emphasis in the history of public relations on organizational issues, 3) Ideological assumptions underlying beliefs that women had no influence in public sphere developments prior to the twentieth century because they were socially confined to the private sphere and played no significant role in development of the public relations profession must be questioned, 4) Among the phenomena investigated and people telling stories, public relations history must be written with attention to a wide variety of social identity dimensions including ethnicity/race, faith/spirituality, gender, sexual orientation, socioeconomic status, and more, 5) The effects of public relations, community building, or any number of interrelated skills practiced in conjunction with the historic development of the field demand scrutiny for ethical implications. More plainly, we cannot celebrate achievements without uncritically examining the side effects. Studying history is important "not merely because it chronicles what has happened but also because it can inform and instruct us in the present, keeping the past alive in successive futures" (Dennis, 2014, p. 284).

Perhaps public relations instructors will choose to share stories about nineteenth-century pioneer women's experiences and contributions during westward expansion across North America to provide additional takes on early community building in our field – with a challenge to the racial underpinnings of westward expansion and manifest destiny. Further study of colonial impulses – and not just in the U.S. – offer lessons for emphasizing ethical, diverse, and inclusive professional public relations today. Recognizing the absence of attention to gender and intersections with other social identities in the telling of public relations history means accepting that power dynamics have limited narratives and that it is time to accept that public relations is a field of practice and study that has been formed by many kinds of people and environments and we are ethically bound to amplify this fact.

References

Ahrne, G., & Brunsson, N. (2010). Organization outside organizations: The significance of partial organization. *Organization*, 18(1), 83–104.

Aldoory, L. (2006). A (re)conceived feminist paradigm for public relations: A case for substantial improvement. *Journal of Communication*, 55(4), 668–684.

Aldoory, L., & Toth, E. L. (2002). Gender discrepancies in a gendered profession: A developing theory for public relations. *Journal of Public Relations Research*, 14(2), 103–126.

Beecher, C. (1865). How to redeem women's profession from dishonor. *Harper's New Monthly Magazine*, November, 31, 708–715.

Bicakci, B., & Hurmeric, P. (2014). The historical development of public relations in Turkey. In B. St. John III, M. O. Lamme, & J. L'Etang (eds), *Pathways to public relations: Histories of practice and profession* (pp. 257–272). New York: Routledge.

Broom, G. M., & Sha, B-L. (2013). *Cutlip & Center's effective public relations* (11th edn). Upper Saddle River, NJ: Prentice-Hall.

Burns, R. (Writer), & Burns, R. (Director) (1992). The American Experience [Television series episode]. In J. Crichton (Executive Producer), *The Donner Party*. Boston, MA: WGBH Public Broadcasting Service.

Byerly, C. (2018). Feminism, theory, and communication: Progress, debates, and challenges ahead. In D. Harp, J. Loke, & I. Bachmann (eds), *Feminist approaches to media theory and research* (pp. 19–35). London: Palgrave Macmillan.

Carty, F. X. (2014). State and church as public relations history of Ireland, 1922–2011. In B. St. John III, M. O. Lamme, & J. L'Etang (eds), *Pathways to public relations: Histories of practice and profession* (pp. 28–40). New York: Routledge.

Crawford, R., & Macnamara, J. (2014). An agent of change: Public relations in early twentieth century Australia. In B. St. John III, M. O. Lamme, & J. L'Etang (eds), *Pathways to public relations: Histories of practice and profession* (pp. 273–289). New York: Routledge.

Crenshaw, K. W. (1991). Mapping the margins: Intersectionality, identity politics, and violence against women of color. *Stanford Law Review*, 43, 1241–1299.

Cutlip, S. M. (1994). *The unseen power: Public relations: A history*. Hillsdale, NJ: Lawrence Erlbaum Associates.

Davis, P. W. (1853). Remarks at the convention. *Una*, September, 135–137.

Dennis, M. (2014). Natives and pioneers: Death and the settling and unsettling of Oregon. *Oregon Historical Quarterly*, 115(3), 282–297.

DiStaso, M. (2019). Undergraduate public relations in the United States: The 2017 Commission on Public Relations Report. *Journal of Public Relations Education*, 5(3), 3–22.

Duffy, M. E. (2000). There's no two-way symmetrical about it: A postmodern examination of public relations textbooks. *Critical Studies in Media Communication*, 17(3), 294–315.

Ertem-Eray, T., & Pompper, D. (2020). Reconstructing the PR history time machine: Missing women and people of color in introductory textbooks. Paper presented at the Association for the Education in Journalism and Mass Communication Conference, San Francisco, CA, August 6–10.

Finneman, T. (Producer) (2016). *Hill podcast: Hidden figures in public relations history* [audio podcast], April 16. Accessed August 15, 2019 from https://bit.ly/2v4FeZQ.

Golombisky, K., & Holtzhausen, D. (2005). 'Pioneering women' and 'founding mothers': Women's history and projecting feminism onto the past. *Women and Language*, 28(2), 12–22.

Gower, K. K. (2006). Public relations at the crossroads. *Journal of Public Relations Research*, 18(2), 177–190.

Gower, K. K. (2007). Introduction. In D. M. Straughan (ed.), *Women's use of public relations or Progressive-era reform: Rousing the conscience of a nation* (pp. 1–8). Lewiston, NY: Edwin Mellen Press.

Grunig, J. E., & Hunt, T. (1984). *Managing public relations*. New York: Holt, Rinehart and Winston.

Grunig, J. E., & White, J. (1992). The effect of worldviews on public relations theory and practice. In J. E. Grunig (ed.), *Excellence in public relations and communication management* (pp. 31–64). Hillsdale, NJ: Lawrence Erlbaum Associates.

Gwartney, D. A. (2019). *I am a stranger here myself*. Albuquerque, NM: University of New Mexico Press.

Habermas, J. (1991). *The structural transformation of the public sphere: An inquiry into a category of bourgeois society*. Cambridge, MA: The MIT Press.

Hiebert, E. R. (2017). *Courtier to the crowd: Ivy Lee and the development of public relations in America*. New York: PR Museum Press.

Hohendahl, P., & Russian, P. (1974). Jürgen Habermas: The public sphere. *New German Critique*, 3, 45–48.

hooks, b. (2000). *Feminist theory: From margin to center*. Cambridge, MA: South End.

Huff, C. (1989). That profoundly female, and feminist genre: The diary as feminist practice. *Women's Studies Quarterly*, 17(3/4), 6–14.

Hurt, R. D. (2004). Miller and Lux, Rachael Calof, Nannie Alderson, and the settlement of the agricultural frontier. In R. W. Etulain (ed.), *Western lives: A biographical history of the American West* (pp. 229–254). Albuquerque, NM: University of New Mexico Press.

Ibraheem, I. A., Ogwezzy-Ndisika, A. O., & Akanni, T. (2014). Shell Oil as a window into the development of public relations in Nigeria. In B. St. John III, M. O. Lamme, & J. L'Etang (eds), *Pathways to public relations: Histories of practice and profession* (pp. 193–205). New York: Routledge.

Jeffrey, J. R. (1998). *Frontier women: Civilizing the west? 1840–1880*. New York: Hill & Wang.

Kern-Foxworth, M. (1990). Ethnic inclusiveness in public relations textbooks and reference books. *The Howard Journal of Communications*, 2(2), 226–237.

Kern-Foxworth, M. (1994). *Aunt Jemima, Uncle Ben, and Rastus: Blacks in advertising, yesterday, today, and tomorrow*. Westport, CT: Praeger Publishers.

Kolodny, A. (1984). *The land before her: Fantasy and experience of the American frontier, 1630–1860*. Chapel Hill, NC: The University of North Carolina Press.

Kruckeberg, D., & Starck, K. (1988). *Public relations and community: A reconstructed theory*. New York: Praeger.

Kunczik, M. (2014). Forgotten roots of international public relations. In B. St. John III, M. O. Lamme, & J. L'Etang (eds), *Pathways to public relations: Histories of practice and profession* (pp. 91–107). New York: Routledge.

L'Etang, J. (2016b). Public relations, activism and social movements: Critical perspectives. *Public Relations Inquiry*, 5(3), 207–211.

L'Etang, J. (2014). Writing PR history: Issues, methods and politics. In B. St. John III M. O. Lamme, & J. L'Etang (eds), *Pathways to public relations: Histories of practice and profession* (pp. xix–xxxviii).Abingdon: Routledge.

Lamme, M. O., L'Etang, J., & St. John III, B. (2009). The state of public relations history. *American Journalism*, 26(1), 156–159.

Lindgren, H. E. (1991). *Land in her own name*. Norman, OK: University of Oklahoma Press.

MacKinnon, C. A. (2006). *Are women human?* Cambridge, MA: The Belknap Press of Harvard University Press.

Malone, M. P. (1991). The new Western history: An assessment. In P. N. Limerick, C. A. Milner, & C. E. Rankin (eds), *Trails: Toward a new Western history* (pp. 97–102). Lawrence, KS: University Press of Kansas.

McPherson, J. (2003). *From the president: Revisionist historians.* Accessed January 14, 2020 from www.historians.org/publications-and-directories/perspectives-on-history/september-2003/revisionist-historians.

Miller, K. S. (2000). U.S. public relations history: Knowledge and limitations. *Communication Yearbook*, 23, 381–420.

Moore, S. (2014). Building certainty in uncertain times. In B. St. John III, M. O. Lamme, & J. L'Etang (eds), *Pathways to public relations: Histories of practice and profession* (pp. 128–143). New York: Routledge.

Morin, K. M., & Berg, L. D. (1999). Emplacing current trends in feminist historical geography, gender, place and culture. *A Journal of Feminist Geography*, 6(4), 311–330.

Morrissey, K. G. (1992). Engendering the West. In W. Cronon, G. Miles, & J. Gitlin (eds), *Under an open sky: Rethinking America's Western past* (pp. 132–144). New York: W. W. Norton & Company.

Munshi, D. (2005). Through the subject's eye: Situating the other in discourses of diversity. In G. Chesney & G. Barnett (eds), *International and multicultural organizational communication* (pp. 45–70). Cresskill, NJ: Hampton Press.

Natanson, H. (2020). An enslaved man was crucial to the Lewis and Clark expedition's success. Clark refused to free him afterward. *The Washington Post*, January 12. Accessed August 15, 2019 from https://wapo.st/2GKKyDV.

Natifu, B., & Zikusooka, A. (2014). Ubuntu, professionalism, activism, and the rise of public relations in Uganda. In B. St. John III, M. O. Lamme, & J. L'Etang (eds), *Pathways to public relations: Histories of practice and profession* (pp. 224–238). New York: Routledge.

Pompper, D. (2010). Researcher-researched difference: Adapting an autoethnographic approach for addressing the racial matching issue. *Journal of Research Practice*, 6(1). Accessed August 15, 2019 from http://jrp.icaap.org/index.php/jrp/article/view/187.

Pompper, D., & Jung, T. (2013). Outnumbered yet still on top, but for how long? Theorizing about male public relations practitioners working in the feminized field of public relations. *Public Relations Review*, 39(5), 497–506.

Public Relations Society of America (PRSA) (n.d.). Working toward a more diverse profession. Accessed February 24, 2020 from www.prsa.org/about/diversity-inclusion.

Rakow, L. F., & Wackwitz, L. (eds) (2004). *Feminist communication theory: Selections in context.* Thousand Oaks, CA: Sage.

Riley, G. (1984). *Women and Indians on the frontier, 1825–1915.* Albuquerque, NM: University of New Mexico Press.

Riley, G. (2006). Sesquicentennial reflections: A comparative view of Mormon and gentile women on the westward trail. In D. L. May & R. L. Neilson (eds), *The Mormon History Association's Tanner Lectures: The first twenty years* (pp. 153–171). Urbana, IL: University of Illinois Press.

Schlissel, L., Ruiz, V. L., & Monk, J. (eds) (1988). *Western women: Their land, their lives.* Albuquerque, NM: University of New Mexico Press.

Schnee, C. (2014). I Claudius, the idiot. In B. St. John III, M. O. Lamme, & J. L'Etang (eds), *Pathways to public relations: Histories of practice and profession* (pp. 144–159). New York: Routledge.

Spaulding, C., & Dodd, M. D. (2014). The public relations and artful devotion of Hildegard Von Bingen. In B. St. John III, M. O. Lamme, & J. L'Etang (eds), *Pathways to public relations: Histories of practice and profession* (pp. 41–55). New York: Routledge.

Szyszka, P. (ed.) (1997). *Auf der Suche nach Identität: PR-Geschichte als Theoriebaustein* (*In Search of identity: PR history as a theory building block*). Berlin: Vistas.

Tantivejakul, N. (2014). The utilization of public relations to avoid imperialism during the beginning of Thailand's transition to modernization (1851–68). In B. St. John III, M. O. Lamme, & J. L'Etang (eds), *Pathways to public relations: Histories of practice and profession* (pp. 160–174). New York: Routledge.

Tilson, D. J. (2014). An alternative view of social responsibility: The ancient and global footprint of caritas and public relations. In B. St. John III, M. O. Lamme, & J. L'Etang (eds), *Pathways to public relations: Histories of practice and profession* (pp. 56–73). New York: Routledge.

Van Dijk, T. A. (1989). *Communicating racism: Ethnic prejudice in thought and talk*. Newbury Park, CA: Sage.

Vardeman, J., Kennedy, A., & Little, B. (2019). Intersectional activism, history and public relations: New understandings of women's communicative roles in anti-racist and anti-sexist work. In I. Somerville, L. Edwards, & Ø. Ihlen (eds), *Public relations, society, and the generative power of history* (pp. 96–112). Abingdon: Routledge.

Vasquez, G. M., & Taylor, M. (2001). Public relations: An emerging social science enters the new millennium. *Communication Yearbook*, 24, 319–342.

Vuolo, B. H. (1975). Pioneer diaries: The untold story of the West. *Ms.*, 3(11), 32–34.

Watson, T. (2013). Keynote speech to the International History of Public Relations Conference, Bournemouth University, June 24–25, June 24. Accessed October 27, 2019 from https://microsites.bournemouth.ac.uk/historyofpr/files/2010/11/Tom-Watson-IHPRC-2013-Keynote-Address4.pdf.

Wehmeier, S. (2015). Historiography (and theory) of public relations. In T. Watson (ed.), *Perspectives on public relations historiography and historical theorization: Other voices* (pp. 85–114). New York: Palgrave Macmillan.

Index

accidents 67, 69, 89
Accredited Public Relations Exam xxiv, 171
Adams, Cecilia E. xxix, 40, 60, 63, 68, 70, 71, 74, 87–88, 103, 111, 125, 128, 130, 133, 142–143, 148
Adams, William 142
advocacy 58, 62–77, 84, 94, 106, 110, 161, 164
African Americans 3, 32, 59, 111, 167
agency 117–134, 164
Aldoory, L. 120, 139
ambassadors 72–75, 103
Ambrose, Steven 34
Americana 32, 163
American Revolutionary War 13
American Society for Encouraging the Settlement of Oregon Territory 36
Annie Get Your Gun 37
Anwarfield 46
anxiety and uncertainty management theory 11
apothecaries 68
archetypes 18, 36, 47, 48
Ardener, E. 14
Ashcraft, K. L. 14
Astor, John Jacob 155
Aunt Jemima 167
authenticity 11
autobiographies xxx, 123

Baker, Joseph Varney 168
Bannard, Margaret 83, 89, 93
bartering 74, 76, 92, 107, 111
Beecher, Catharine 90, 140, 166
behavioral consistency 11
Belknap, Keturah 60–61, 70, 109, 130, 139
Bentele, G. 6, 8

Berger, P. L. 17
Bernays, Edward xxi, xxiv–xxv, 12, 13, 165
Bible 105
Bingham, George Caleb 119
biographies xxv, 13, 162; *see also* autobiographies
bison 151
Bivins, T. H 139
Black Elk 152
Black Lives Matter 162
Black Public Relations Society 167
Blank, Parthenia xxix, 40, 60, 63, 68, 70, 71, 74, 87–88, 103, 111, 125, 128, 130, 133, 142–143, 148
Bodnar, J. 43
bonding experiences 85
bonds 140
Boone, Daniel 119
boundary spanners 16, 85–87, 122
Bournemouth University 7, 169
Bread Riots 59
bridgers 16
Brown, Tabatha 91
budgets 92
Buffalo Bill Cody's Wild West Show 37
Burns, Ken xviii
Burt, E. 13
Buss, H. 70
Butruille, S. G. 41, 57, 70, 105, 125, 129
Byerly, C. 166

Cabrera, E. 14
California Trail 3
Captain Grey's Company, or Crossing the Plains and Living in Oregon 123
care 82; ethics 84; giving 83; "good" 83; receiving 83; and relational leadership 120; *see also* care perspective; caretaking

care perspective 82–83, 97
caretaking 58, 62–77, 84, 94, 161, 164
Carr, E. H. 17
Carter, K. 92
Cayuse, the 37, 74, 108, 147, 151–152
Cayuse War 151–152
charisma 120
charitable institutions 8
charitable work 107
Cherokee, the 73
Chicago School 62, 80–81, 89, 138, 155
childbirth 70
children: Cayuse 108; looking after 69; Native American 152
Children's Farm Home School 87
cholera 39, 69
Christianity 36, 105, 107
Christian values 105
Chudacoff, H. P. 59
churches 101, 102, 105
citizenship 86
civilizing function 101–113, 160, 164
civil service 90
Civil War xxiii, 3, 31, 32, 39, 58–59, 106, 111, 112
Clark, William xvii–xix, 34, 37, 102, 151, 162, 167
cleaning 63–66
clusters 16
Coalition for Western Women's History 18
codes of ethics 102
Colby, Mary 132
collaboration 120
collective memory 29, 32–33, 43–46, 49
colonialism xix, 163
colonization 5, 15, 161
commemorations 43, 71
commercial enterprise 92–95
commitment 12
common goals 10
communication 6; and community 81; face-to-face 10; interpersonal 10; organizational 11, 14; public xiii, 13, 20; strategies 10; *see also* feminist communication theory
communitarianism 10–12, 89, 137–138, 142, 156
community 57, 62, 81, 155; engagement 11; investment 12; maintenance 81; planning 86–87; project managers 88–89; relations 10, 81; service 82, 84
compromise 10
computer games 33

conflict intermediaries 71–72
Conscription Act 59
cooking 63–66
Coontz, S. 58
Corps of Discovery expedition xvii–xix, 34, 102, 151, 162, 167
credibility 12
critical race theory 8, 163
"cult of true womanhood" 58, 59, 83, 160
cultural tradition 17
culture 5, 11, 33, 36–38, 47, 48, 73, 76, 91, 119, 131–132
Custer's Last Stand 46
Cutlip, S. M. xxiii, xxiv, 32

Davidson, S. 16
daybooks xxx–xxxi, 96
deaths 71, 73, 147
decision making 118, 123–129
deconstructionism xxv
Dennis, M. 45
determinism 14
Dewey, J. 89, 90
diaries xxviii, xxx–xxxi, 5, 18–20, 47, 96, 121, 125, 127, 166
diarrhea 140
Dick, E. 131
DiStaso, M. 165
distrust 16
diversity 6
division of labor 58, 60–62, 66–67
domesticity 43, 45, 83, 166
dominant ideology 17
Donation Land Claim Act of 1850 4, 38
"drudge" 131, 133
Duffy, M. E. 168
Dukes, Ofield 167
Duniway, Abigail Scott 122–123, 129, 133

ecological balance 33
economic depressions xix, 38, 43; *see also* Great Depression
economic management 92
education 87, 89, 91; *see also* schools
Effective Public Relations xxiv
efficiency xxiv
Ellison Goltra, Elizabeth Julia 67, 146, 148
emigrants 34
Emigrants' Guide to Oregon and California 32
emotional connection 137–156, 164
empathy 120
England 13

entrepreneurs 92–95
Episcopal Church 168
equal rights 14
equity 6
ethical arguments 156
ethical decision making 102
ethical practice 7, 9
ethical standards 102
ethics: care 84; codes of 102
ethnic inclusion 167
Evans, S. D. 126, 133, 141, 146, 147
expansionism xix–xxi

face-to-face communication 10
Fairbanks, Avard T. 44
family xxviii, xxxi, 39, 90, 92, 124–125
family-friendly policies 14
Faragher, J. 47, 73, 144
Farman, Ella 119
farming 93–94
Fawkes, J. 156
Feltskog, E. N. 118
female friendships 140–141
female missionaries 36, 106–108
female socialization 140
female subculture 138–139
femininity 47
feminism 8, 166–167
feminist communication theory 14, 166, 172
feminist historical geography 14–15, 120, 167
feminist movement 118
feminist theory 12–14, 165–166; *see also* feminist communication theory; feminist historical geography
feminist values 21
feminization 21
ferry crossings 92–93
financial costs 92–93
financial public relations 92
fire fuel 63
Fisher, B. A. 16
Fleischman, Doris E. xxi
flora 143, 144
formality 11
Foss, S. K. 47
Foucault, Michel xxii, 18
Fowler, W. W. 106
"frontier democracy" 118
frontierswomen 18, 20, 34, 94, 108, 132
Fuller, Emeline 154
fundraising 109–110
fur trading 30

gender: differences 15; inequalities 12, 13, 17, 82; and leadership 120; and power 162; ratio 84; roles 13, 17, 43, 45–46, 57–60, 76–77, 119–120, 132, 160, 162
gender-appropriate behavior 58
gendered organizing 14
gendered salary gap 14
genocide 154
Germany 8
Gilligan, C. 82
"glass ceiling" 14
Godey's Lady's Book (magazine) 36
gold 152
Gold Rush xvii, 39
Good Old Days 46
graves 71
"Great Community" 81
Great Depression 44, 46
Great Emigration 38
"great man" theory 13–14
Greeley, Horace xx, 32
Gregson, N. 77
grounded theory approach xxx
group consciousness 46
Grunig, J. E. 7, 8, 10, 95, 161
Grunig, L. A. 11, 21
Gudykunst, W. B. 11
Gustavson, C. G. 14
Gwartney, D. A. 128, 150

Halbwachs, Maurice 45, 46
Hall, Stuart 12
Hammond Hadley, Amelia A. 63, 65, 67, 73, 77, 85, 103–105, 131, 143–145, 147, 148
Hanna, Jane (Jennie) Paul Eakin 64, 67, 69–70, 74, 77, 85, 125, 127, 133, 147
Harris, Barbara 168
Hastings, Lansford W. 32
Heath, R. L. 139
Heidegger, M. 82
Hiebert, E. R. xxv, 162
historiography xxii, xxiii, 6, 7
history: learning xxi–xxii; and power relations xxii, 15; of public relations xiii–xxvii, 3,5–9, 12–13, 15, 17–18, 20–21, 48–49, 76–77, 80–82, 84–85, 95–96, 102, 119–120, 133, 160–172; revisionist xxii–xxiii, 167; Western xix, xxv, 18, 33–35, 38, 166
History of Public Relations: From the 17th to the 20th Century xxiii

Hollywood films 33, 91
Holmes, K. L. 85
Holtzhausen, D. 102
Homestead Act of 1862 xvii, xx, 29–32, 48, 94, 101, 102, 126
home-work-life balance 14
Hon, L. C. 15, 21
Horner, P. V. 110
household items 18
housing 83
hubs 16
Hudson Bay Company 3
Hunt, T. 7, 95, 160
hyper-masculinity 46, 49

identity-affirmation 46
Indian Removal Act 153
indigenous peoples xviii, 15, 43, 101–102, 149–154; *see also* Native Americans
industrialization 7, 43
Industrial Revolution 8, 167
infectious diseases 69, 151; *see also* cholera; measles
information exchange 127, 139
inter-connectedness 16
interconnectivity 139
interdependence 16
International History of PR Conference 7
International Public Relations Association (IPRA) 84, 103
interpersonal communication 10
intimacy 140
investor relations 92
Iowa News 108
IPRA *see* International Public Relations Association

Jackson, Andrew 58, 153
Jameson, E. 20, 35, 89
Jefferson, Thomas xix, 162
Jeffrey, Julie Roy 13, 18, 35, 57, 86, 90, 91, 103, 121, 123, 141, 150, 156, 170
Jordan, T. 131
journalists 80
Journal of Public Relations Research 7
journals xxviii, xxx–xxxi, 5, 18–20, 47, 96, 121, 127, 166

Kalapuyan, the 152
Kant, Immanuel 83
Kern-Foxworth, M. 168
kinship ties 95, 141
knowledge 18
Kolodny, A. 48

Korean War 13
Kruckeberg, D. 62, 80–81, 96, 137, 155, 156
Kuhn, T. S. 17

labor 58, 60–62, 66–67
Lamme, M. O. 13–14, 18
landscape: changing 153–154; recording 142–145, 155
"languagescape" 48
Lavender, D. 39
leadership 117–134, 164; and gender 120; styles 120; and suffrage 120–130
leaky pipeline theory 14
Lee, Ivy xxiv, xxv, 12, 13, 162
Lee, Jason 36
Leeds-Hurwitz, W. 17
legitimacy 10, 102
leisure-time activities 142
Leonard, E. D. 58
L'Etang, J. 5, 7, 12, 48, 119, 163
letters xxx, 5, 39–40, 89, 127–128, 132
Lewis, Meriwether xvii–xix, 34, 37, 102, 151, 162, 167
Lewis & Clark: The Journey of the Corps of Discovery (documentary) xviii
liaison 72–75
Lincoln, Abraham 30
Lindgren, H. E. 165
links 16
Little House on the Prairie 91
"little woman" stereotype 131, 133
lived experiences 20, 35, 47–48, 82, 85, 118, 142, 160, 163, 165
livestock 66–68, 156
living conditions 86
logging 154
logs xxvii
Lonesome Dove 38
Loughary, Harriet A. 61, 93, 127–128, 133, 146
Louisiana Purchase xvii, xix, 30, 162
Luckmann, T. 17

Maanen, John Van xxviii
macronetworks 16
Manen, Max Van xxviii, xxix, xxx, 12, 20
Manifest Destiny xvii–xx
marriage 40, 90, 117, 165
married women xx, 31, 84, 107, 126
Maslow's hierarchy of needs 9
mass media xxiii, xxiv, 7, 13, 32, 80, 107–108, 162, 164

Mathes, S. 112
McMillen, Joseph 142
McMurtry, Larry 38
measles 108
media relations 87
medical profession 107
medical treatment 68
meeting houses 89–91, 161
memory 49
Merskin, D. 36
micronetworks 16
midwives 68–71
Miller, J. W. 89, 93
mining 154
mission stations 108; *see also* missions
missionaries 36–37, 106–108, 147; and Native Americans 36–37, 106–108, 110, 151–152
missionary wives 36
missions 36–37; *see also* mission stations
modernism xxv
monuments 43–45, 49, 162
moral orientation 82
moral standards 105
moral superiority 107
Mormon faith 167
Morrissey, K. G. 17, 76
Mumby, D. K. 14
Munshi, D. 163
mutuality 12
mutual understanding 10
Myers, Joseph 153
Myres, Sandra L. 35

national identity 46
nationalism xvii, xxvi, 33
nation building 86
Native Americans xix, xxix, 5, 19, 33; assimilation 152; bartering with 74, 76, 107, 111; children 152; encounters with 72–76, 111–112, 146–149, 153; extermination of 151–153; and land ownership 29–30, 101; and missionary work 36–37, 106–108, 110, 151–152; perceptions of 46, 106–107, 111–112, 146–149, 154–155; persecution and discrimination 151–152; portrayal of 119
network building 123–129
networking 10, 11, 16
network theory 15–17, 124
neutrality 17
New Northwest, The 123
New Republic, The 38
new social history xxviii

New York Tribune xx, 108
Newell, J. A. 139
normativity 102
Northwest Passage xvii, 162, 167
Norwood, V. 47
nostalgia 46
nursing 68–71

Oakley, Annie 37–38
objectivity 17
openness 10, 12, 16
oppression 45, 162
oral culture 47
oral histories 19
Oregon xxix
Oregon–California Trails Association 71
Oregon City 38, 74–75
Oregon Country/Territory xvii, xxix, 3–4, 19, 29–32; gender ratio 84
Oregon Fever 38
Oregon Historical Society 43
Oregon Native Daughters 43
Oregon Native Sons 43
Oregon Pioneer Association 43
Oregon Trail 3, 5, 12, 15, 29, 38–42, 48, 121; development as a commercial road 72
Oregon Trail (computer game) 33–34
Oregon Treaty xvii, 30
organization: and environment 11; partial 11, 167–168; *see also* organizations
organizational communication 11, 14
organizational management 82
organizations: feminist communicology of 14; types of 10; *see also* organization
organizing processes 86–88
Overland Trail 3, 11, 18, 34, 35, 47, 67, 101, 151, 155

Pacific Fur Company 30
Pacific University 88, 91
paintings 13
partial organization 11, 167–168
"particularism" 102
"Parting of the Ways" junction 40–41
partnerships 128
Pascoe, P. 91
patriarchy 3, 15, 35, 58, 90
people of color 6, 8, 111, 123, 167–168
personal items 18
persuasion techniques 7
Philo, C. 77
Pioneer Mother Movement 44–45
place names 154

poetry 13
polis 7
Polk, James K. xvii
popular culture 5, 33, 36–38, 48, 73, 76, 91, 119, 131–132
Portland 84
positivity 10
postcolonial theory 163
postmodernism xxii, xxv, 102
power 15, 18, 162
"Prairie Madonna" stereotype 131, 133
prayer 101, 103, 109
pregnancy 60, 70
Prescott, C. C. 33, 45
press agentry xxiii, xxiv, 7, 96
private sphere 13, 45, 58, 86, 105, 108, 118, 163–164
Proctor, Alexander Phimister 45
profit-centred industry 7
Progressive Era 87, 118, 162
Progressivism xxiv
promotion 95
"protohistory" 8
"PR progress myth" xxv
PRSA *see* Public Relations Society of America
public communication xiii, 13, 20
public engagement 11
public interest 76
public opinion 10
public relation-like activities 95
public relations xiii–xviii, 5; antecedents 8; definition xii–xiii, xxii, 6–8, 84; five-stage framework 7–8, 161, 171; four evolutionary models 7, 95, 161, 170–171; history xxiii–xxvii, 3, 5–9, 12–13, 15, 17–18, 20–21, 48–49, 76–77, 80–82, 84–85, 95–96, 102, 119–120, 133, 160–172; practitioners 9, 16, 156; professionalization 6, 7; students 9, 163; textbooks xxiii, xxv, 133, 164, 168–169; U.S.-centric standpoint 7, 8
Public Relations Commission on Undergraduate Education 9
Public Relations Review 7, 21
Public Relations Society of America (PRSA) xii, xxiv, 7, 75, 102–103, 163, 168,
public space 86
public sphere 13, 58, 95, 118, 163–164
public trust 12

race 111–112
racism 45, 155, 162

railroads 8, 30, 32, 38, 149
reality 17
reflections xxviii, 5
relational leaders 120
relationship building 10–12, 16, 73, 75, 84, 87, 108–111
relationships 10, 11; *see also* relationship building
relativism 6
religion 101–113
religious meetings 105
religious worship 103
Reminisce 46
reminiscences xxviii, xxx, 18–20, 121, 166
reservations 151, 152, 153
resource dependency theory 102
revisionism xxii–xxiii
revisionist history xxii–xxiii, 167
rhetoric 47
Riley, Glenda 18, 32, 35, 72, 77, 89, 90, 91, 106–107, 112, 152, 163
Rose, G. 15, 77
Rudd, Lydia Allen 71, 74, 77, 86–87, 125–126, 133

sabbath 103–105
Savage, Kirk 45
Schill, Michael H. 45
Schlissel, Lilian 35, 67, 87, 89
"schoolmarms" 34, 91
school programs 83
schools 89–91, 161; *see also* school programs; Sunday schools
scientific paradigm shifts 17
"seedbed era" 8, 162, 171
"selective experiences" 5
self-censorship 70
self-confidence 94
self-sufficiency 94
Seneca Falls Convention 118
Shoshone, the 153
Simonsen, K. 15
single women 31, 40, 91, 107, 112, 125, 141; *see also* unmarried women
Sioux, the 73
slavery 32, 111–112
Snake River Massacre 153
social activities 105
social change 96–97
social cohesion 137–156, 164
social constructionism xxii, 17–18
social development 5
social identity 6, 35, 38, 43, 102, 163, 167

social justice 13
social life 89
socially disadvantaged groups 17
social networking 11, 16
social reform 105
social responsibility 96, 169
social spatiality 15
social standards 102
Southern women 59
Spalding, Elza 36, 37, 121
Spillman Cooper, Arvazine A. xxix, 59, 63, 69, 72, 73, 77, 87, 94, 140, 146, 147
spiritual life 105
Spokane, the 110
Stansell, C. 144
Starck, K. 62, 80–81, 96, 137, 155, 156
State Equal Suffrage Association 122
stereotypes: African Americans 167; American male identity 76; gender 9, 18, 36, 38, 86, 91, 119, 132, 170; indigenous people 154–155
Stewart Knight, Amelia 59–60, 67–68, 70, 74, 76, 77, 92, 93, 130
Stogdill, R. M. 117
strategic planning 129–131
strategic thinking 118
Stuart, Robert 30
suffrage 120–123
Sunday schools 36, 105, 109
Szyszka, P. 166

task sharing 10
Taylor, M. 7–8, 161
teaching 90–91, 95; Sunday schools 36, 109
Thomas, Julia 71, 77, 129–130, 146, 149
Toth, E. L. 120
"Trail of Tears" 153
transformational leadership 120, 122
transparency 11
transportation revolution xix
travel costs 39
tribal cultures 152
Tronto, J. 83
trust 139; public 12; and relationship building 12, 16
truth 17
Tualatin Academy 88
Turner, Frederick Jackson 34–35, 38, 46
TV programs 33

Uncle Ben 167
undertakers 68–71
University of Oregon 45, 91, 162
unmarried women xx, 95, 117, 125; *see also* single women
Unruh, J. D. 73, 147
urbanization 43
U.S. Bureau of Land Management 41
U.S. Supreme Court xxiii
Utter-Van Odum Massacre 153

vaccination 151
Vasquez, G. M. 7–8, 125, 161
Virginian, The 91
voting rights 118, 123
Voto, R. 102
Vuolo, B. H. 18

wagon trains 39
Walker, Mary Richardson 110–111
Ward Massacre 153
Ward, Elizabeth 121
waterways 151
Watson, Tom 7
Weaver-Hightower, R. 45
Webber, B. 11
West, the: and gendering 33–38; imagery 32–33; as multicultural space 35
Whitman, Marcus 151
Whitman, Narcissa Prentiss 36, 37, 108, 110, 121, 128, 147, 150, 151, 160
wild animals 151
Willamette Valley xviii, 4, 12, 38, 45, 80, 83–84, 89, 93, 96, 152–153
Williams, Raymond 17
Winters, Rebecca Burdick 71
Wisconsin Herald 108
women of color 123, 167
women's clubs 108
women's rights 118, 122–123
women's stereotypes 9, 18, 36, 38, 86, 91, 119, 132, 170
Wood, Molly 91
woods 153–154
World War II 44

York (slave) 167

Zelizer, B. 49

Lightning Source UK Ltd.
Milton Keynes UK
UKHW020757010822
406672UK00006B/714